Playing t...

A Baden-Powell Compendium

ROBERT BADEN-POWELL

Playing the Game

A Baden-Powell Compendium

Edited by Mario Sica

PAN BOOKS

First published 2007 by Macmillan

First published in paperback 2008 by Pan Books
an imprint of Pan Macmillan Ltd
Pan Macmillan, 20 New Wharf Road, London N1 9RR
Basingstoke and Oxford
Associated companies throughout the world
www.panmacmillan.com

ISBN 978-0-330-44235-0

Typeset by Intype Libra Ltd
Printed and bound in Great Britain by
Mackays of Chatham plc, Chatham, Kentt

Contents

Playing the Game

Foreword

As part of his legacy to future generations my grandfather left not only the two greatest youth movements in the world, the Scout and Guide Movements, but also a vast collection of writings that survive to this day. In the course of his long life Robert Baden-Powell wrote many books, articles and letters and gave many speeches. This unique anthology pulls together some of these that focus on his life and two of the subjects most dear to him – the Scout method and the cause of international peace. I therefore have the greatest pleasure and pride in introducing this book to you.

Some of the chosen texts you may be familiar with but most I am sure will be new to you. All, though, will give you a personal insight into this extraordinary man and his equally extraordinary life. He wrote often about his life – his childhood and youth, through to his army career and national fame with the creation of Scouting and his final years. You will find here a selection, helping to form what amounts to an autobiography. Again, on numerous occasions he unpacked and explained what Scouting was about and how it achieved its purpose to people perhaps not as familiar with it as we are today. For those of us who have been involved in the two Movements since our youth it will refresh our memories on the true purpose and principles of what we are trying to do.

The third section will, I am sure, be a revelation to many and a salutary reminder. Contrary to what others may have written or believed over the years, Scouting was not founded as a military youth wing or a recruiting ground for the army in the years before the First World War. Far from it. As the book will show, Scouting and Guiding have both been major contributors to world peace, forged through membership of two worldwide Movements that exist in every corner of the globe.

And finally throughout you will find various small quotations – quirky, unusual, different and funny – that show Baden-Powell's wit and skill with words.

Scouting and Guiding succeed where politicians and religious leaders often fail. They enable young people to develop and achieve their own potential, providing opportunities that would otherwise be denied. They give many a real start in life and a hope for a better future. Through working in small groups, through outdoor activity, through coming into contact with the youth of other nations, young people appreciate and come to know their God and love their neighbour. Scouting and Guiding are not just

Foreword

about meetings once a week — they are a way of life that transcends all barriers.

As Scouting celebrates its first centenary, there is much reason to give thanks. As it moves into its second century it does so in hope, knowing that while it must continue to change with the times to continue to be relevant to young people, it does so while remaining true to its Founder's vision and principles.

Bade Powen

3rd Baron Baden-Powell of Gilwell
Vice-President of The Scout Association

Books are like a gigantic treasure chest stuffed full of gold and precious stones and pieces of eight — and a bit of nonsense too. It is tremendous fun exploring the chest and deciding for yourself what is valuable and what isn't, what you want to keep and what you don't like.

The Wolf Cub's Handbook (15th), 162

Introduction

In 1907 Robert Baden-Powell founded the Scout Movement. His most famous book, *Scouting for Boys*, was published the following year. It has since been through thirty-five editions, is still in print and has been translated into some thirty languages. But Baden-Powell wrote much more than *Scouting for Boys*, and the contents of this compendium are drawn from a multiplicity of books, magazines, speeches and letters. Much of what he wrote can be classified under three headings: his own life, the Scout method, and – increasingly in the latter part of his life – international peace and understanding. In fact, Baden-Powell was nominated for the Nobel Peace Prize in 1939, but after the outbreak of war, this was deemed an inopportune year in which to award a prize for peace.

Scouting is so deeply rooted in its Founder's life that, soon after the first experimental camp at Brownsea, Baden-Powell repeatedly used events from his own life to illustrate an educational point in his books and articles. When he was invited to write a fully-fledged autobiography, however, he turned down the idea, saying he could not feel inspired to do so. 'I don't see,' he wrote in 1923 in reply to one such proposal, 'that my reminiscences have really any general interest except so far as they refer to the Scout and Guide Movements — and all this part is already well known.'[1]

Nevertheless, in 1930, by which time he had become world famous and had already written twenty-four books, he was prevailed upon by the publishers Pearsons to write *Lessons from the 'Varsity of Life*. Like many of Baden-Powell's books, it was put together almost at random, in this case largely during a voyage to Australia by way of the Atlantic Ocean, the Panama Canal and the Pacific. During the long days at sea, with his wife Olave at his side as his adviser, secretary and typist, Baden-Powell relived various episodes of his life. After much work, the book came out in the first months of 1933, first serially in *Pearson's Magazine*, then in book form.

Despite his considerable achievements, Baden-Powell refused to be put on a pedestal, and his autobiography is written in a light-hearted, even occasionally flippant tone, although he never forgets his role as Chief Scout of the World: he includes some edifying passages, and the book reveals his idealism and profound sense of duty. Yet he always saw life as a game, to be played with scrupulous fairness, and the world as a playing field. He held an ironic view of those who take life too seriously, especially in the

Introduction

pursuit of money or career: it was a God-given gift, and at its end, when the shadows lengthen and the 'evening comes', one should be able to say that one had done one's best, and that one's life was at least partly spent in making others happy.

It is from this delightful book that many of the extracts in the first section are drawn. However, readers unfamiliar with the Chief Scout's eventful life could be tempted to think of his autobiography as no more than one stroke of luck after another. To redress the balance, and to give a full picture of both his achievements and his exceptional qualities, passages from his other books, among them *The Downfall of Prempeh*, *The Matabele Campaign*, *My Adventures as a Spy*, *Indian Memories*, *Sketches in Mafeking and East Africa* and *Adventures and Accidents*, are also included.

The second section draws on *Aids to Scoutmastership*, itself an anthology representing perhaps the most complete compendium of the Scout method, but also includes extracts from *The Wolf Cub's Handbook* and other writings, largely Baden-Powell's many contributions to Scout magazines. It will soon become clear that Scouting is more than just a set of games and activities designed to entertain young people. It is a distinctive educational method that aims at developing their talents and abilities.

Scout training rests on a set of values simply expressed in the Scout Law and Promise. The Law is not a theoretical statement of principles, but a code of behaviour. It draws up a moral profile in positive terms. The Promise expresses the boy's or girl's commitment, freely undertaken, to observe the Law and to be a Scout or Guide. It makes him or her a full member of the community to which they belong and of the worldwide family of the Movement. The training itself is based on self-education. 'Self-education, that is, what a boy learns for himself, is what is going to stick by him and guide him later on in life, far more than anything that is imposed upon him through instruction by a teacher.'[2] It means that the boy, instead of conforming to a model proposed, and indeed often imposed, by adults, becomes the main actor in his own personal growth. The Leader's role is limited to 'giving him the ambition and keenness to learn for himself'.[3] Drawn from a body of volunteers who take the Scout Promise and practise Scouting and its value system before teaching it, the Leader's example is crucial. A Scout Leader is very much an older brother – not a father figure or a teacher – who can guide and advise the youngsters.

The Scout method is formed by a number of interdependent elements that are not generally original or exclusive to it. Baden-Powell's originality lay rather in the way in which he put them all together. As he once put it, 'Scouting is a medicine composed of various ingredients and, unless they are mixed in their proper proportion according to the prescription, the patient must not blame the doctor if the effects are unsatisfactory'.[4]

The third and final section draws on Baden-Powell's extensive writings on peace, most of which were originally published in *The Scouter*, the UK Scout Leaders' national magazine, or in *Jamboree*, the magazine of the Boy Scouts International Bureau. Today, Scouting is unquestionably seen as a force for peace, yet Baden-Powell's initial inspiration was resolutely imperial. In the first edition of *Scouting For Boys* he says that 'the surest way to keep peace is to be prepared for war'. In his mind Scouting was an important part of Britain's preparedness. This in itself is not particularly surprising, given Baden-Powell's years of service as a soldier of

Introduction

Queen Victoria's Empire. What is striking, however, is the subsequent evolution of his thinking.

As Scouting spread across the world at a surprising pace, Baden-Powell was quick to see in the Movement 'a genuine factor for the maintenance of peace', realizing that it was possible to base the concept of world citizenship on the very existence of the Movement in different countries. Then came the First World War. Baden-Powell visited the front in Flanders and was deeply struck by the horrors of trench warfare. He refrained from written comment during the war itself, but after it was over he could not help revisiting what he had seen and his views irrevocably changed: 'there is something wicked and profane about war'. From then on, he made peace his mission and the 4th Scout Law was extended to encourage international brotherhood: 'A Scout is a friend to all and a brother to every other Scout, no matter to what *country*, class or creed the other belongs.'

Throughout the twenties and thirties, Baden-Powell continued to concentrate on building his own 'League of Youth', which would be called upon to establish the foundations of a new world order, based on goodwill, international understanding and peace. To this end, Scouts and Guides were encouraged to camp abroad whenever possible, and pen-pals schemes were actively pursued. World Scout Jamborees were held every four years and Guide World Camps every two years. In the thirties, he even started Goodwill Cruises, where he and Olave led groups of Scout and Guide leaders and other adult members of the Movement on a ship calling at various ports where they were received by local Scouts and Guides.

Robert Baden-Powell died aged eighty-four in January 1941.

Playing the Game

The world was again riven by war, but Scouts and Guides continued to spread the message of international peace. Today the Movements he founded have grown to 28 million Scouts and 10 million Guides in two hundred and sixteen countries and territories. There could be no better epitaph than his own final message to the Scouts:

> *Try to leave this world a little better than you found it and, when your turn comes to die, you can die happy in feeling that at any rate you have not wasted your time but have done your best.*

Mario Sica, Rome, 2006

NOTES
1 Quoted in Reynolds 1942, 240. For abbreviations in footnotes, see Sources and Abbreviations, p. 420.
2 SFB (26th), 243.
3 HQG, October 1913.
4 *Jamboree*, January 1922.

Part I

The Adventures
of My Life

How to get rich*

I have had in my sojourn on earth as good a time of it as any man, so I can speak with some knowledge.

A writer in the *Manchester Guardian* who is unknown to me lately described me as 'the richest man in the world'.

That sounds a pretty big order, but when I come to think it out I believe he is not far wrong.

A rich man is not necessarily a man with a whole pot of money but a man who is really happy. And I am that.

I have known lots of millionaires who were not happy men; they had not got all they wanted and therefore had failed to find success in life. A Cingalese[1] proverb says: 'He who is happy is rich but it does not follow that he who is rich is happy.'

The really rich man is the man who has fewest wants.

Almost any biography will have its useful suggestions for making life a success, but none better or more unfailing than the biography of Christ.

I have over and over again explained that the purpose of the Boy Scout and Girl Guide Movement is to build men and women

* LVL, 12–13.

as citizens endowed with the three Hs – namely, Health, Happiness and Helpfulness.

The man or woman who succeeds in developing these three attributes has secured the main steps to success in this life.

I was asked the other day if I could define in a few words, say fifty, my idea of the best step to take in life.

I replied that I could do it in three – make A HAPPY MARRIAGE, meaning that he who succeeds in gaining the lasting affection of a really good wife has won the biggest step in life.

By happy marriage I don't mean a jolly honeymoon of a few weeks or months and then mutual toleration, but a honeymoon that lasts through the years. *Experto crede!*[2]

Yet one more item is needed to complete success, and that is the rendering of service to others in the community. Without this the mere satisfaction of selfish desire does not reach the top notch.

Have you ever realized what the word 'Scout' spells and means? It is quite worth remembering:

– S *martness*

– C *ourtesy*

– O *bedience*

– U *sefulness*

– T *rustworthiness.*

I hope that every Scout will carry out those points in his daily work.

The Scout, 21 April 1934

The Adventures of My Life

*My double life**

Another excuse for my venturing to write is that I have had the rather unique experience of having in my time lived a double life.

I don't mean exactly what you would infer from this!

Life Number One

No, I mean that I first started out in life, after leaving school, as a young officer in the Army, and, by extraordinary luck coupled with an unaccountable love for my work, I gained rapid promotion through all the successive ranks.

There was in this life the romance of seeing strange lands at my country's expense, through serving successively in India, Afghanistan, South Africa, West Africa and Egypt. There was the campaigning, the sport, and the comradeships; there were hardships and sicknesses and partings, the shadows which enabled one the better to appreciate the sunshine.

Big jobs as well as little fell to my lot; as Adjutant, as Squadron Commander, and finally as Colonel commanding my Regiment, I had in turn what I thought the most enjoyable bits of responsibility that could fall to any man, and in which I was in close touch with my men.

But bigger jobs came to me, of which I will tell in a later chapter, such as, for instance, raising a contingent of native scouts for the Ashanti expedition, acting as Chief Staff Officer in the

* LVL, 13–15.

campaign in Matabeleland, commanding that grand lot of men and women who held Mafeking in the Boer War, and, biggest of all, organizing the South African Constabulary for the settlement of that country after the campaign.

Eventually I reached the top of the tree in my branch of the Service as Inspector-General of Cavalry, with its inspiring opportunities of preparing our horsemen for the Great War when it came.

Thus, at the comparatively early age of forty-two I found myself a Major General, and at fifty-three, after a marvellous run of luck, I had completed my career as a soldier and retired on a pension.

Life Number Two

Then I started my life Number Two, beginning an altogether new life, one on an entirely different plane, but, like Number One, it includes Scouting.

I married her who was to be my right hand in bringing up, not only our own children, but the vast family of Boy Scouts and Girl Guides which then came into being.

We have enjoyed the extraordinary experience of seeing this Movement grow from the tiny acorn of twenty boys encamped on Brownsea Island[3] into a Brotherhood and Sisterhood which embraces almost every civilized country in the world.

The Adventures of My Life

The Scout Promise

On my honour I promise that
1. *I will do my duty to God and the King.*
2. *I will do my best to help others, whatever it costs me.*
3. *I know the Scout Law, and will obey it.*

Scouting for Boys, 1908

NOTES
1 Of Ceylon (presently Sri Lanka), its principal language and ethnic group (also spelled *Singhalese*).
2 The exact Latin quotation is *Experto credite* ('Believe him who has tried'), from Virgil, *Aeneid*, XI, 283.
3 An island in Poole Harbour, Dorset, on the South Coast of England, where the 1907 experimental camp was held (p. 257).

1. My Education*

You should not depend altogether on what is taught you in school. The teacher can't teach you everything, but when you have been shown by him how to learn useful knowledge it is up to you to go on and learn things for yourself.

The fellows who teach themselves are the fellows who get on in life. So teach yourself and don't wait to be taught.

PYOC, 10–11–12

* LVL. 16.

What was my preparation for this life? What my education? My education came from several sources – home, school, travel, sport, etc.

Now, some of you will think: 'Yes, that's all very well, but you (meaning me) probably had a good start with lots of money and tons of luck.'

I certainly had tons of luck. But luck is a thing like pluck, you may have some of it come to you, but you can make it to a very large extent for yourself.

But I certainly had no money. When your father is a clergyman with fourteen[1] children, and you are the last but two, there is not much money flying around for you.

*My mother**

The alliance between my mother and myself was of the nature of a loving comradeship which lasted for over fifty years.

My father was a clergyman and when he died he left my mother a widow with ten children to bring up, and very little money to do it with. Seven sons and three daughters, the youngest only a month old.

She was, however, a very clever woman and a very plucky one. With a very small income and little help from outside, she managed to train and bring up this large family under difficulties and anxieties which it would be difficult for anyone to realize who had not gone through them.

---

* Unpublished manuscript in SAA, with HQG, November 1914 and LVL, 17.

Thanks to her care and interest in each of us not only were there no failures, but we all of us made our way successfully in one career or another.

For myself I know that my mother had a very powerful influence over my life owing to her close sympathy and wise counsel on almost every subject. The whole secret of my getting on lay with my mother. She expected a letter from me every week when I was on service abroad and the letter had to be accompanied by sketches. These she used to examine and criticize in a way so practical and encouraging (she was a very good artist herself) that I took to drawing with great keenness and though I never had any lessons I managed to make a small income out of my pictures for the newspaper press and magazines.

When I started the Scout Movement in a tentative way, she naturally took the deepest interest in its progress, and with her enterprise and experience she urged me to go on with it, recognizing from the first the educational possibilities which underlay it, such as I had hardly foreseen myself. So it was largely thanks to her that the Scout Movement made its start in the world; and with her life as an example one could not but feel — in spite of the difficulties met with at the first inception of such a scheme — one had only to stick to it and look forward to the great possibilities that lay ahead to obtain success in the end.

No man can do more than his best. If everyone practised that principle throughout his life, then when, towards the end of it, he looks back, as he is bound to do, on what use he has made of it, he needs have few regrets of time misspent and opportunities lost.

Jamboree, April 1940

The Adventures of My Life

Early ambitions*

When I was only eight I became a reformer, and a red-hot socialist. I wrote *Laws for me when I am old*.

> *I will have the poor people to be as rich as we are (which was not saying much). Also they ought by right to be as happy as we are. All who go across the crossings shall give the poor crossing-sweepers some money, and you ought to thank God for what he has given us. He has made the poor people to be poor, and the rich people to be rich, and I can tell you how to be good. Now I will tell it to you. You must pray to God whenever you can but you cannot do good with only praying, but you must also try very hard to be good.*

26 February, 1865

My grandfather, Admiral Smyth, wrote on this: 'Surely your intention "when you are old" to make the rich and poor share alike in purse is only following the wake of Jack Cade who cleared the way by taking the heads of the lawyers. This gentleman decreed, when he took London Bridge, that henceforth all should be treated alike, and they were, for he lost his own head and his decree became fulfilled.'

> *Our desire is to help the boy — and mainly the poorer boy — to get the fair chance, which in the past has too often been denied him, of becoming a self-respecting, happy and successful citizen, imbued with an ideal of service for others.*

SYM, 38

* LVL, 17–18.

Playing the Game

*Charterhouse**

When I was thirteen I was granted a Foundation scholarship at Charterhouse.

I was not a clever boy, nor, I grieve to say, was I as industrious a boy as I ought to have been. According to the school reports I began fairly well in my conduct but deteriorated as I went on.

The other day I wanted to inspire my son, Peter, to work harder at school and win good reports from his masters, so I pulled out my own old school reports and invited him to inspect them. 'Now look at this' – I said – 'um – er – well p'raps not that one.' (In it Monsieur Buisson had said of me – 'Fair – could behave better.') 'Well then this – No.' (In it Mr Doone recorded me as 'Unsatisfactory' and my classical master as 'taking very little interest in his work'.)

When, in spite of these uncomplimentary remarks, I succeeded in getting into the Sixth Form, my new classical master, the well-known Dr T. E. Page, generously reported that I was 'satisfactory in every respect'; but the mathematical authority countered this by saying that I 'had to all intents given up the study of mathematics', and it was further stated that in French I 'could do well, had become very lazy, often sleeping in school' and in Natural Science that I 'paid not the slightest attention'.

Thus my form-masters generally do not appear to have had a very high opinion of my qualities. The headmaster, however, that characterful educationist, Dr Haig-Brown, managed in spite of their criticisms to see some promise in me, and reported that my 'ability was greater than would appear by the results of my form work, and he was very well satisfied with my conduct'.

* LVL, 18–19.

This spark of encouragement afterwards fanned itself into a flame of energy when later on I found it really necessary to work.

The test of success in education is not what a boy knows after examination on leaving school, but what he is doing ten years later.

HQG, August 1922 (rep. BPO, 104)
(one of B.-P.'s 'shaving paper notes')

Out-of-school education*

In addition to what I learned in school – which wasn't an overwhelming lot – there was a great deal that I learned *at* school, outside the classroom, which *was* of value to me. On the playing fields one got corners knocked off, one found one's place and gained something of character. And though the games themselves would not last one for middle age, they had their value in the stage of preparation and their lessons held good.

Also I learned more still in my holidays, from my brothers.

The woods†

When I was a small boy at Charterhouse, outside the school walls was 'The Copse', a long stretch of woodland on a steep hill-side, extending for a mile or so round the playing field.

* LVL, 22–3 and 27, with LS, 24.
† LVL, 24–6, with LS, 24–6.

Playing the Game

It was here that I used to imagine myself a backwoodsman trapper and scout. I used to creep about warily looking for 'sign' and getting 'close up' observation of rabbits, squirrels, rats and birds.

As a trapper I set my snares, and when I caught a rabbit or hare (which wasn't often) I learned by painful experiment to skin, clean and cook him. But knowing that the Redskins were about, in the shape of masters looking for boys out of bounds, I used a very small non-smoky fire for fear of giving away my whereabouts.

Incidentally, also, I gained sufficient cunning to hide up in trees when danger of this kind threatened, since experience told me that masters hunting for boys seldom looked upward.

Thus, without knowing it I was gaining an education to be of infinite value to me later. It proved not only a help to me in the hunting of big game and also in the conduct of scouting, but incidentally it started in me the habit of noticing small details or 'sign' and of putting this and that together and so reading a meaning for them — in other words the invaluable habit of observation and deduction.

That Copse lore appealed and was self-taught, and for that reason it stuck. Moreover, it went beyond the development of health of body and of mind, it helped me as a youngster to find my soul. It was in an elemental way, but that solitary creeping and 'freezing' in observation of the birds and the beasts and the butterflies made one a comrade instead of an interloper in the family of Nature, it brought some realization of the wonders that surround us, and it revealed too, through opening eyes, the beauties of the woods and the sunsets. The hikes on the open road brought Nature lore and human side into proper mutual relations, both through historical relics at the wayside and through the intercourse with men of the road.

Then sea cruises and rock climbing widened and confirmed the lessons of the Copse, and later on led one to appreciate across the oceans and among the eternal snows the good things the Creator has set for our enjoyment on a wider scale in the wilder parts.

Watch that lad going down the street, his eyes are looking far out. Is his vision across the prairie or over the grey-backed seas? At any rate, it isn't here. Don't I know it!

Have you never seen the buffaloes roaming in Kensington Gardens? And can't you see the smoke from the Sioux Lodges under the shadow of the Albert Memorial? I have seen them there these many years.

Through Scouting the boy has now the chance to deck himself in a frontier kit as one of the great Brotherhood of Backwoodsmen. He can track and follow signs, he can signal, he can light his fire and build his shack and cook his grub.

Aids, WB, 38–9

But though all such things as these can, in combination, give a sense of efficiency and capability for higher enjoyment of life, conscience will give voice to the knowledge that there is yet something needed to make the whole complete. That something is to be found in the use of that efficiency for the service of one's fellows and for imparting some of one's own joy to become the joy of others.

Playing the Game

*Travel and Sport**

The remaining schools through which I passed came later, after my actual schooldays were over – namely Travel, Big Game Hunting and Active Service.

Through travel I gained the opportunity of seeing how other nations live and how we, in our own country, compare with them. And more particularly I gained from those whom I met in my travels new views, fresh experiences, and a widened outlook which were very much needed items in my education.

Then through sport in the jungles I got nearer to Nature, which is a soul-opening experience, and, incidentally, I gained practice in tracking and stalking as well as in camper-craft and in facing risks, which were all invaluable for successful scouting.

Then on Active Service I completed my education by practice in the real thing.

Scouting†

Through the whole of my career in the Army there was a vein – a fad or whatever you like to call it – that obsessed me and which, while adding zest to my work, came to be of use for the service. Later on it proved the connecting link between my two otherwise dissimilar lives.

This was scouting.

* LVL, 27.
† LVL, 27–9.

The Adventures of My Life

Scouting includes a rather wide range of work. Briefly, it is the art or science of gaining information. Before or during war, information about the enemy's preparations, his strength, his intentions, his country, his circumstances, his moves, etc., is vitally essential to a commander if he is to win success. The enemy, therefore, on his part, naturally keeps such details as secret as he can.

Thus the job which falls to the fellow that has got to find these out is a difficult one and risky. If he does it in disguise he is called a spy, and is liable to be shot, while in uniform he is the more conspicuous as a scout and equally liable to meet his end.

To do effective work demands a good knowledge of military tactics and organizations. It demands also, to a very high degree, the qualities of personal initiative and imagination, as well as of the four Cs, which I have elsewhere said go to make a soldier, namely, Courage, Common sense, Cunning and Cheerful Co-operation.

> *We can get great pleasure out of work well done, even it is only polishing up a kettle successfully.*
>
> GG, 177

If you look back on your past life which bit of it attracts you most?

For my part, although my life has been to a large extent a series of enjoyments, when I ask myself which bit of it I most enjoyed, memory, without any hesitation, flies back to blazing sunshine on a hot, parched, thorn-scrub plain in Rhodesia, where the only shade from the scorching heat was got by hanging your coat over a little bush, where one's clothes were in rags, one's food a small portion of horse and a double handful of flour (which for want of time we usually mixed with water and drank down), and where we were tired and worn out with constant night marching against a crafty foe.

Veld[2] sores, roughly dressed with a fingerful of grease out of a wagon wheel, adorned our faces and hands. Our horses were drooping bags of bones, and they were tired, very tired.

And yet — we were fit and hard, there was new adventure, new excitement or anxiety every day, and we were good tried comrades all. It was all a glorious care-free adventure.

And then the nights; those clear frosty nights under the dark overhead vault, with its stars big and brilliant, twinkling humorously and watching you as you creep along in your crafty, silent stalk (with all the possibility of being yourself at the same time stalked).

You feel your way in the bitter darkness, suspicious of every rock or bush, with all your senses on the strain, eyes, ears and nose, to catch sight, sound or scent of an enemy. On you creep, lying low; pausing; creeping again with deadly patience, in a blindfold game of hide and seek. You are alone, dependent wholly on your own scoutcraft for guidance, for safety, for your life, but above all for not coming back empty-handed.

Risks? Of course, there are risks. They are the salt that gives the savour to it all.

The Adventures of My Life

Don't let your camping be the idle, boring picnic that it can become when carried out on military lines. Scouting and backwoodsmanship is what we're out for, and what the boys most want. Let them have it hot and strong.

HQG, July 1917

NOTES

1 B.-P.'s count includes the offspring of his father, Professor Powell's first marriage, as well as some brothers and sisters who died at a very young age. Professor Powell died in 1860 when B.-P. was only three years old.

2 This word (meaning *field* in Dutch and Afrikaans) indicates the open country of Southern Africa, with high grass, few bushes and almost no trees.

2. Dabbling in the Arts

*Play-acting at Charterhouse**

I am convinced that the play-acting which was encouraged among us boys by that broad-minded and far-seeing Headmaster, Dr Haig-Brown, was of great value to us in after-life.

It was not necessarily with a view to going out on the stage, however, that the Headmaster encouraged us to act but rather as a useful bit of general education.

For instance, it brought us to appreciate for the first time something of the values and beauties of poetic expression. It taught us to memorize speeches, to express ourselves without self-

* LVL, 32.

conscious awkwardness before an audience, to articulate clearly, to use apt phrases, so to modulate voice and gesture as to grip and hold our hearers; moreover it taught us that valuable asset of being able to gauge their responsiveness; all in fact that was helpful later on in public speaking.

Play-acting is very good fun – and besides speaking clearly the great step to success is to play your part as naturally as you possibly can, just as if you were not in front of a lot of other people but actually doing the things that you are pretending to do. I needn't half talk! Once when playing the part of a man dressed as a monkey I fell asleep on the stage, and the other actors had to give me a prod as well as my cue. This took place on the night before my examination in tactics, and is evidence that my nerves were not unsettled by the prospect of the morrow.

The man who holds the average boy's attention for more than seven minutes is a genius.

Note written in 1909, published in *The Scouter*, May 1939

Conjuring*

Conjuring? Yes, I've done a bit of that, too, but in my experience I found that the simplest tricks went down better than the most carefully apparatused ones.

But all tricks, whether simple or not, should be most carefully

* WSCD, 39–41.

rehearsed over and over again, as the slightest mistake will make you look a fool. It is, of course, quite another matter if you make what looks like a mistake and yet bring off the trick successfully all the same. In that way you take in your audience and they are all the more amused in the end.

I once performed a trick where I covered a lady with a black cloth, and informed the audience that before they could count thirty she would have disappeared.

I counted aloud up to twenty, and there she sat motionless in her chair. On and on I counted, purposely looking more and more anxious and counting more and more slowly till we got nearly to thirty, and then I came forward and apologized and said they must excuse me, as I was only a beginner.

Everybody, of course, felt very sorry for me, and I went back to the lady and whipped off the covering, and there stood a donkey!

A difficulty is no longer a difficulty when once you laugh at it – and tackle it.

SFB, DE, 236; YKE, 64, and LS

Contortionism*

Some fellows are more lissom in their joints than others, and if you happen to be gifted this way it helps you very much in your stunts.

* WSCD, 37.

I used to do the trick of squatting down on the floor and putting one leg over the back of my neck. It looked most uncanny. I was doing it in a play one night and I got stuck! I couldn't get my leg back again; so I said in an undertone to the girl who was acting with me:

'Pull my leg, for goodness sake, pull my leg!'

She misunderstood my meaning and thought that she had to chaff me, so she only said:

'Well, you do look a guy sitting like that. What are you playing at? A monkey with a toothache, or what?'

She wasn't at all helpful or encouraging till she saw what was the matter, and eventually helped me out.

Scene painting*

On joining the regiment one of the first questions asked me by the Adjutant was: 'Can you act, or sing, or scene paint?' This struck me as curious and incongruous. I thought that he would only care for my ability to drill, to ride, or to shoot. But later on I realized the inner meaning of the idea. I began as scene-painter in our regimental theatre, and in that capacity was afterwards invited up to Simla for the theatre there. It was not on account of my excellence as a painter, but on account of the rapidity with which I was able to work at scene-painting owing to my ambidexterity. It was easy for me to slam away with a paint brush in each hand because I unfortunately do not know which is my better hand, the right or

* IM, 93.

left, so I use them both. In this way I did the work at double the pace of the ordinary painter; the quality may not have been good but the quantity was all there. I even went so far on occasion as to strap a brush on to each foot, and sitting on a crossbar between two ladders I managed to paint a woodland scene in record time with four brushes going at once! At least it was meant to be a woodland scene, but I think rather required a notice on the programme to that effect, before people quite understood what it represented. I was a futurist before my time.

Life without an appreciation of beauty is like a dull day without sunshine.

LS, 76

3. Adventuring on Water

The spirit of adventure is inherent in almost every boy, but adventure is hard for him to find in the crowded city.

The Scouter, October 1932

With my brothers*

Although I badly missed the guidance of a father, I, as seventh son, got a good training at the hands of my brothers during my holidays. These all had the sporting instinct strongly developed

* LVL, 57–8; YFBS, 15; ATM, 16–17.

and were good comrades together, first-rate swimmers, footballers, oarsmen, etc.

All were good at devising things that they could not afford to buy, even to building a boat.

We built our own boat, made our fishing, rabbit and bird-trapping nets, and thus caught and cooked our own food to our hearts' and stomachs' content.

In all of this I, as junior, had to take my share of the work, especially that part of it which would naturally be delegated to a junior, such as gutting the fish and rabbits (a really filthy job!), some of the cooking, and very much of the washing up.

Well, you know what it is when you begin as a Scout to cook your food: it is not quite a success at first. Mine was not, either. The dinner was not good; I know it, because I ate the whole of it myself — not because I liked it, but because I had got to. My brothers could not eat it, so they made me do so, just as a reminder that I must learn to cook better.

> *Once you have got into that habit [of observing to a hair's breadth] you will be accurate and exact in all things: exactly on time and punctual, neat and exact in your clothing, and accurate in all that you say.*
>
> *Remember that accuracy will pull you through to success where others, less careful, fail. So practise accuracy all you can until it is a regular habit with you.*
>
> PYOC, 43

36

The Adventures of My Life

*A river cruise**

As money came in we were able to buy a collapsible boat. Among
other expeditions, three of us made the journey in it from London
as far as we could get her to float up the Thames, practically to its
source. We got right away up in the Chiltern Hills where no boat
had ever been seen before. We carried our cooking kit, tent and
bedding with us and camped out at nights, getting our supplies of
food from farms or villages as we went along, and catching fish
from the stream.

When we reached the source of the river we carried the boat
over the watershed and launched her again on the stream which
ran down to the westward and which in a few miles became the
Avon.

Through Bath and through Bristol we journeyed, rowing, sailing, poling or towing, as circumstances required, until we reached
the mighty waters of the Severn.

Across this we sailed, with centre board down, in our canvas
cockle-shell, till we successfully reached Chepstow on the other
side. Here we made our way up the rapids of the Wye through its
beautiful scenery, to our then small home in Wales near Llandogo.

From London to Wales, almost all the way by water, with lots
of adventure and lots of fun!

Another time I made a canoe trip from Oxford down the
Thames to Weybridge and up the Wey to Godalming. Another
time we went across Scotland, voyaging along a canal, from sea to
sea. Each time it was grand fun.

* SFB, 70 (from ATM, 121–2); WSCD, 107; LVL, 26.

Playing the Game

A camp if it is used merely as an excuse for loafing and slackness is almost worse than no camp at all.

HQG, October 1919

'Save that boat-hook!'*

The one adventure which remains in my memory most clearly came one day when we were sailing out of Portsmouth harbour in a light breeze, with a very strong tide running against us and a chop on the water.

To avoid the tide, we hugged the Haslar shore, but at the critical moment of that course we passed into the lee of the fort and an eddy of wind took us aback. Before we knew what was happening, we felt a frightening bump and a heave. We heeled over, stuck hard and fast on the stone groyne running out from the fort.

It was a dangerous situation, but our skipper did not lose his head. He gave orders calmly, as if the mishap were part of our ordinary programme. And the crew jumped to obey him.

As for me, I was frankly scared. I realized that we were in a very serious predicament, and trembled.

As we worked, the boat was screwing herself about on the cruel stones, creaking with so sinister a sound that it seemed she must break up at any moment.

She was nearly on her beam-ends,[1] and we younger boys looked around us, felt how vast the waters were and how small we were — and put a new desperation into our labours.

* AD–AC, 5–9; HQG, May 1915; YFBS, 15–16.

Then, with a wave of hope, I saw two big wherries racing towards us, followed by a powerful tug.

'Now,' I thought, 'we may be all right. We shall get a few hefty fellows on board with a good warp which they can pass to the tug, and in a jiffy we shall be off and afloat.'

My relief lasted for just one minute. When I pointed out our would-be rescuers to the skipper he said angrily, 'If one of those fellows puts a foot on our deck knock him overboard. We don't want their help.'

As they came near he bawled to them that we did not need assistance. Our trapped boat groaned on the stones with what to me was a new note of despair.

My brother explained crisply as he laboured that if the 'wreckers', as he called the wherries, once passed a rope to our vessel they could claim salvage against it.

'We can't afford it,' he said; but what he meant was that our pride would not allow it.

Under my brother's sharp orders I worked with every ounce of my strength, but all the while the violent lurches of the boat were adding to the panic which I was trying to smother.

Then a new shock hit us. The boat began to heel right over to the water, and it seemed inevitable that disaster had arrived. I came to the end of my tether, shut my eyes and waited numbly . . .

A voice shouted in my ear. It was our skipper's.

'Save that boat-hook, you lubber! What are you dreaming about?'

I opened my eyes. My brother was pointing angrily at a boat-hook which was slipping overboard close to me.

The command (while I was rather waiting for a sign to get into a life-belt and take to the boat) did me good. I slid to the gunwale as the hook fell into the sea, and began to make grabs for it.

And as I did so, I found that I was not afraid any more. If, I thought, my brother could concern himself with little things at this moment, then our plight could not be so desperate. Death, perhaps, was not at our elbows after all.

I caught the boat-hook, and pulled it aboard, ready now to use it as a weapon against any wrecker who dared to board us.

As I looked round eagerly for further orders, the boat began to sway again. Slowly, slowly it moved . . . until it had, as if by a miracle, regained an even keel.

Surely we were heaving clear of the rocks? A moment of suspense, and — yes, we were off! We were afloat!

We handled the sails with an energy that surprised even ourselves. There was a favourable puff of wind, and we were under way.

We sighed deeply, looked at each other with faces that were perhaps a little white, and then burst into the laughter which often follows tension.

'Well, we fooled the wreckers, eh?' grinned the skipper.

Afterwards we treated the incident lightly, as nothing but a little joke, but one moment of it made an indelible impression on my young mind.

That was the moment when I had been giving in to fear but

had been inspired to take a new grip on myself by my brother's brisk order to attend to a detail.

> *If you are feeling down and out, wretched and in pain, just remember that, in the end, clouds roll away always to make room for the sunshine. Twist up the corners of your lips, if they are down, and make them smile.*

ATM, 176

Pirates in Malta*

In ancient days Malta was a regular lair for pirates with its innumerable little sheltered creeks and bays, and placed, as the island was, right out in the middle of the Mediterranean where trading ships were continually passing to and from the ports along the coast.

Even now you can see the caves where the pirates lived, in overhanging cliffs. They must have had rare old times until the Knights of St John came along and drove them out in 1530. Even then they tried to get back again, and were only finally defeated and driven off after very severe fighting under their splendid pirate chief, Dragout.[2]

So when I came to be quartered in Malta when I was a young officer I read all about those gallant old ruffians and visited their cave dwellings in the ravines. I got to admire them so much that —

* Unpublished note in SAA.

don't, for goodness' sake, tell anybody about it – I BECAME A PIRATE MYSELF!

With about a dozen other fellows worse than myself, we hired a small steam yacht one day when there was a big yacht sailing-race going on round the island. In this race each Regiment entered a yacht.

So we sailed out with our 'Jolly Roger' – the black flag with white skull and cross-bones – flying, and made for a hidden bay near which the yachts would pass. On the way, as we were coasting along, we saw a single figure walking on the beach. Through our glasses we recognized it as being a fat little major of one of the regiments. The order was given: 'Press gang away!' In a few moments our dinghy was lowered with three or four hefty men in her. They dashed to the shore, seized the harmless wanderer and brought him forcibly on board. (I am bound say he did not offer much resistance when he realized what was up and he soon made himself the life and soul of our party.) At length we reached the little cove where we carefully ensconced our ship. The great idea was to sally out directly an unsuspecting yacht came by and to board her and threaten to spoil her chance in the race unless she handed over some of her lunch to us.

After a long wait in which we found ourselves getting desperately hungry, the lookout startled us all to life with: 'Ahoy there! Here she comes!' Up steam and out we dashed. There she was, a big yacht booming along under full sail. We closed on her to within hailing distance and then from the small gun we had on board we fired a shot across her bows in the true pirate fashion and ordered her to heave to. Not a bit of it. She simply took no notice but went booming on. That was a bit too thick! So our next shot was sent plumb through her mainsail. This *did* make her haul her wind and stop for us. Then to our dumbfounded confusion we realized that she was not one of our friends' yachts at all, but belonged to a particularly irate and nasty-looking Maltese nobleman!

It was hours before we could placate him, though we crawled on our bellies in apology – and it ended up in our having to pay for a new mainsail.

Meantime, while we were arguing, the yacht race went sailing by and so we never got at our looked-for prey; and we gently hauled down the 'Jolly Roger' and made for home sadder and wiser and very much hungrier men than we started out.

And it served us right too!

Canoe travelling in Canada*

When I was in Canada[3] I had to travel a good deal by canoe . . .

The backwoodsmen use canoes which they build for themselves out of wood that grows on the spot. They make a strong framework of the lightest wood they can find, and over this they put a covering made of strips of bark taken from the birch-trees.

These strips are not nailed on to the frame but stitched on with string that is made from the long roots of the spruce-trees, and the seams are made watertight with gum, which is the juice out of the fir-trees growing round.

I remember, one day, when some friends and I were paddling

* YKE, 181–2; OWF, 95–100; RTS, 238; AD–AC, 163–4 (from BSBS, 72–3).

in our birch-bark canoe across a good-sized lake where there were a lot of small islands, among the woods, we suddenly ran upon a sunken tree, and one of its branches pierced a small hole in the thin birch-bark side of the canoe and the water began to pour in. While one of us plugged up the hole with his cap, the other paddled the canoe as fast as he could to the nearest island, and when we got there the canoe was already half-full of water. We just reached it in time to prevent the canoe sinking, and got safely ashore.

We hauled her up on a flat, smooth rock, and got our gear out of her and rolled her over, bottom upwards, so that the water could run out and we could get to the hole from outside. It was only a small slit, which we were able easily to mend. This was done in quite a neat way.

Ben and I scraped away with our knives some of the 'gum' or natural pitch with which the seams of the canoe were caulked. Jim meantime had made a little fire with driftwood. Then Ben took a bit of rag, which he had used as a bandage for a wounded hand, and stitched it over the hole in the boat with a few stitches of spruce root; and fixed it there with a little bit of gum which he melted down with a red-hot stick taken from the fire.

In this way he made a watertight patch over the leak in a very few minutes, and we soon had the canoe afloat again.

We launched the canoe to see whether it was watertight, and so soon as we found it was so, we put back our baggage, got into the boat, and continued our journey. Within ten minutes of the disaster we were on our way again as happily as ever, but we kept a sharper look-out than we had done before for snags and rocks just below the surface of the water.

The whole job of repairing our ship only took ten minutes, but it showed how quick and resourceful a backwoodsman can be.

The child wants to be doing things, therefore encourage him to do them in the right direction, and let him do them in his own way. Let him make his mistakes; it is by these that he learns experience.

HQG, January 1916 (rep. BPO, 59)

NOTES
1 A *beam* is any of the heavy, horizontal crosspieces of a ship; a ship *on the beam-ends* is one tipping so far to the side as to be in serious danger of overturning.
2 Turghud Ali, known in the west as Dragout, was a Tunisian pirate active in the sixteenth century.
3 In September 1910.

4. Big Game

Big game Kodak-ing is taking the place of big game shooting, as the recognised form of sport.

LVL, 107, BBA, 98

An elephant hunt in Africa*

We were on leave at Knysna in South Africa, on a hunting expedition in the forest, which was very beautiful with wild mountain

* LVL, 88–90; AD–AC, 109–12.

scenery. Deep in the forest we made our camp and started to tramp after elephants.

To judge from the accounts of the inhabitants the danger lay in the elephants tramping after us!

However, we were not beset by the animals. We walked for miles and miles without seeing any. We were in a ghastly jungle of tree-ferns over one's head, entangled, with a dense growth of creepers, creeping ferns and thorn bushes, forming a regular maze of narrow, well-worn elephant paths running in all directions.

The danger of these paths is that if the elephants suddenly get frightened they come tearing down them, and you might just as well be in a narrow alley with a motor-bus running away down it. There is no getting out to either side, and the elephant, in his fright or rage, is delighted to trample you under his great feet.

Some time afterwards the great elephant hunter, Selous, visited the spot and when he saw the almost impassable jungle he made tracks out of it again as fast as he could, thankful to get away from such a hopelessly dangerous place before any elephants spotted him.

We being perfectly ignorant of elephants and their ways went boldly in where an angel would have feared to tread!

From a small open hill we at last saw a herd of elephant feeding in low bush on the opposite hillside, their great rounded backs and flapping ears gleaming in the sun.

We crept and struggled for an hour through thick fern jungle. This was composed chiefly of tree ferns — that is, ferns growing in great branches on the top of short, thick stems, but about six feet high. This was splendid cover for us, as we could walk between the stems, but were completely hidden from view by the thick roof of ferns above us.

Moreover, by looking between the stems, we had a chance of seeing the elephants' legs before their owners saw us. But the elephant does not see very well, and like many other wild animals seldom discovers you if you stand perfectly still; you must be careful, however, to keep down wind of him; he is very quick to smell you, even at some distance away. In the forest, of course, it is very difficult to tell which way the air is blowing, it feels dead still down in all that undergrowth; so one cannot easily tell when one is down wind.

Gradually, as we crept on, we began to hear the elephants in front of us at work tearing down branches of trees to eat the leaves. There was a lot of crashing and cracking of timber, and a regular kind of conversation going on of gurgling, rumbling sounds, with an occasional snort or blast like a trumpet. Suddenly there was a noise to our right, then a crash to our left, close by. As yet we could see nothing. Then there was a rumbling gurgle behind us. We were right in among them. Still we could see nothing, owing to the dense bush, and yet the animals sounded, some of them, as if quite close. We crouched low and waited and listened to the curious noises made by the herd, which was evidently quite unconscious of our close presence. We could hear the little young ones with their shriller cries evidently asking for a higher branch to be pulled for them, and then would follow a tearing, swishing crash as old mother elephant reached up with her great strong trunk and dragged down a leafy tree-top. Then followed such a mumbling, gurgling and munching by the hungry youngsters.

Presently, as we were creeping forward towards a dark point in the undergrowth, which looked like a shady tunnel in the jungle, it moved! It was the leg of an elephant close in front of us, not more than ten or twelve yards away, just the other side of a big thick bush.

This bush he was tearing at with his trunk — the branches over our heads were jerking and swishing about; we were staring expectantly to get a sight of his body or head, and suddenly we got it — only for a moment! But it was not in the place where we had been looking — it was much nearer.

Suddenly there was a movement in the bush high above the spot where I was looking for them. A branch was suddenly dragged down with a slatey coloured trunk coiled round it and then for a second there appeared two great white tusks and the huge head and ears of a wild elephant. In a moment it was hidden again by waving branches.

Two other elephants were close by me on either side but quite invisible except when they moved. Even then they were difficult to distinguish from the trees in dark shadow around them.

I could not see enough to shoot at, and even if I had I doubt whether I should have fired; this was not from any motive of caution but because I was so fascinated in watching them and, well, I have always felt that, if one may say so, an elephant is too big a thing and too sacred a thing for a puny man to slay.

On they went, crashing, munching, rumbling and squeaking. Then, suddenly, there was a complete and tense silence. Not a sound. I guessed that they had niffed us or heard us, and were standing alert.

But the silence was broken by my tracker who said: 'They've

gone.' And so they had. They had slipped away without a rustle, without cracking a twig, on tip-toe as it were.

We got on their spoor, but found that they had started off at a great pace and, as elephants when alarmed run for thirty or forty miles without a stop, we gave up the chase as hopeless.

> *Don't stay in the mud because the others stick there; look for your stepping stones and make your way out of it.*
>
> RTS, 61

*Hippos**

I don't mind confessing that I have a weakness for hippos. If I kept a mascot I think that, though he doesn't exactly lend himself to being a pet, I should certainly like to have a hippo as mine.

Of course, he isn't quite what you would call beautiful – but there he is – he is not commonplace at any rate, he is quaint. I can watch him by the hour and . . . love him!

Unable to gratify my lust for a hippo as a pet in an English home I have to content myself with the next best thing – the skull of one as a memento.

> *If you look at a real wolf, he wears a big grin on his mouth. So, too, the boy-Cub should always be smiling. Even if you don't feel like smiling – and sometimes you may feel more like crying – remember that Cubs never*

* LVL, 93–5.

cry. In fact, Cubs always smile, and if they are in difficulty, in pain, in trouble, or in danger, they always grin and bear it.

WCH, 43–4

Lions*

It was about four in the morning. We were sleeping peacefully, the camp-fires were burning low, and even the most hungry of our 'boys' were dozing; one of the dogs awakened me by continual growling and uneasiness; then the disturbance was added to by a neighbouring goat startling the night with a shrill bleat of alarm; in another moment there was a sudden rush as of the wind, a crash, and a confused trample of flying hoofs as our herd of four oxen burst from their corral and rushed into the surrounding bush.

In a second everybody was awake and moving. I rushed from my tent, hog-spear in hand, to find all the 'boys' in an unwonted state of excitement, with but one word in their mouths: 'N'gonyama' (lions).

It appeared that, attracted by the scent of the roasting hippo and of our cattle and ponies – and pony is to a lion as turtle soup to an alderman – a roving band of lions had made a rush through our camp, and the cattle had in consequence stampeded, followed by their aggressors.

While we were yet discussing the situation a shrill bellow of

* LVL, 98–100; AD–AC, 41–6; PYOC, 74–8; RTS, 84–5.

pain echoed through the bush at a short distance from the camp, and told us of the fate of one of our poor beeves.

At dawn we dispatched three boys to ascertain the worst, while we prepared ourselves to follow up the lion and exact what vengeance we could.

Of course every boy in the camp wanted to join in the expedition, but we selected only a dozen or so of the best trackers and most reliable men.

We had hardly finished our coffee when the three men whom we had sent out returned to camp in solemn procession, bearing the wet skin, the shank-bone, head and horns of the dead bullock.

They had disturbed the slayers at their banquet within half a mile of camp and had found one lion and two lionesses devouring our beef, while another, a grand old lion, having finished his breakfast, had retired to allow the younger ones to have a chance.

We started off without delay to visit the scene of the repast. Arrived there, we took up the trail of the lions, whose soft feet left but an indistinct spoor in the yielding sand. Every few hundred yards they would notice that the lions had paused to listen and had then changed the direction of their retreat; the new line was of course immediately taken up, but for a long time we went on without being rewarded by sight or sound of our foes.

At last, as we were advancing stealthily in line, ready for anything to our front, a sudden rush and scurry through the bushes was heard on our right; a glance at the ground showed that our quarry had in its zigzag course passed back close to our flank; again and again this manoeuvre was carried out without our catching a glimpse of any of them.

At length the great heat of the sun began to make itself felt;

but if it had told on us we knew it must tell doubly on the lions, who are but poor workers by day, especially after a heavy meal.

The tracks too now began to give us every encouragement to persevere; the instinct (common to all animals, man included) that they were being followed now seemed to have possessed the lions; they had galloped for short distances with frequent changes of direction, halted for a short rest, then up and on again with despairing energy.

At last our leading tracker, sneaking along with his eyes well forward, suddenly 'froze' like a pointer, almost as if petrified. In one brief moment this living bronze statue was photographed on my mind, and the next moment a crash through the bush told us that we had come upon the lions during their siesta.

But still we failed to get even a glimpse of them. The fright that our sudden appearance caused among them impelled them to make their escape in different directions, and thenceforward we proceeded to follow up the big lion, who had taken a line of his own.

On and on under the heat of the day we went, pounding through heavy sand, endeavouring to avoid treading upon crackly sticks and being caught by the 'wait-a-bit' thorns.

At length the bush became thinner and thinner: we were approaching the end of it, and the daylight gleaming between the trees showed that we were coming to open ground beyond. If we could only persuade him to take to the open we were almost sure of a shot.

Suddenly there was a crack, a whisper, a shout, and a general rush for the open. There he is, five hundred yards away, bounding through the grass and scrub – a great lanky yellow cat with arched back and tail, making as fast as he can for a small isolated cover of thorn-bushes.

We all went after him, the boys as excited as ourselves. Gradually we string out. The best runners gain pride of place while others drop behind. Although good for two hundred yards, I was never up to a quarter of a mile even at Charterhouse, and here, weighted by a rifle and ammunition, I was easily passed by the long-legged and well-trained native hunters.

However, the best of us were not quick enough to get within distance of this lion before he had in safety gained his cover. Boys were therefore posted at all corners to wait for his coming out.

But he didn't come out. So a plan was then made, at the suggestion of our chief tracker, who was an old Zulu warrior, by which we could make sure of getting him.

Umpula (this was his name) swore the idea had worked successfully once before.

This clump of bush was very like a big patch of furze bush which you may see on any common, very thick and prickly above but with several runs of various wild animals forming passages and tunnels through it underneath.

The plan was that I should creep into a tunnel on all fours, with my rifle, and the Zulu would follow close behind me. So soon as I saw the lion I should shoot at him, but aiming low so that the bullet, even if it missed him, would kick up such a cloud of dust that the lion would not see us very clearly as he rushed at us; and then lie flat. The Zulu would put his big shield over both of us and as the lion charged us he would stick him in the tummy with his assegai.

I thought it a splendid scheme excepting the part where I came in! And I didn't at all like the idea of that creeping game. It looked to me uncommonly like offering lunch to the old brute after having already provided him with an ample breakfast.

At this moment I felt horribly inclined to give in to myself. But I am glad to say that I stuck to it. Moreover, though I was afraid of the lion, I was still more afraid of the contempt of my Zulu.

So I put on a sickly grin and dragged myself on hands and knees into the dark hole in the bush. Meanwhile Umpula was following almost on top of me with his shield projecting over my head like a small verandah.

On we went, worming our way through the dark tunnel with its many side passages, any one of which might be the lion's retreat. On and on we crawled.

As we got farther in my hair got more than ever inclined to stand on end until, on turning a corner in the tunnel, I saw before me . . . daylight at the other end! Then my pluck returned; the lion was not there, and I crawled into the open on the other side feeling a perfect hero.

'All clear' sounded joyously in my ears while my tongue was proclaiming to Umpula 'What a pity, the lion sneaked away without our having seen him.'

When you are in a funk you must not on any account show it. Then is the time to whistle and smile as if you liked it.

The bravest of all are those who, while feeling funky, are so strong-minded that they conquer their fear and don't allow it to show itself to others.

PYOC, 77 and 79

Playing the Game

*Stalking with a camera**

Big game Kodak-ing is taking the place of big game shooting, as the recognized form of sport. Where big game hunters used to compare notes over their rifles they now do so with no less interest over their cameras. After all, it is much better sport and more satisfactory all round to stalk animals and 'shoot' them with the camera rather than with the gun. It implies more crafty stalking and as great daring and skill as ever.

The trophies, especially if gained with a movie camera, form a far more exciting record both for yourself and for your friends than any dead horns and hides.

It is tending to make the big game hunter more of a naturalist than a butcher, and it leaves the fauna still intact for our sons to hunt in their turn, in the same fashion, and so to learn the invaluable lessons one gains in the school of the jungle.

Why do I like Africa? Well, because you can get away from cinemas and jazz, motor-buses and crowds, noisy streets, stuffy with petrol-exhaust fumes, and all the artificial life which we call civilization.

No, give me the open veld and its glorious sunshine, where you live face to face with Nature, the mountains and the jungles, and the wild folk that live in them. That's where I've just been, in Kenya and Tanganyika, and that's where I want to be again.

AA, 73

* LVL, 107; BBA, 98–9.

5. An Old Wolf's Favourites

For those who have eyes to see and ears to hear the forest is at once a laboratory, a club and a temple.

RTS, 181

Squirks, a mischievous panther*

The only other wild pet that I had was a small panther, named Squirks. I had heard of a panther in a certain part of the Kadir and was out looking for him on an elephant.

Peering down into the grass jungle through which we were

* LVL, 102–3; OWF, 22–6; IM, 242–4.

moving I saw what I took to be the paw of a panther sticking out from behind a tussock of grass. So I fired where I judged the body of the animal to be.

This startled the paw, which sat up and looked at me. As it moved I saw that it was a complete panther on a very small scale, a baby panther, so I made the elephant kneel down, and I quickly slid to the ground and picked it up.

He was just like a huge yellow kitten, about the size of a full-grown cat, dark on the back and light almost to white underneath, and he was covered with black spots, which on his back were big, black rings close together, getting smaller down his sides until they were mere black dots.

I said to him, 'Who are you?' and be answered back with a sort of snarl which sounded like 'Squirks!' so Squirks became his name.

I brought Squirks back to my camp and showed him to Jack, my puppy.

Neither of them liked the other at first, but after a time they grew to be great friends.

I was sleeping out in the open that night on a native bedstead with my puppy and this new acquisition alongside me. In the night he started squalling in panther language but soon settled down again quietly alongside the puppy, with whom he was already friends.

Next morning we found the pugs of a panther having walked round and round my bed, evidently in connection with the squawkings – possibly its mother, but she had not summoned sufficient courage to rescue her off-spring.

So Squirks lived with me for nearly a year and was a most

cheering mischievous comrade, as tame as a dog, but in no way reliable.

Squirks and Jack played together all day long. After some months Squirks began to grow big, much bigger than Jack. His jaw became strong, and his claws became long, and in his play he rolled the poor dog over and over, and in his mouthing and clutching caused him much more pain than pleasure, and so poor Jack began to get tired of games where he always got the worst of it, and he finally gave up playing with Squirks altogether.

But Squirks was naturally gay and light-hearted, so when he found Jack no longer wanted to play with him, he took to playing with himself, and would chase his own tail round and round the lawn, and then dash into the house and rush over tables and chairs, upsetting everything.

He used to go for walks with me just like any dog would do. One day when out walking I met some ladies whom I knew. I stood talking to them with the panther and dogs at heel. Presently the breeze caught the lace edging of a lady's petticoat, which at once attracted the interest of Mr Squirks. He pricked his ears, his head gradually went more and more sideways as he gazed with fascination on the twinkling lace. 'What is it?' he thought. 'Is it alive? No. Yes, it must be. I believe the darned thing is laughing at me.' Phit – chumm! and he suddenly sprang, claws and all, at the lace. The lady whisked her skirt out of the way with a scream. This was too much; he set to work to claw the whole thing in dead earnest, and I don't know where he would have stopped if I had not got him by the collar and hauled him off by main force.

Once, when I had been ill, I was lying out on a stretcher in the garden. Squirks was then getting nearly full-grown, and I used to love to watch him playing about, he was so active and graceful, and his glossy yellow and black hide made him very handsome.

Presently I saw Mr Squirks quietly creeping towards me. Nearer and nearer he came, crawling more and more slowly all the time, with his green eyes watching me, and his tail nervously twitching from side to side. It was different from his usual way, and I hardly knew whether he was coming at me in fun or in earnest.

I was not able to move, so I let out a yell for help. He had now crouched down to the ground a few yards away from me, and then suddenly, like an arrow from a bow, he sprang through the air with a mighty bound and landed plump on top of me, half squashing me with his weight. There it crouched on my chest, grinning down into my face at very close quarters. Luckily, at that moment my big Afghan servant ran up and, seizing the brute, dragged him off. He soon showed me that Squirks' roughness was all well meant, and that he merely wanted me to play with him.

But after this adventure I kept Squirks tied up by a long chain to his collar, the other end being attached to a tree. He used to love to climb up in the tree and lie on it along a big branch.

When I was leaving India many people volunteered to take over Squirks. I gave them twenty-four hours' trial of him, but in every case he was returned with thanks. He was too strong and too mischievous, so I finally passed him on to my Indian servant.[1]

Boys want variety. Don't be surprised when they get tired of one thing. Be prepared with the next.

HQG, November 1911

The Adventures of My Life

*My mare Hagarene**

Hagarene was a real beauty. It was out in India that I got her.

I had been home ill, and had just got back to India to find that my Regiment was on its way to the front in Afghanistan, away up beyond the North-West corner of the country. I had to get myself a horse, and to follow the Regiment as quickly as I could.

I saw an advertisement in the newspaper of this mare for sale owing to her owner going home to England. So I telegraphed that I would buy her, and asked for her to be sent by train to meet me at the end of the railway which led to Afghanistan. I got there the same day, and, of course, was awfully anxious to see what she looked like. When she was taken out of the horse-box she looked a beauty, just as her master described her in his letter to me.

He also said: 'You must be careful when mounting her as she is rather difficult, but once you are on her back she is excellent.'

Well, she had been for two days boxed up in the train, and had had no exercise, and so I expected that she would be more than ever difficult to get on to. However, I was very keen to see what she was like, so we put the saddle on her, and very gingerly I prepared to mount. After much fondling and sugar-feeding I suddenly and quietly slipped on to her back. Not a move! She didn't seem to mind in the least. I thought to myself, 'Oh! It is just some clumsy beggars find her difficult. It only wants a little "horse-sense" and it will be all right.' M'yes; I got to learn more of her very soon!

However, now that I was successfully in the saddle I thought

* OWF, 84–94; IM, 230–31.

we could go for a short ride, and so I gave her a hint to go on. But she stood absolutely stock still. 'My dear,' I said to her inwardly, 'I want you to go on, please,' and gave her a gentle squeeze with my legs. No result; she just stood like a rock. '*My dear*,' I said with greater firmness, '*I want you to go on. D'you hear?*' and I gave her a punch with both heels to show her that I meant it.

I don't quite know what happened: there was a sort of earthquake, and I suddenly found myself standing on my feet on the ground facing her, and the mare standing still looking at me. I never quite knew how I got there. There was no desperate struggle about it; I was simply landed there, by her, without any effort. It showed me, however, that she knew more than I did about how a rider could be chucked. She had performed what is known as a 'buck'.

So I had her exercised for a bit at the end of a long rope, so as to work off her energy and temper; and then I tried again. This time there was no doubt about her dislike to anyone getting on her back. She fought and struggled with the groom who was holding her head while I was bobbing around looking for a chance of nipping on to her. At last I managed it, and sat very tight, expecting another earthquake; but not a bit of it! This time she was quiet the moment she found I was securely in the saddle and directly I asked her to go on she went like a lamb, and was delightful to ride.

But that was her drawback; whenever I wanted her there was a tremendous tussle between her and her groom. It was only a week or two later I found out the secret.

I was away scouting by myself a long way from the rest of the column when by accident I dropped my revolver. So I jumped off to pick it up. Then suddenly the awful thought occurred to me,

'How shall I ever be able to mount her again, with nobody to hold her head!'

Well, something had to be done, so I plucked up my courage and tried to do it without any help.

Hagarene did not show the slightest annoyance at my getting up. I tried it over again, and then discovered that she had no objection to my mounting; what she did object to was anybody holding her head while I did it. So never again did I let the groom hold her, and she was always quite nice and friendly in consequence.

Well, when I say that, I mean she was quite friendly with *me*. But once I wanted one of my men to take a message for me, so I told him to jump on my horse and ride with it. He jumped on all right, but somehow Hagarene didn't like him, and she jumped him off in double quick time.

But she never was nasty to me after our first meeting, except once and that was – well, I think really that she forgot herself for the moment.

We had just come in from a long field-day, men and horses tired and thirsty. It was my duty to see that the men rode their horses to the watering trough before taking them to the stables. I was sitting lazily on Hagarene, and she had had enough work to make her feel glad that the parade was over. Suddenly she performed that earthquake stunt again, shot me up out of the saddle so that I fell on to my hands on the ground while my feet were still up in the saddle. Then, just as before, she stood perfectly still, so that I pulled myself back into the saddle without having tumbled right off! It was a near shave of being fined, because if an officer falls off his horse on parade he has to pay a fine to the mess. But I was not fined this time because I did not come right off – my feet were never on the ground.

Dick, my 'first charger'*

Dick. True, he was a rum 'un.

A big, well-shaped, chestnut-coloured horse, with an ugly old head and rather a small eye. Well – that is an important point. You can tell a lot about a horse from his eye; a horse with a sleepy eye is generally a quiet old thing, while one with a big, open eye is a jolly, honest beast: but beware of the animal with a small eye – he is often nasty-tempered, cunning, and sulky. Well, although Dick had a small eye, he wasn't really nasty-tempered, at least, not always; he was more *short*-tempered . . . that is, he would get angry if you did anything that he didn't like.

For instance, he grew some rather long hair on his heels. He was touchy about this. He rather fancied himself with hairy heels; I didn't. So I told my Indian groom to pull or cut these hairs. But Dick wouldn't allow it. He looked out of the corner of his little eye and put back his ears as much as to say, 'Don't you dare to touch my heels!' and lifted one of them ready to give a sledge-hammer back-kick to the man if he tried it on. So we sent for a farrier who was accustomed to shoeing horses and to playing about with their feet. He came with his mate, and went into the stable to argue the point with Mr Dick.

Dick at once saw that they had got some game on against him,

* OWF, 76–83; RTS, 32–3.

so he resolved to have a row. He edged away from them into the corner of his stall and prepared to fight them. He saw that they expected him to lash out and kick at them, so he made up his mind to spring a surprise on them, and, instead of kicking backwards, he swung round and reared himself up on end to pounce down on them and strike them down with his fore feet.

But he had forgotten one thing. There was a rather low beam across the top of his stable, and when he reared up he caught his head an awful crack on the beam, and he dropped down in a heap on the floor – stunned. The farrier cried, 'Come on, Jim, let's clip him while he's silly!'

So they tied his feet together, in order that if he came to he could not strike out at them, and they then cut his hair quite comfortably.

He recovered consciousness in about a quarter of an hour and was led about staggering as if he were drunk. For some weeks he had to have cold water trickling on his head, and he finally recovered entirely; but he had cracked his skull and one could feel the break across his forehead.

And, mind you, Dick was not bad at heart. He was a great friend of mine, and I taught him lots of little tricks. For one thing, he would stand for hours without moving away if I left him with orders to stop there. On one occasion this was jolly useful to me.[2]

Dick was my 'first charger'. That is, although he was my own property, I was not allowed to use him for purposes except for riding on parade or just quiet riding, must not drive him to harness, or ride him hunting.

Well, one day when I was riding him near our camp, I saw a

fine wild boar scampering across the fields. This was too much for me. I called to my Indian groom to hand me my spear, and on I went on it, forgetting all rules and orders, to catch that pig. After a great gallop we got close up to him, and I reached forward to lunge the spear into him, when Dick stopped short and stood up on end. He very nearly sent me flying to the ground by doing so. The reason for this was that among other tricks I had taught him was that whenever I made a low bow to anybody he was to rear up on his hind legs and paw the air. So, when I stooped over to stab the boar, Dick thought I was bowing, and played his part accordingly; and stood up.

The pig might easily have escaped us while Dick was playing the ass, but the pig was clever, and he said to himself, 'Now's my time to kill those two,' so instead of running away he turned and came for us.

As he rushed at us I prepared to receive him on my spear, but as I had to lean over to do this up went Dick again, my spear missed, and the boar got a good cut with his tusks into Dick's hind legs, fortunately missing his stomach. A second time the same thing happened. But when he came at us yet again I gave Dick such a dig in the ribs with my spurs as made him jump into the air instead of rearing, and as the boar passed under him I jabbed the spear down into his back and killed him.

But the awful thing was how to face the Colonel and explain the wounds in my first charger's legs.

'Please, Sir,' I said, 'a boar attacked me, and I *had* to defend myself!'

'Yes, that's all very well,' said the Colonel, 'but how did you come to have a spear in your hand when riding your first charger?

The Adventures of My Life

Let me see, isn't that the horse that helped you to catch A.44 when he ran away? Yes. Well, youngster, don't go riding your first charger after pig again.'

> *When you are trying to get boys to come under good influence you are as a fisherman wishful to catch fish. If you bait your hook with the kind of food that you like yourself, it is probable that you will not catch many. You therefore use as bait the food that the fish likes.*
>
> *So with boys: if you try to preach to them what you consider elevating matter, you won't catch them. The only way is to hold out something that really attracts and interests them.*

SFB, OFP (28th) and Aids, WB, 30–31

NOTES

1 A different version of the end of Squirks is given in OWF, 26: 'One day, when I was away, he attempted to jump out of the tree, but unfortunately his chain caught up over a branch and hanged him, and that was the end of jolly old Squirks.'
2 See 'The search for A.44', p. 70.

6. Spying and Scouting*

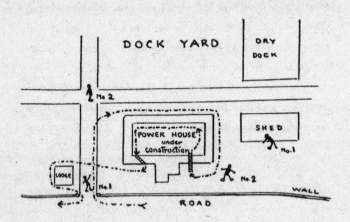

Every Scout ought to prepare himself to be a good citizen of his country and of the world.

SFB, DE, 262

The search for A.44†

I had not been long with my Regiment after leaving school when we were ordered to Afghanistan, and while camped out there a sudden storm of wind and rain blew half our tents down and

* LVL, 110.
† RTS, 31–2 (after OWF, 76–83); LVL, 111; IM, 147–9.

hurled a large tarpaulin up into the sky, and it eventually fell among the horses picketed out in the horse lines. The animals were naturally terrified.

They had strained at their head and heel ropes and, the ground being wet, had torn the pegs out and were rushing all over the place.

Some of them had the sense to form up amongst the other horses and had remained there until fastened up again, others returned when the trumpeters sounded 'Feed', but a number had galloped off into the country.

Next day, when daylight broke, the Regiment was busy rounding them all up until only one was missing – the best horse in the Regiment, A.44, ridden by the Regimental Sergeant Major.

There was considerable excitement about this, especially as the Colonel was very angry over its loss.

So I started off on Dick, my horse, to try and find him. It had been raining and snowing all night, so I soon found his tracks and followed them, sometimes in mud, sometimes in snow. They led me off into wild country among the mountains, often over rocky stony ground where tracking was most difficult.

After some hours of work, and after going over some miles of country, the tracks led straight to a mountain where it was much easier for me to go on foot. Dick would stand for hours without moving away if I left him with orders to stop there. So I got off Dick and told him to wait there, and off I went scrambling up the rocks and gullies, until at last, taking my eyes off the track and looking upwards, I spotted the runaway horse up on the skyline at the top of a small mountain.

Poor old A.44 was shivering with cold, apparently dazed and

very badly cut about the legs with the iron tent peg which was still hanging on to his head rope.

It took a long time to get him down the mountain-side again, but when at last we reached the foot, there was Dick calmly waiting for us – and I was soon heading home in triumph, leading my prize.

Poor A.44 never got over it – he was never the same horse again, and at last got a bad fever and died. But the Colonel was very pleased with what Dick and I had done in getting him back.

It is something to be good, but it is far better to do good.

SFB, OFP and GG

A tell-tale glove*

While we were stationed in Baluchistan, near Quetta, the General at manoeuvre-practice posted a line of outposts and defied the cavalry to get information of what was going on behind their lines.

It was an all-night business, and a very dark and cold night at that.

Among others I was told off to try and find out where the enemy were posted and if possible to get through their lines and report anything I could find out.

Naturally the sentries were very much on the *qui vive*, and a

---

* LVL, III–12; IM, 159–60.

good many of our scouts were observed by the sentries and either captured or driven back. Some of us managed to find out a good deal as to the location of the enemy's outposts and were then glad to lie down and have a sleep on some heaps of *bhoosa* (chopped straw). Waking up some hours later from the cold, I thought it might warm me up to go and try again to get more information.

Then again patient creeping which I had practised in the Copse at school came in useful. Knowing pretty well where the sentries were posted, I was able to evade them and to crawl past them to one of the supports.

Having had all their excitement in the earlier part of the evening in driving us back, they apparently supposed we had retired for good and therefore the look-out was not so sharply kept as in the earlier part of the night, I had therefore no difficulty in getting past the support, and then in keeping along in rear to find the position of other supports, and eventually by following one of their visiting patrols I found the exact location of the reserve.

Having got as far as I could I marked the spot by planting a stick in the ground with one of my gloves on top of it, and then crept my way out again to my own force, just as dawn was breaking.

Next day at the conclusion of the operations we officers had to give our respective versions to the General of what we had done.

I explained where I had been and was told by the officer commanding the outposts that I had a touch of the Ananias[1] about me – or words to that effect – as it would have been impossible for anyone to go where I had been.

So I told them of my glove, which was then found at the spot indicated.

Scouts never grumble at hardships, nor whine at each other, nor swear when put out.

SFB, OFP (4th) and (for Guides) GG, 66

My first spying expedition*

The Colonel sent for me one morning and said that he was going to form a flying column of mounted troops and guns to be ready to move across country into the Boers' territory, in the event of Sir Charles Warren's expedition meeting with resistance in Bechuanaland.

As a preliminary, he wanted accurate information as to possible passes by which he could move over the Drakensberg Mountains which formed the frontier between Natal and the Boer Provinces of the Orange Free State and the Transvaal and *I was to go and get this information*. It had to be done in absolute secrecy.

There were two well-known passes through which roads ran into the Transvaal and Orange Free State respectively. Naturally these would be held by our adversaries. There had been in old days other passes through the mountains, but these had been purposely blown up and destroyed by our engineers, in order to prevent raids into Natal by the natives of Basutoland. I was to find out whether any of these could readily be made available in an emergency.

* LVL, 114–17.

My expedition took me a month, involving a ride of six hundred miles. I rode one horse and led a second, which carried my blankets and foodstuffs. I grew a scraggy beard and must have looked an awful ruffian. At any rate my disguise was evidently effective, for one day* I happened to meet the Major of my Regiment in a town through which I was passing, and which he was visiting on leave. He was a grumpy old customer.

Quite forgetting my appearance, I greeted him with the customary 'Good morning, Major.' He turned and looked at me for a moment, and apparently thinking I was a tramp out for money, he growled savagely: 'Get out,' and went his way; and I went mine, with the contented feeling that I was not likely to be taken for a British officer, and only reminded him months later of our brief meeting!

I generally put up at farms where I happened to find myself at nightfall, and my usual excuse for wandering about in this fashion was that I was a newspaper correspondent seeking information, with a view to recommending it for immigrants, and I thus got to know a good many Boers, as well as British farmers, and their varied opinions about each other and about the prospects of the country.

I found that the map which I took with me for guidance was a very inaccurate one, and therefore I took it upon me to add a bit of surveying to my activities, and made a number of corrections which would be useful from a military point of view.

One of these, at any rate, was not taken notice of by the authorities to whom my reports were afterwards shown, for when

* LVL, 115; MAAS, 37–8.

the Boer War came on, and Redvers Buller fought the battle of Colenso, he believed a certain mountain to be on the far side of the Tugela River, as the old map showed it, whereas I had found it to be on the near bank. Apparently, this error had not been corrected in the Government map, in spite of my pointing it out.

Also, I had expressly said in my report that, in the event of our column from Natal being driven back in its effort to advance northward, it should fall back south of the Tugela and not attempt to hold Ladysmith. Had that line been taken in the Boer War, I feel that Sir George White's division would not have been held up as it was by the Boers for over four months.

> *Common sense is almost the most useful and valuable thing you have got in your character.*[2]
>
> PYOC, 19

It has often been argued that the Zulus could do longer marches than the ordinary British soldier. Of course the latter is handicapped by wearing heavy clothes and equipment, but even without these, and without the practice, I doubt whether he could hold his own with the average Zulu on a walking tour.

On a particular day I started out from Greytown at the same time as a fine young Zulu and his bride. I cantered off at my usual loping pace, and then pulled up after an hour or so, to off-saddle, graze the horses, and have a meal myself; before long, the Zulu pair came trotting by, and went ahead of me. Later I overtook them again going merrily along, and again when I halted they once more overtook me.

This went on throughout the day, and when I eventually arrived at my destination forty miles from starting, there they were, quite cheery, and probably able to go on the next day at the same rate.

> When you see an impossible-looking job before you, go at it, 'grin and tackle it', as the Scout motto tells you, and ten to one you will come out triumphant in the end, and all the more happy because it was difficult.
>
> The Scout, 1 June 1918

Spying in foreign countries*

My first essay in spying was so interesting that I repeated the experience so soon as I could get the opportunity.

When quartered in England I took every opportunity I could of travelling abroad. I attended manoeuvres wherever I could, as an ordinary tourist going abroad the country, until finally employed for such work.

Fooling a German sentry†

On one occasion I wanted to ascertain what value there was in the musketry training of a foreign infantry. Also it had been reported that they had recently acquired a new form of machine gun which

* LVL, 117.
† MAAS, 113–16.

was a particularly rapid firer and very accurate in its effects. Its calibre was known, and its general pattern (from photographs), but its actual capabilities were still a matter of conjecture.

On this occasion I thought the simplest way would be to go undisguised. Without any concealment I went to stay in garrison towns where I happened to know one or two officers. I obtained introductions to other officers, and gradually became their companion at meals and at their evening entertainments. They mounted me on their horses, I rode with them on their rounds of duty, and I came to be an attendant at their field days and manoeuvres; but whenever we approached the rifle ranges I was always politely but firmly requested to go no further, but to await their return, since the practice was absolutely confidential. I could gain no information from them as to what went on within the enclosure where the rifle range was hidden.

Two of my English friends one day incautiously stopped at the entrance gate to one of the ranges, and were promptly arrested and kept in the guard-room for some hours, and finally requested to leave the place, without getting much satisfaction out of it. So I saw that caution was necessary. Little by little, especially after some very cheerful evenings, I elicited a certain amount of information from my friends as to what the new machine gun did and was likely to do, and how their soldiers could of course never hit a running target, since it was with the greatest difficulty they hit the standing one at all. But more than this it was impossible to get.

However, I moved on to another military station, where as a stranger I tried another tack. The rifle ranges were surrounded by a belt of trees, outside of which was an unclimbable fence guarded by two sentries, one on either side. It seemed impossible to get into or even near the range without considerable difficulty.

One day I sauntered carelessly down in the direction of the range at a point far away from the entrance gate, and here I lay down on the grass as if to sleep, but in reality to listen and take the rate of the shooting from the sound and also the amount of success by the sound of the hits on the iron target. Having gained a certain amount of data in this way, I approached more nearly in the hope of getting a sight of what was going on.

While the sentry's back was turned I made a rush for the fence, and though I could not get over, I found a loose plank through which I was able to get a good view of what was happening.

While engaged at this, to my horror the sentry suddenly turned on his tracks and came back towards me. But I had been prepared against such eventualities, and jamming back the plank into its place, I produced from my pocket a bottle of brandy which I had brought for the purpose. Half of it had been already sprinkled over my clothes, so that when the man approached he found me in a state of drunkenness, smelling vilely of spirits, and profuse in my offers to him to share the bottle.

He could make nothing of me, and therefore gently but firmly conducted me to the end of his beat and thrust me forth and advised me to go home, which I did in great content . . .

A man who is in the habit of drinking wine or spirits in strong doses every day is not the slightest use for Scouting, and very little use for anything else.

SFB, OFP, 2

Playing the Game

Look on the bright side of things instead of the gloomy one.

Last Message to Scouts, January 1941

Butterfly hunting in Dalmatia*

Once I went 'butterfly hunting' in Dalmatia. Cattaro, the capital, lies at the head of a loch some fifteen miles long, and in some parts but a few hundred yards wide, in a trough between mountains. From Cattaro, at the head of the loch, a zigzag road leads up the mountain side over the frontier into Montenegro.

Batteries had been built upon these mountain tops, and it was my business to investigate their positions, strength and armaments.

I went armed with most effective weapons for the purpose, which have served me well in many a similar campaign. I took a sketchbook, in which were numerous pictures – some finished, others only partly done – of butterflies of every degree and rank, from a 'Red Admiral' to a 'Painted Lady'.

Carrying this book and a colour-box, and a butterfly net in my hand, I was above all suspicion to anyone who met me on the lonely mountain side, even in the neighbourhood of the forts.

I was hunting butterflies, and it was always a good introduction with which to go to anyone who was watching me with suspicion. Quite frankly, with my sketchbook in hand, I would ask innocently whether he had seen such-and-such a butterfly in the

* MAAS, 78–88.

neighbourhood, as I was anxious to catch one. Ninety-nine out of a hundred did not know one butterfly from another – any more than I do – so one was on fairly safe ground in that way, and they thoroughly sympathized with the mad Englishman who was hunting these insects.

They did not look sufficiently closely into the sketches of butterflies to notice that the delicately drawn veins of the wings were exact representations, in plan, of their own fort, and that the spots on the wings denoted the number and position of guns and their different calibres.

Some examples of secret sketches of fortresses which have been used with success are shown on the following pages:

This sketch of a butterfly contains the outline of a fortress, and marks both the position and power of the guns. The marks on the wings between the lines mean nothing, but those on the lines show the nature and size of the guns, according to the key below. The marks of the wings reveal the shape of the fortress shown here and the size of the guns.

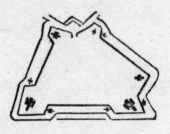

FORTRESS GUNS.
FIELD GUNS.
MACHINE GUNS.

The position of each gun is at the place inside the outline of the fort on the butterfly where the line marked with the spot ends. The head of the butterfly points towards the north.

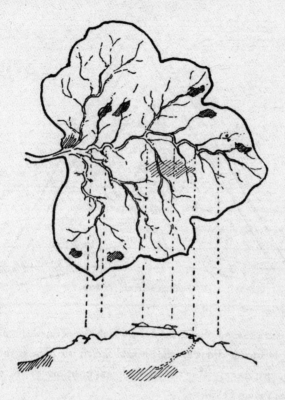

A smart piece of spy-work. Veins on an ivy leaf show the outline of the fort as seen looking west (point of the leaf indicates north).

Shows 'dead ground', where there is shelter from fire.

Shows where big guns are mounted if a vein points to them.

° ° Shows machine guns.

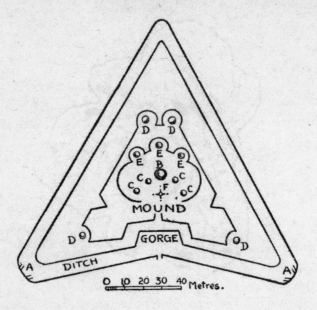

Here is another of the methods by which I concealed the plans of the forts I made. First of all, I would sketch the plan as shown in the picture above, giving the strength and positions of the various guns as shown below:

a. Kaponiers with machine guns.

b. 15-cm gun cupola.

c. 12-cm gun cupolas.

d. Q-F disappearing guns.

e. Howitzer cupolas.

f. Searchlight.

Having done this, I would consider the best method of concealing my plans. In this case it was decided to transform the sketch into that of a stained-glass window, and if you will carefully examine the picture above you will see how successfully this has been done. Certain of the decorations signify the sizes and positions of the guns. These signs are given below, together with their meaning.

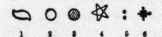

1. 15-cm gun.
2. Howitzers.
3. Q-F disappearing guns.
4. 12-cm guns.
5. Machine guns.
6. Searchlight.

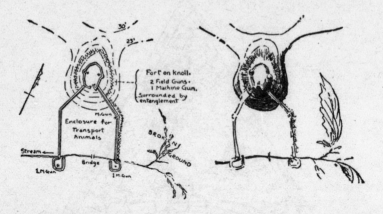

Another example of this method of making secret plans is shown here.

This sketch was made, giving all the particulars that I wanted. I then decided to bury it in such a way that it could not be recognized as a fortress plan if I were caught by the military authorities. One idea which occurred to me was to make it into the doorway of a cathedral or church, but I finally decided on the sketch of the moth's head. Underneath in my notebook I wrote the following words: 'Head of Dula moth as seen through a magnifying glass. Caught 19.5.12. Magnified about six times size of life' (meaning scale of 6 inches to the mile).

> *I do not suggest Nature study as a form of worship or as a substitute for*
> *religion, but I advocate the understanding of Nature as a step, in certain*
> *cases, towards gaining religion.*
>
> RTS, 178

Posing as an artist*

A map had been sent me by my superiors of a mountainous district in which it had been stated that three forts had recently been
built. It was only known generally what was the situation of these
forts, and no details had been secured as to their size or arma-
ment.

On arriving at the only town in the neighbourhood, my first
few days were spent strolling about looking generally at the mountains amongst which the forts were supposed to be. I had meantime made the acquaintance through my innkeeper of one or two
local sportsmen of the place, and I inquired among them as to the
possibilities of partridge or other shooting among the mountains
when the season came on.

I told them that I enjoyed camping out for a few days at a time
in such country for sketching and shooting purposes. I asked as to
the possibilities of hiring tents and mules to carry them, and a
good muleteer was recommended to me, who knew the whole of
the countryside, and could tell me all the likely spots that there
were for camping grounds.

Eventually I engaged him to take me for a day or two in

* MAAS, 108–12.

exploring the neighbourhood, with a view to fixing on camping grounds and seeing the view. We went for a considerable distance along a splendid high road which led up into the mountains. As we got into the high parts he suggested that we should leave the road and clamber down into the ravine, along which we could go for some distance and then re-ascend and rejoin the road higher up.

He then explained that this was a military road, and that it would be desirable to leave it for a space in order to avoid the guard-house upon it, where a sentry was posted with orders to allow no one beyond that point.

We successfully evaded the guard-house according to his direction, and eventually found ourselves on the road again, in a position well up towards the top of the ridge, but on our left as we progressed up the road was a steep minor ridge which we presently proceeded to ascend.

When we were near the top he said to me with a knowing grin:

'Now if you look over there, you will see before you exactly what you want.'

And as I looked over I found below me one of the new forts. It was exactly what I wanted to see spread before my eyes like a map. I simply had to take a bird's-eye view of it to get its complete plan.

Beyond it on another ridge lay another fort, and almost behind me I could see part of the third, while beyond and above were still more forts up on the heights. I had got into a regular nest of them. My position on the ridge gave me a splendid view of mountains and referring to them I said:

'Yes, indeed, you have brought me to exactly the right spot.'

But he grinned again maliciously, pointing down to the fort, and said:

'Yes, but that is the best view of all, I think.'

He seemed to grasp my intentions most fully. Far below the forts lay the straits which they were designed to protect for the vessels steaming through them. I started at once to make a sketch of the panorama, carefully omitting that ground where the forts lay, partly in order to disarm my friend's suspicions, and partly to protect me in the event of my arrest.

Presently my companion volunteered to go down to the fort and bring up his brother, who, he said, was a gunner stationed there, and could give me every detail that I could wish about their guns.

This sounded almost too good to be true, but with the greatest indifference I said I should be glad to see him, and off went my friend. The moment that he was out of sight I took care to move off into a neighbouring *kopje* where I could hide myself in case of his bringing up a force of men to capture me.

From here I was able to make a pretty accurate sketch of the fort and its gun emplacements on the inside of the lining of my hat, and when I had replaced this I went on as hurriedly as possible with my sketch to show that I had been fully occupied during the guide's absence.

Presently I saw him returning, but as he was only accompanied by one other man, I crept down again to my original position and received them smilingly.

The gunner was most communicative, and told me all about his guns and their sizes and what were their powers as regards range and accuracy. He told me that once a year an old vessel that was about to be broken up was towed along behind a steamer down the straits to afford a target to the defence forts as she passed on. He said regretfully:

'We are number three fort, and so far, no vessel has ever successfully passed one and two; they always get sunk, before they reach us,' and he gave me the exact range and the number of rounds fired, which showed that their shooting was pretty good.

Many other details I found out as to the number of the men, their feeding and hospital arrangements; and a few days later I was able to take myself home with a good stock of valuable information and the good wishes and hopes of my various friends that I some day would return to shoot the partridges. But I am certain that one man was not taken in by my professions, either as an artist or as a sportsman, and that was the muleteer.

One pair of trained eyes is as good as a dozen pairs untrained.

ATS, 3

Tea and a Turk*

Reports had got about that some wonderful new guns had been installed in one of the forts on the Bosphorus and that a great deal of secrecy was observed in their being put up. It became my duty to go and find out any particulars about them.

My first day in Constantinople was spent under the guidance

* MAAS, 131–4; LVL, 118–19.

of an American lady in seeing the sights of the city, and when we had visited almost all the usual resorts for tourists she asked whether there was anything else that I wanted to see, and to a certain extent I let her into my confidence when I told her that I would give anything to see the inside of one of these forts, if it were possible.

She at once said she would be delighted to take me to see her old friend Hamid Pasha, who was quartered in one of them and was always willing to give her and her friends a cup of tea.

When we arrived at the gate of the fort the sentry and the officer in charge would on no account allow us to pass until the lady said that she was a friend of the Pasha, when we were at once admitted and passed to his quarters.

He was a charming host, and received us with the greatest kindness, and after showing us his own quarters and the many curiosities he had collected he took us all round the fort and pointed out its ancient and modern devices for defence, and finally showed us its guns. Two of these, in a somewhat prominent position where they could easily be seen from outside, were covered with canvas covers. My excitement naturally grew intense when I saw these, and I secretly begged the lady to persuade him to allow us to look at them, and he at once acquiesced, thinking I was an American, and, grinning all over his face, said, 'These are our very latest development.'

I almost trembled as the covers were drawn off, and then I recognized guns, truly of a modern make but not very new nor powerful, and then he gave away the whole secret by saying: 'These are the same old guns that have been here for years, but we thought it advisable, in view of some moves by a certain neighbouring power, to let them suppose that we had re-armed ourselves with something very new and very formidable, and therefore we are letting it be known that we are keeping these guns a dead secret and covered from view of any spies.'

Don't let your patriotism be so narrow as to count your own country as the only pebble on the beach. Recognize that there are other nations too, all with their good points, and with their interests and ambitions. Aim to be good friends with them and to co-operate rather than hinder their wishes. What we want in the world is peace, happiness and prosperity for all. And we can get it if all men become friends instead of rivals.

Baden-Powell's Broadcast to America (6 July 1937), in *Jamboree*,

October 1937

*The forts on the Dardanelles**

On another occasion it fell to my lot to inspect some of the defences of the Dardanelles, and I found this could best be done from the seaward. This involved my taking passage in an old grain steamer running between Odessa and Liverpool, and my voyage in her was one of the most charming and original that it has been my lot to take.

A tramp steamer loaded down with grain until its cargo is almost running out of the ventilators is – contrary to all expectations – quite a comfortable boat for cruising in. The Captain and his wife lived in comfortable cabins amidships under the bridge;

* MAAS, 134–5; LVL, 118.

the after deck was stocked with pigs and chickens, which fed liberally on the cargo. The Captain's good lady was a Scotch woman, and therefore an excellent cook and a motherly hostess.

Everything was most clean and comfortable, and the Captain most thoroughly entered into my various schemes for observing and examining the defences of the coast as we went along.

He allowed me practically to take command of the ship as regards her course and anchoring. From side to side of the Dardanelles we wandered, and when we came abreast of one of the forts that needed study we anchored ship and lowered a boat for me to go 'fishing'.

This erratic procedure naturally invited investigation, and several times he was visited by patrol boats from the forts, telling him to clear out. He drew their attention to loud hammering going on in the bowels of the ship, informing them that his engines had broken down, and so soon as these were mended he would gladly get on his way again; meantime could they advise his nephew in the boat yonder what was the best bait to use for fish; his 'nephew' meantime being busy angling in another sense of the word, that is by observing the different types of the guns employed and sketching their position and the radius of fire allowed to take them by the splay of their embrasures; also we took soundings where necessary and made sketch maps of possible landing places for attacking or other purposes.

Have a place for everything and have everything in its place. If you are not sure which is the right place for a thing, think, 'Where, if I wanted it, should I go to look for it?' That place is the right one.

GG, 156

Playing the Game

*Hoodwinking a Turkish sentry**

A big new Turkish fort had been recently built, and my business was to get some idea of its plan and construction. From my inn in the town I sauntered out early one morning before sunrise, hoping to find no sentries awake, so that I could take the necessary angles and pace the desired bases in order to plot in a fairly accurate plan of it.

To some extent I had succeeded when I noticed among the sand-hills another fellow looking about, and, it seemed to me, trying to dodge me. This was rather ominous, and I spent some of my time trying to evade this 'dodger', imagining that he was necessarily one of the guard attempting my capture.

In evading him, unfortunately, I exposed myself rather more than usual to view from the fort, and presently was challenged by one of the sentries. I did not understand his language, but I could understand his gesture well enough when he presented his rifle and took deliberate aim at me. This induced me to take cover as quickly as might be behind a sand-hill, where I sat down and waited for a considerable time to allow the excitement to cool down.

Presently, who should I see creeping round the corner of a neighbouring sand-hill, but my friend the 'dodger'! It was too late to avoid him, and the moment he saw me he appeared to wish to go away rather than to arrest me. We then recognized that we were mutually afraid of each other, and therefore came together with a certain amount of diffidence on both sides.

* MAAS, 123–6.

However, we got into conversation, in French, and I very soon found that, although representatives of different nationalities, we were both at the same game of making a plan of the fort. We therefore joined forces, and behind a sand-hill we compared notes as to what information we had already gained, and then devised a little plan by which to complete the whole scheme.

My friend took his place in a prominent position with his back to the fort and commenced to smoke, with every appearance of indifference to the defence work behind him. This was meant to catch the sentry's eye and attract his attention while I did some creeping and crawling and got round the other side of the work, where I was able to complete our survey in all its details.

It was late that night when we met in the 'dodger's' bedroom, and we made complete tracings and finished drawings, each of us taking his own copy for his own headquarters. A day or two later we took a steamer together for Malta, where we were to part on our respective homeward journeys – he on his way back to Italy.

As we both had a day or two to wait at Malta, I acted as host to him during his stay. As we entered the harbour I pointed out to him the big 110-ton guns which at that time protected the entrance, and were visible to anybody with two eyes in his head. I pointed out various other interesting batteries to him which were equally obvious, but I omitted to mention other parts which would have been of greater interest to him.

He came away from Malta, however, with the idea that, on the whole, he had done a good stroke of business for his Government going there, and convinced of his luck by getting hold of a fairly simple thing in the shape of myself to show him around.

Playing the Game

Play fair yourself and insist on fair play in others.

SFB, DE, 224

Shot as a spy*

I have now nothing more to add about spying, because I was apparently eventually caught and shot as a spy during the Great War.

The following is the complete account of my death as reported in the American press.

The first intimation of it was the following cable: 'Sunday papers report Baden-Powell shot in Tower London as German spy upon return from Germany. Was caught with maps of fortifications which he was trying to dispose of to the enemy. Mr Walterbury, returning to Pittsburgh, tells of the above knowledge gleaned from brother, an English officer who was present at the trial and saw him shot to death.'

The press account of the unhappy episode reads as follows:

BADEN POWELL SHOT AS A SPY.
January 15th, 1916. Pittsburgh, Pa.

Shot to death by English soldiers on his return to England as a German spy.
That is what happened to Major-General Robert Stephenson Smyth Baden-Powell, hero of the defence of Mafeking in the Boer War, and organ-

* LVL, 124–7.

izer of the Boy Scouts, when he went back to London and was caught with papers in his possession, showing maps of Great Britain's fortifications that he is said to have been selling to the enemy of England. — This statement is made by a man who says he is a Britisher and that the execution was witnessed by his brother.

'My story is a true one,' he declared to-night. 'I can tell you nothing else. My brother saw the execution with his own eyes. My brother explained that Baden-Powell marched to his place of execution without a quiver, and, as the cover was being placed over his eyes, said only these words: "May God have mercy." If reports be true, and I am sure that my brother is to be relied upon, England has put into his last sleep one of the bravest soldiers who ever headed her armies in foreign lands.'

It was really worth being shot as a spy to gain so sweet an epitaph as that.

Apropos this slight mix-up of my nationality the case is rather on a par with that of my being burned in effigy by the factory girls of a Scottish city on the night of the relief of Mafeking — just an awkward little case of mistaken identity between President Kruger[3] and myself.

I have, however, quite recently had a possible explanation of this from General Smuts,[4] who told me that after the Boer War an old back-veldt Boer at Rustenburg said he was a bit confused in his mind as to the relationship between 'Oom Pole' (Kruger) and one called 'Baden Pole'.

I don't happen to have been in Germany during the War although I have been assured on good authority that I was there.

Playing the Game

A naval officer, for instance, told me only recently that he had escorted me home during the War when I came from Norway. He knew the name of the ship that I had travelled in (one that I had never heard of myself) and that his patrol boat took special care to prevent my being captured or torpedoed *en route*.

The German Staff also knew that I was in Germany and issued some special orders for my capture.

I think the foundation for these rumours may probably have lain in our War Office, where sometimes it was found useful to start a hare to see whether and how far confidential information leaked out.

Quick disguise*

A tremendous lot of your success in spying naturally turns on the disguise adopted. I don't mean by that merely the actual theatrical 'makeup', but the ability to assume a totally different character from your own and also the repression of any little mannerisms you may happen to have, or the adoption of some special one for the occasion. This may mean a limp in your walk, a habit of sniffing, a croaky voice, etc.

A very important point in your makeup is to alter your appearance as seen from behind.

I was at one time under the surveillance of a detective who changed his appearance each day; one day he was a soldierly-looking man; the next an invalid with a patch over his eye; and so

* LVL, 127–8.

on; but I recognized him as being the same man when I watched him from behind, and saw him walk.

Sometimes it may be necessary to make a quick change of appearance as I have had to do more than once.

You know how, when you are addressing a man, you notice his necktie more than anything else — and probably his hat.

I was interviewed one day* by a newspaper man at a railway station. A few minutes after the ordeal I found myself close to my interviewer in the crowd, where he was re-telling the incident to a brother journalist who was also anxious to find me — and I was not anxious to be found.

'He is down there in one of the last carriages of the train. You will know him at once. He is wearing a green hat, a red tie, and a blue serge suit.'

Fortunately I had a grey overcoat on my arm, in the pocket of which was my travelling cap and comforter. Diving into the waiting room I effected a quick change into these, crammed my hat into my pocket, and tottered back, with an invalid's shuffle, to my carriage. I re-entered it under the nose of the waiting reporter without being suspected, and presently had the pleasure of being carried away before him unassailed.

Besides making your body strong you've got to make your mind clever. The first step is to let nothing escape your notice and, when you have seen or felt or smelt, to put this and that together.

ATM, 131

* LVL, 127–8; MAAS, 31–3.

Playing the Game

*The value of hide-and-seek**

The game of Hide-and-Seek is really one of the best games for a boy, and can be elaborated until it becomes scouting in the field. It teaches you a lot.

I was strongly addicted to it as a child, and the craft learned in that innocent field of sport has stood me in good stead in many a critical time since. To lie flat in a furrow among the currant bushes when I had not time to reach the neighbouring box bushes before the pursuer came in sight taught me the value of not using the most obvious cover, since it would at once be searched. The hunters went at once to the box bushes as the likely spot, while I could watch their doings from among the stems of the currant bushes.

Often I have seen hostile scouts searching the obvious bits of cover, but they did not find me there; and, like the elephant hunter among the fern trees, or a boar in a cotton crop, so a boy in the currant bushes is invisible to the enemy, while he can watch every move of the enemy's legs.

This I found of value when I came to be pursued by mounted military police, who suspected me of being a spy at some manoeuvres abroad.[5] After a rare chase I scrambled over a wall and dropped into an orchard of low fruit trees. Here, squatting in a ditch, I watched the legs of the gendarmes' horses while they quartered the plantation, and when they drew away from me I crept to the bank of a deep water channel which formed one of the boundaries of the enclosure. Here I found a small plank bridge by

* MAAS, 91–3.

which I could cross, but before doing so I loosened the near end, and passed over, dragging the plank after me.

On the far side the country was open, and before I had gone far the gendarmes spied me, and after a hurried consultation, dashed off at a gallop for the nearest bridge, half a mile away. I promptly turned back, replaced my bridge and re-crossed the stream, throwing the plank into the river, and made my way past the village to the next station down the line while the horsemen were still hunting for me in the wrong place.

There is no pleasure that comes near to that of preparing your own meal over your little fire of wood embers at the end of the day, and no scent like the smell of that fire.

There is no view like that from your lair on the woodland hill-side. And there is no sleep like that in the open with a warm blanket or a good thickness of paper beneath you.

RTS, 121

To hide in the open*

It is quite possible for a hider, if he is clever and properly dressed, to hide himself out in the open. When I say properly dressed, I mean that if he has clothes that are the colour of the ground about him, he can by sitting perfectly still escape notice of his pursuers. Even a soldier in red, if he stands against a red wall, is not noticeable at a short distance, provided that he keeps still.

* OWF, 50; MC, 93; ATS, 44.

But if he goes and walks about in a green field, of course you would spot him at once a mile away.

I have myself sat on a hill-side along a lot of stones and rocks dressed in khaki, which was of the same colour, and so long as I did not move I was in full sight of the enemy and yet unseen by them. I noticed that after I had been on the sick list and resumed my scouting expeditions, the enemy caught sight of me much more quickly than they used to, though I took just as much care, and remained just as motionless; and I then came to the conclusion that this was due to the fact that I had, in accordance with the doctor's advice, taken to wearing a flannel cummerbund wound round my waist – and the only flannel at that time procurable was of a brilliant red. This was what caught their eye.

Searching for water*

I was once acting as scout for a party in a desert country where we were getting done up from want of water. I had gone out two or three miles ahead to where I thought the ground seemed to slope slightly downwards, but except a very shallow dry watercourse, there was no sign of water. As I was making my way slowly back again, I noticed a scratching in the sand, evidently recently made by a buck, and the sand thrown up was of a darker colour, therefore, damper, than that on the surface.

I thought to myself that the buck would not scratch there for nothing, so, I dismounted and scooped up more with my hands,

* ATS, 32–3; MC, 332–3.

and found the undersoil quite moist, so water was evidently near and could probably be got by digging. In fact a little deeper the water began to ooze in.

But at that moment two pigeons sprang up, and flew away from under a rock near by; full of hope, I went to the spot, and found there a small pool of water, which yielded sufficient for the immediate requirements of the party.

Had I not noticed the buck-scratching or the pigeons flying up, we should have had a painful toil of many miles more before we struck on the river which we eventually did come to.

The open-air is the real objective of Scouting and the key to its success.

Aids, WB, 70

Tracking*

From all that I have been saying about Observation you can probably realize how all-important for scouting is the art of tracking.

It has been said that scouting without tracking is like bread and butter without the bread. With a scout tracking becomes habitual; subconsciously he is looking for and reading signs all the time even when engaged in other things.

Scouting is an art which you can go on practising for ever, and though you keep improving you seldom reach the acme achieved by native trackers, like those in the Sudan or the bushmen in

* LVL, 134–5.

South Africa, who are brought up to it from infancy, using tracks as their newspaper in hunting and in war.

Even more important is the ability to read the meaning of the tracks.

When I went scouting with Fred Burnham[6] he was quicker than I in noticing 'a sign', but in pointing it out to me he would say: 'Here, Sherlock, what do you make of it?'

I was sent to join a column on the march in Matabeleland, and riding along with the Commanding Officer I noticed the fresh tracks of natives, evidently moving in our neighbourhood. These became so intriguing that I asked the Colonel whether his scouts had brought in any information. He replied that he had no scouts out, as it wasn't worth tiring men and horses in the country where no enemy were visible.

I was horrified and assured him that if he did not see them he would in a very short time feel them, since as far as I could see they were all round us.

Mercifully they did not attack us and later I found from this *impi*,[7] when it surrendered, that they had allowed the column to go through that part of the country undisturbed because they did not want to draw attention to their presence there where they were getting good feeding; but, having seen the column wandering about with its Commander riding in front, they had given him the nickname as 'The bellwether[8] leading his flock'.

I know nothing more enjoyable or more cheering and health-giving than a good old tramp every weekend.

RTS, 118

Example of practice in deduction[*]

A simple deduction from signs noticed in my work one morning on a stormy mountain path in Kashmir.

Signs observed: tree-stump, about three feet high, by the path. A stone about the size of a coconut lying near it, to which were sticking some bits of bruised walnut rinds dried up. Some walnut rind also lying on the stump. Farther along the path, thirty yards to the south of the stump, were lying bits of walnut shell of four walnuts. Close by was a high sloping rock, alongside the path. The only walnut tree in sight was 150 yards north of the stump.

At the foot of the stump was a cake of hardened mud which showed the impression of a grass shoe.

What would you make out from those signs? My solution of it was this:

A man had gone southward on a long journey along the path two days ago carrying a load and had rested at the rock while he ate walnuts.

My deductions were these:

It was a man carrying a load, because carriers when they want to rest do not sit down, but rest their load against a sloping rock and lean back. Had he had no load, he would probably have sat down on the stump, but he preferred to go thirty yards farther to where the rock was. Women do not carry loads there, so it was a man. He broke the shells of his walnuts on the tree-stump with the stone having brought them from the tree 150 yards north — so he was travelling south. He was on a long journey, as he was

[*] SFB, 165.

wearing shoes, and not going barefooted, as he would be if only strolling near his home. Three days ago there was rain, the cake of mud had been picked up while the ground was still wet – but it had not been since rained upon, and was now dry. The walnut rind was all dry, and confirmed the time that had elapsed.

There is no important story attached to this, but it is just an example of everyday practice.

Nothing is impossible, except putting the tooth paste back into the tube.

Quoted in letter to Heather, 11

*Scouting by night**

A great part of one's scouting work was done by night. This again is an art which requires a lot of practice such as we seldom get at home. Personally I believe that I have done more work by night than by day when on active service, and certainly when engaged in scouting.

For one thing, in Matabeleland and Zululand at any rate, one had to make one's way very close to the enemy's positions under cover of darkness, and then go into hiding during daylight where one could watch the enemy's proceedings unobserved, getting away again after nightfall.

It often followed that one had then to guide a column by night and to get it into position for an attack by daybreak. One felt a

* LVL, 137.

horrid lot of responsibility on one's shoulders when doing this lest one should take a wrong line or lead the whole body into an ambush.

Such leading needs every ounce of concentration one can put into it. I was not constitutionally rude but I was never so rude to anybody in my life as when one young officer, thinking I looked lonely walking along by myself, came up with me and, meaning well, started a merry and bright conversation. My response was not courteous and he fell back to his place feeling a little hurt.

Landmarks by night are very different from those by day, and that is a thing that a beginner does not realize. Then there are those infallible guides the stars, infallible until the important night when they are invariably covered by clouds; and then you thank goodness that you made notes of landmarks as well.

> *The attitude of the Scoutmaster is of greatest importance, since his boys take their characters very much from him; it is incumbent upon him, therefore, to take the wider view of his position than a merely personal one, and to be prepared to sink his own feelings very much for the good of the whole. That is true discipline.*
>
> SFB (26th), 298

Out-scouted by a girl*

I was taken down a peg in my boasted tracking by a young lady in England. She was the daughter of the late Lord Meath. As we

* LVL, 135–6.

were walking in the gardens of Sion House she suddenly pointed to footprints on the path and asked what they meant.

I said indulgently: 'A common or garden cat has recently passed this way.'

'Yes, even I could tell that,' she replied, 'but I can further tell what was the colour of the cat – can you?'

Thus put on my mettle I set to work to examine any twig or spray that might have caught a hair from the animal, much on the principle by which Zadig[9] was able to say that a roan horse of sixteen hands high had passed through a wood.

But search as I would I could find no clue that would indicate the colour of that cat. My companion looked at the track again closely, and said, 'Yes, I am not mistaken. It was a light tortoiseshell cat.'

I also looked more searchingly on the ground but it gave back no helpful sign. At long last I confessed myself beaten. 'Now how did you arrive at the colour?' I asked. 'I saw the cat,' she replied.

If you stick to it pluckily and say, 'What does a little irritation matter – I'm going to stick it out and make the best of it and will show those weak-kneed girls their duty,' they will follow your lead.

Remember they look to you to see what they ought to do. If you grumble, they will do the same. If you put a grin on and say, 'Never mind disappointments: I am going to make a success of it,' they will do the same.

From a letter written in 1931 to his daughter Betty, then aged
fourteen and a Patrol Leader.

The Adventures of My Life

NOTES

1 In the Bible, a notorious liar who fell dead together with his wife when Peter the Apostle rebuked him (Acts 5: 1–10).

2 'Common sense is as rare as genius' (R. W. Emerson, 1803–82, *Essays*).

3 Paul Kruger (1825–1904), President of Transvaal from 1883 to 1900 and political leader of the Boers during the war against Britain, was affectionately known by his own people as 'Oom Paul'.

4 Jan Christian Smuts (1870–1950), South African general and statesman, was one of the young Boer commanders in the Boer War and played a role in the peace of 1902. Then, having reconciled himself with the British, he became one of the leading personalities of the Empire. He was twice (1919–24 and 1939–48) Prime Minister of the Union of South Africa.

5 This happened at the Austrian military manoeuvres at Schwarzenau. The date was 30 August 1892.

6 A well-known American scout, whom B.-P. met and worked with during the Matabele campaign (see below, p. 165).

7 A Zulu word meaning a large force of Zulu or native warriors. See also below, p. 131.

8 The leading sheep of a flock on whose neck a bell is hung. The term is also used to mean a leader of a foolish, sheeplike crowd.

9 A reference to the well-known example of deduction in Voltaire's *Zadig* (1747), quoted by B.-P. in WCH, 85–6.

7. First Steps in Soldiering

Scouting comes in very useful in any kind of life you like to take up, whether it is soldiering or business life in a city.

SFB, OFP, 1st, and YFBS, 35 and 39

*Oxford declines me and I enter the Army**

From Charterhouse I had gone to Oxford, but my learning was apparently not considered of sufficient merit to admit me to Balliol or Christ Church, where I desired to go. My hopes were in vain and I had for the time to take up my position as an unattached member.

* LVL, 142 and IM, 3–4.

Within a few days of my joining I went up for the Army examination to test my possibilities in that line, but without any special hope of passing in my first attempt. Indeed I took the whole thing airily as a trial canter over the course.

A few weeks after the examination, I was on board the *Gertrude*, a yacht belonging to Professor Acland, Regius Professor of Medicine at Oxford, an old friend of my father's. One of the guests on board was the Dean of Christ Church, who accosted me one morning with the news that, according to the newspaper, a namesake of mine had passed his exam for the Army. And there, in black and white, was my own name!

To my astonishment I found that I had passed, and not only passed but that I was very near the top of the list. I had gone in for both examinations, for cavalry and for infantry, and I had come out unaccountably high up in each. I did not know then, and I have not been able since to imagine how this came about. I can only suppose that the examiners must have misread my examination index-number, and that some other clever young fellow is now eking out a precarious existence as an author or a play-actor, who ought really to have been in the position occupied by myself. But such is life, and I do not regret it.

Instructions, and especially orders, are apt to have different and even opposite effects with boys. Order a boy not to smoke and he is at once tempted to try it as an adventure; but give him the example, show him that any fool can smoke but a wise Scout doesn't, and it is another matter.

HQG, July 1910 (rep. BPO, 15–16)

Playing the Game

*Arrival in India**

Successful candidates were all drafted to Sandhurst for a two years' course of instruction before actually joining the Army, but by some strange luck the first six were excused this preliminary and were at once gazetted to regiments. Thus, although I left Charterhouse only in June, I had my commission in September and was in India, a full-blown officer of the 13th Hussars, in November.

I can remember to this day the smell of India which assailed our nostrils before we had set foot ashore at the Apollo Bunder, and, though it is very many years ago, I can well remember the bother which my companion and I had in getting our baggage safely ashore, loaded on to a bullock-wagon and conveyed from the docks to the hotel. We had donned our best uniforms and were not a little proud of ourselves in the early part of the day; but as hour followed hour in that soggy heat we seemed to melt into the thick tight-bound cloth, and we wished we had something more seasonable to wear. By nightfall we were dog-tired and our pride had all leaked out, and under the cover of darkness we willingly climbed up on to the pile of baggage on our bullock-cart and allowed ourselves to be ignominiously carried through the back streets of Bombay to the hotel.

Sink personal ambition. Be prepared to take such a place as duty directs.

Letter expressing the Principles of Life, 1902,
quoted in BPBB (9 May)

* IM, 13.

*The cholera belt**

I was lucky enough to make a success of my very first parade, the day after I joined, and in this wise. My troop was ordered to parade in close rank, and I was given by my Captain the simple task of walking round to inspect the men and to see that each of them was wearing a cholera belt. Shirts were thrown open and I walked down the front rank, finding each man dressed as he should be. As I turned at the end to come up the rear rank with my eyes downcast from sheer shyness at commanding a parade, I just caught with the tail of my eye a movement at the opposite end of the troop, as a man stepped from the rear rank into the front rank which I had just examined.

I only knew the name of one man in the troop at that time, because he had been detailed to bring me my horse, and this happened to be the man who stepped across. I took no notice of the move, as I had to debate in my mind whether or not it might be a bit of orthodox drill that, when the officer arrived at the rear rank, one of its number should step into the front rank. As I passed along the rear rank examining their belts I pondered the matter over, and came to the conclusion that I would risk matters and call this man out.

On arriving at the front again, I called:

'Private Ramsbotham, step to the front. Have you got your cholera belt on?' There was a blushing, confused reply of, 'No, sir.' I did not punish him, as I was not clear what powers of punishment I had; but I said, with much fear and great gruffness, 'Take

* QTW, 5–7.

care you don't allow it to occur again' and dismissed him. But the punishment which he afterwards got from his own comrades in the way of jeers at being caught out by a freshly-joined subaltern was far heavier for him to bear than any that I could have inflicted.

Insist on discipline and strict obedience. Let [the boys] run riot only when you give leave for it, which is a good thing to do every now and then.

SFB, OFP (28th), and Aids, WB, 51

A soothsayer's method*

Once I had a lot of money stolen out of my bungalow. I thought it must have been done by one of my servants.

I had lost three hundred rupees, which had been stowed in a bag in a cupboard in my room. None of the servants knew anything about it when asked, but it was obvious that no stranger could have come in without their knowledge, so instead of sending for the police I called in the assistance of one who is far more dreaded by natives – that is, the soothsayer. In this case the test they had to go through was for them to chew a handful of rice, but without swallowing it. Then, when the soothsayer gave the order, after a couple of minutes' chewing, every man spat out his mouthful on to his plate and the medicine man went round and examined each mouthful. If it was wet from the chewing the

* MSK, 126–8; IM, 284–5.

owner of it was judged to be innocent; but if it was dry in spite of the chewing that chewer was guilty.

In my case, however, the soothsayer said that as a first step he would have a prayer meeting of the servants in one of their houses to implore the deity to explain what had become of the money, and if he could not tell them the soothsayer himself would apply the ordeal which could not fail to show the delinquent. The prayer meeting, however, decided the case. The soothsayer presently came to me and said that their God had made it manifest that I was bringing a false charge. The servants were all loyal to me; the money had never been stolen but was there in the house. It was probable that some mischievous *jinn*, or devil, had come in the night and had transferred my money from the cupboard into my gun case, where I should now find it.

This was a place where I never had my money, but I looked – and there it was! Of course, the thief, whoever he was, had feared the ordeal when he heard it was to come off, and had quietly replaced the money in this odd place and had bribed the soothsayer. The latter, therefore, went away the richer by a double fee – one from me and the other from the grateful servants, with whom he had connived.

But now, how could chewing rice show up a guilty man? Well, I don't know that I am right, but I think it is this way. When a man is in an awful funk, his mouth gets dry, he is unable to moisten the rice in his mouth because the saliva won't come and wet it.

Knowledge without character is mere pie-crust.

Jamboree, July 1921

Playing the Game

Officers' ragging[*]

In India, as elsewhere, ragging breaks the monotony of existence, especially for the victim. A fellow seldom gets ragged without having given some cause for it; either he is dirty and wants washing, or he has got some characteristic which needs toning down. I got plenty of it and I know how good it was for me. I have often heard it spoken of by outsiders as bullying, but personally I have never known it take that line.

I remember a horrid game we had at the School of Musketry at Hythe. Certain of us formed ourselves into a fire brigade for the purpose of saving life in the event of a conflagration, and we took every opportunity of keeping ourselves fit for work by practice. As soon as we saw a party of officers comfortably settled to whist[1] in the ante-room after mess, or congenially playing billiards together, a cry of 'Fire!' was raised, and immediately one party detailed for catching the victim rushed out and took up position below the mess-room window, while the second party as rescuers, shouting 'Smith's on fire!' would rush and seize Smith from amongst his friends and carry him to the window and throw him out, to be caught by those below. In the many times that we did it, it only happened once that we threw a man out of the wrong window. The party were waiting for him at the next; they got nothing and he got a bad fall. But we were not a bit sympathetic, beyond explaining to him that it was our mistake and not his.

A new and original game was introduced into the mess by a brother of our Colonel who came to stay with him. We believed

[*] IM, 166–170; RTS, 70.

him to be a quiet, harmless planter from Bihar,[2] and so he seemed throughout the evening both during and after dinner, when he remained watching us playing the fool in various ways for our own amusement. But evidently our ways did not strike him as original, and he therefore invited us to play the great game of 'The Bounding Brothers of the Bosphorus' and when he had once shown us we joined most heartily in the sport. The game had few rules about it, but a certain amount of etiquette. The apparatus required was that all the furniture should be piled in a heap about the centre of the floor and a writing table placed a couple of yards from it. You were expected then to clap your hands three times, that was the etiquette of the game, then run at the table and turn head over heels on it on to the pile of furniture, shouting as you did so: 'I am a bounding brother of the Bosphorus!' That was all. Quite simple, but how it hurt when you landed on the upturned leg of a chair or the side of a table!

Good humour is as catching as the measles.

WSCD, 142

The ways of snakes*

Snakes are one of the great drawbacks to life in India in the rainy season. They get swamped out of their holes then and are apt to prefer a dry house to a wet garden. Often too in the summer, when

* IM, 226–8.

everything is baking hot, they like to slide into the cool, wet bathroom and lie alongside your tub. If they were harmless it would not matter, but so many of them are nasty poisonous fellows. The hooded cobra is common, and so is the krait, a little thin chap of active habits. He has a pleasant way of lying stretched out perfectly straight along the edge of a rug, so that you don't notice him till you step on him as you are going to bed! He is very clever at climbing up a door, wriggling up between a half-open door and the door-post until he gets to the top, and there he stretches himself out along the top of the door and falls out on to you when you shut it!

There was a great hubbub one evening, and one of my grooms was brought into the house to be doctored. He had put his hand into a hole in the wall where he kept his horse-brush and had been bitten by a cobra who was lying in there; an immense cobra, judging from the pain of the bite. To cut and suck the wound was the work of a moment for me — except that I got somebody else to do the sucking. Then I reluctantly got out my treasured bottle of old brandy and poured some of it down his throat and had him walked up and down with orders that he must be heartily smacked and kept awake at any cost. More brandy was administered and the result was that instead of showing any signs of dying he got into the singing stage, and then became abusive, and finally wanted to fight any man, black or white, who would care to face him.

As he seemed now in a promising condition for living, we left him and sallied out to find the snake. We jabbed and pried the bale without result, and finally, after rigorous search, we discovered a little scorpion there which had been the cause of all the trouble. The subsequent smacking which that groom got was not entirely meant to save his life, but in some sort to get a return for the bottle of brandy lost to me and for the trouble and anxiety he had caused.

> *Discipline is not gained by punishing a child for a bad habit, but by substituting a better occupation that will absorb his attention and gradually lead him to forget and abandon the old one.*
>
> SFB, OFP (28th)

The Afghan war and the field of Maiwand*

In 1880 we were at war with the Afghans under Ayub Khan. It happened this way.

After a British expedition had taken Kabul, Abdurrahman was now made emir (1880), on condition that he remained an ally of the British; but Ayub Khan, a son of the late emir Yakub Khan, had meantime raised a force in Persia and advanced from Herat against Kandahar. A British force, consisting of about 2,500 British and native troops under General Burrows, went out to oppose him. They met near Maiwand in a heavy mist and our force was surrounded and defeated with heavy loss. In this fight 961 of our officers and men were killed and 168 were wounded or missing.

♦♦

* IM, 123–4, 134–8.

I had a very interesting three days' outing at Maiwand with a reconnoitring squadron.

A few miles from Kokoran we came across the marks of gun wheels where our guns had made their escape from the massacre. They had come round the end of a spur of mountains, which made rather a long detour, and it was said that the Afghans had come a shorter cut through the mountains and so harassed their retreat. Therefore we made a bee line for the mountains to see if we could discover the short cut, and before long we came on wheel marks, which we afterwards discovered were those of Ayub Khan's guns. Following these up we came to a pass in the mountains which the Afghans had used, but of which our people had no knowledge. It was a wonderfully picturesque, steep, rocky gorge, and as we passed through it we could see a number of ibex on the cliffs above us watching our progress. The battlefield was a big, open, sandy and stony plain, and we camped about a mile from it.

Everything was very much as it had been left after the fight. Any amount of dead horses were lying about, mummified by the sun and dry air. There had been no rain and apparently very little wind since the battle was fought, and the foot-marks and wheel tracks were perfectly clear in every direction.

Lines of empty cartridge cases showed where the heaviest fighting had taken place: wheel-tracks and hoof-marks showed where the guns had moved, dead camels and mules showed the line of the baggage train. Dead men lay in all directions; most of them had been hurriedly buried, but in many cases the graves had been dug open again by jackals. Clothes, accoutrements, preserved food, etc. were strewn all over the place. In one spot the whole of an Afghan gun team, six white horses with pink-dyed tails, had been killed in a heap by one of our shells.

The British brigade, in marching early in the morning, had sent out a reconnoitring party to visit the only watering place in the desert to the westward and this patrol had returned saying there were no enemy there. It was therefore at once assumed that no enemy were in the neighbourhood, but, as subsequently transpired, the patrol had not been to the right place and the enemy were there all the time. That morning a heavy mist hung over the plain and the Afghan army had crossed just in front of the advance of the brigade, neither party being aware of the other's presence. Our advance guard, seeing a few men retiring into the mist, had fired after them. This had brought the Afghans back to attack us.

Unknown to the British a deep ravine ran in a horse-shoe form almost entirely round the spot on which the brigade was standing. The brigade formed a square to receive the attack, expecting to see the enemy coming across the open, instead of which the Afghans poured down the ravine by thousands unseen, and then suddenly made their attack from three sides at once. Some Bombay cavalry, ordered out to charge them, swerved under their attack and charged into the rear of our own men, and the native infantry broke and ran with them through the ranks of the Berkshire Regiment, the 66th. These stuck to their post as well as they could but were driven back, and then held one position after another to cover the retreat of the remainder, but in the end were practically wiped out in doing so. They made their last stand at a long, low mud wall and ditch. It was at this spot that one of the men waved his hand cheerily to the Horse Artillery getting their guns away, and cried that historic farewell: 'Good luck to you. It's all up with the bally old Berkshires!' They were all killed here, and the shortest way of burying them was to throw down the wall on the top of them.

I had to make two maps of the battlefield for General Wilkinson and the Commander-in-Chief. The Colonel also asked me to do one for him to send to Sir Garnet Wolseley. I brought back some mementoes from the battlefield, a shell, also the hoof of a horse of E Battery, Royal Horse Artillery – it belonged to the one pulling the gun which went to the front and fired to the Afghan rearguard and so began the battle. I have also a belt stained with blood and a leaf out of Sir Garnet Wolseley's pocketbook, which was found by one of the officers.

Camping is the great point in Scouting which appeals to the boy, and the opportunity to teach him self-reliance and resourcefulness, besides giving him health.

SFB, WB, 109

The dangers of Kandahar*

Kandahar itself, which I visited many times, was a strange place and more than a trifle dangerous. All the officers and men went about armed, most officers carrying a hog-spear, some of them revolvers. I had a long stout stick with a lanyard to it, and a beautiful smile which I expected would disarm anybody! But amongst

* IM, 131–4; PYOC, 125–6.

the crowd there were very often fanatics or Ghazis who were only too anxious to stick their knives into a European, as they believed that if they were then killed in consequence of their act they would go straight to Heaven. The soldiers had to carry revolvers or bayonets when they went for a stroll. Even when a man was going only ten yards from the barrack-room to get water from the stream he would carry a drawn bayonet in his hand. It was a very necessary precaution, as the fanatics generally pounced on them without warning.

We got up a small theatrical performance, *The Pirates of Penzance*. We had no room in which to rehearse, so it had to be out of doors. But there was always the danger of the Ghazis rushing down on us at any moment with their nasty great knives, awfully unpleasant things. So each performer brought his sword with him to rehearsal, and these weapons we stuck up in the ground to mark the boundaries of our stage, and they were at the same time handy in case of an attack.

Don't expect to find any man perfect: he is bound to have defects. Any ass can see the bad points in a man. The thing is to discover his good points and keep these uppermost in your mind so that they gradually obliterate his bad ones.

The Scouter, August 1929 (rep. BPO, 128)

* IM, 150–2.

Playing the Game

*The evacuation of Kandahar**

When at last we received orders to leave Kokoran and Kandahar the 13th was ordered to form the rearguard and to parade at a certain hour so as to move off from Kokoran immediately in the rear of the infantry, but the Colonel had told me to find out the best road to follow, and I found that by one particular short cut we could save at least two hours' marching.

So he ordered the regiment to delay its departure accordingly. The General heard of this and asked his reason. When the Colonel gave it the General said that his staff officers knew the country perfectly well and would not have given the order for parade for that hour had it been possible to economize time as he suggested. The Colonel replied more politely but generally to the effect that he did not care what the staff officers' ideas to the contrary were, he knew better and proposed to rest his men and horses until the last moment: and he used my short cut accordingly, and we were exactly at the right time at the appointed place. I mention this little incident because it was from it that I date my ultimate promotion at the hands of Sir Baker Russell.

On the day we were to march from Kokoran our mounted sentries were relieved by those of the Afghan army of Abdurrahman, and it was an amusing contrast to see the Hussars, who for this occasion were dressed in full kit, relieved by rough-looking 'catch-'em-alive-o' warriors who while on duty carried umbrellas to protect themselves from the sun. After we had marched out some distance I suddenly recollected that we had left in our mess a coloured print from the *Graphic* of Millais' *Cherry Ripe*. I somehow did not want it to fall into the hands of the Afghans, so I rode back and fetched it away with me, and for a long time afterwards it decorated my tent and bungalow; so, accidentally, I was the last Britisher to leave Kandahar.

Hobbies are an antidote to Satan's little games.

Aids, WB, 80

*Learning how to drive a train**

It was when my regiment travelled down from Northern India to Bombay for embarkation to South Africa. We were moved by rail, in troop trains. These trains generally travel by night so as to interfere as little as possible with the ordinary day traffic, and the men are disembarked into rest camps by day. The train joggles along from station to station in a leisurely way, going into sidings even to let goods trains pass.

So it may be imagined the journey was not altogether an exciting one, and I was getting as bored as most people with it when the brilliant idea struck me that although I was godson of the founder of locomotives I did not know how to drive one. No opportunity like the present. So I got on terms with the driver and took my place on the foot-plate, and was very soon, in my own estimation, quite a capable driver.

I rather fancy from what I got afterwards that our Colonel woke up realizing that the train had suddenly exchanged her

* IM, 83–4.

demure progress for a new life, and was rocking and tearing along at 70 miles an hour.

He asked the reason and got the answer that probably I was at the lever. There was no communication cord in that train!

But the thrill came when we ran down the *ghats*. The *ghats* are the cliffs and gorges which lead from the great plateau of India down to the coast level. The railway zigzags down these at pretty steep gradients round hairpin corners, over lofty bridges and viaducts. Flying down these with the brakes on, is something like an emotion, but the climax comes when before you in the moonlight you see the sudden black abyss of a chasm with nothing across it but for a brief moment you wonder whether it is there or has been carried away, and you feel inclined to yell with exultation as she jumps on to it with a spring and a roar and screams across the depths.

Opportunity is a tramcar which has very few stopping places.

SFB, OFP (22nd)

On the Staff*

In due course I got a footing on the Staff in a humble capacity, as ADC to General H. A. Smyth, Commander-in-Chief in South Africa.

At this time the Governor of the Cape was Sir Hercules Robinson, afterwards Lord Rosmead. He was a typical Colonial

* LVL, 143–6.

Governor, very British, a diplomatist, and a sportsman, and managed to look all three.

❦

Lady Robinson on her part looked a typical duchess, stately and very sure of her own mind. And she caused for me one of the most terrifying experiences it has ever been my luck to go through.

I wanted to secure her patronage for a concert I was getting up and called at Government House for the purpose. I was a very shy young officer and hoped to the last moment that she might not be at home. But there she was and I was shown in.

Although she used them to scrutinize me Her Ladyship did not need lorgnettes to see that I was in a powerful funk. She put me through a close catechism as to my feelings towards each in turn of the many charming young ladies of the Cape, and appeared to think less and less of me as we went through the list without any exciting discovery.

Finally, when I was reduced to a nervous rag she asked: 'What about this concert? Are you going to sing one of your imitations of a Prima Donna?' Thinking to please her I said yes. 'Then sing it now,' was her order.

There was no way out of it. I halted, I hesitated, but I had to do it. Can you picture it? Alone and helpless under that pitiless gaze I started miserably to sing in my ridiculous high falsetto those runs and trills which had made me such a hero to myself on the stage.

There was precious little of the hero about me now. But gradually I warmed a little to my work and was in the middle of a *tour de force* which trilled to the top notes of my compass when the door opened and in marched a footman followed by a portentous butler bringing tea. I didn't know whether to stop or what to do. What I most wanted was that the earth should open and swallow me up. As it was I brought my performance to an end within the next bar or two, and exercising all my dramatic powers I explained to her, for the benefit of the butler, that that was the sort of thing we might expect at the concert.

Then she gave me tea and I soon found that under that, to me, alarming exterior, there was a soul full of humour and a heart full of kindness.

Before you go to camp, and the whole time you are away, say to yourself: 'I am going to make this the most enjoyable camp there ever was for the other Cubs.'

WCH, 141

NOTES

1 A card game played with a full pack of fifty-two cards, normally by two pairs of players; a forerunner of bridge.
2 A state in north-east India (capital Patna).

8. Zululand

When men can learn to see with each other's eyes and to give unself-seeking friendship to their neighbours, the chances of war must subside and the foundations of peace will be laid about the world.

Jamboree, October 1935

My luck was in

An alarming telegram* came through from Zululand to say that the Usutus were up. They had defied the police; some troops from

---

* LVL, 147.

Natal had been sent to back up the civil force and had been driven back with loss. Generally the fat was in the fire.

The Governor of Natal (and incidentally of Zululand) was disturbed in his mind. He wanted more troops as a backing, but being by title 'Commander-in-Chief' of Natal he did not want military generals butting in. However, General Smyth saw that if there were to be troops there must be transport and supplies and organization and hospitals and remounts, and that every hour's delay meant wider outbreak, so without ado he despatched all necessary orders and promptly embarked with his Staff for Natal and Zululand.

Here again my luck was in. The post of Military Secretary was just then vacant, waiting for a Field Officer to be appointed from England. I was gazetted to act as such in the interim although I was below the rank of Field Officer.

John Dunn*

I shall never forget my first meeting with a Zulu army.

I was going with our troops on the march in Zululand when we met a group of warriors with a white man riding at their head. It was John Dunn, followed by a few of his head-men. John Dunn was an old Scottish trader who had lived since his boyhood among the Zulus, and was so liked and trusted by them for his honesty and courage that he had become the chief adviser to Cetywayo.

Even when the Zulus broke out in war against the British and

* LVL, 147–9.

Cetywayo, thinking himself invincible, expected to invade and capture the whole of Natal, no harm was offered to Dunn. He even went so far as to try to persuade that great Chief that his outbreak was bound to end in disaster.

If one of his own people had dared to tell him this, Cetywayo would have promptly killed him but he had too great a respect for Dunn.

All the same he did not accept his advice, and he lived to regret it when his vast army was finally smashed up in the battle of Ulundi, and he himself was taken prisoner.

It was after this defeat that the Zululand was divided up into eight provinces by Lord Wolseley, and each province placed under a different chief — of whom John Dunn was made one.

When we met John Dunn he informed us that he was bringing his *impi* or regiment along to join our force in our advance against the remainder of the Zulu nation.

Expect a great deal of your boys and you will generally get it.

HQG, September 1911 (rep. BPO, 25)

A Zulu impi*

Shortly afterwards I heard a sound in the distance which at first I thought was an organ playing in church, and I thought for the moment that we must be approaching a mission station over the brow of the hill.

* LVL, 149–50; WSCD, 75–7 (identical in ATM, 76–8); Aids 61.

But when we topped the rise we saw moving up towards us from the valley below three long lines of men marching in single file behind their *indunas* (chiefs), and singing a wonderful anthem as they marched.

Both the sight and the song, sung by four or five thousand warriors, were intensely impressive.

Then the men themselves looked so splendid. They were as a rule fine, strong, muscular fellows with cheery, handsome faces of a rich bronze colour, and very smartly decked out with feathers and furs and cows' tails.

They wore little in the way of clothing and their brown bodies were polished with oil and looked like bronze statues. Their heads were covered with ostrich plumes and they had swaying kilts of foxes' tails and stripes of fur; while round their knees and elbows were fastened white cows' tails as a sign that they were on the warpath.

They carried huge shields of ox-hide on the left arm, each regiment having shields of its special colour, while in the right hand they carried two or three throwing assegais flashing in the sun for hurling at an enemy, and a broad-bladed stabbing assegai which they kept for hand-to-hand fighting; while in their girdles was slung a club or axe for polishing off purposes.

At a given moment every man would bang his shield with his *knobkerry* (club) and it gave out a noise like a thunderclap.

At times they would all prance like horses, or give a big bound in the air exactly together. It was a wonderful sight, and their drill was perfect.

Behind the army came a second army of *umfaans* (boys), carrying on their heads the rolled-up grass sleeping-mats, wooden pillows, and water-gourds of the men.

These boys were going on the march and looking on at battles, giving first aid to the wounded, and cooking the men's food, and were all learning how to become good warriors later on.

As we knew there were four great *impi* of this kind against us, we felt that we were lucky in having at any rate one such force on our side, and under such a man as John Dunn. He and his scouts were invaluable.

An old Scout is full of resource, that is he can find a way out of any difficulty or discomfort.

SFB, OFP and YFBS, 39 ('A good Scout . . .')

A flying column*

General Smyth, on arrival in the country, lost no time in getting to work. Following up Major McKean's success in the Southern part, he established a line of fortified posts to prevent the enemy from returning there, and arranged to attack the different hostile *impis* in detail before they would complete their concentration together.

But the first and most urgent business was to effect the relief of Pretorius, a magistrate who was besieged in his house by the Zulus. A flying column was at once formed for the purpose,

* LVL, 150–52.

consisting of 400 mounted infantry and Dragoons, two guns, 200 Basutos and native police, and John Dunn's 2,000 Zulus.

This force was placed under command of Major McKean and he took me as his Staff Officer.

We started off on the 7th July and covered the first fifty miles in two days, with the enemy hovering around us, not daring to attack at first, but on the second day they charged our rearguard killing four of our men. They were, however, easily repulsed.

The brave Zulu girl*

After the fight it was a filthy wet night which will always remain in my memory. We were travelling light without tents, but with a few mule wagons carrying rations and forage.

McKean and I bivouacked under one of these wagons, but it was only a pretence of a shelter, for the ground underneath was soft wet mud and very cold, while the rain ran steadily through the bed-boards of the wagon and dripped on us in a continuous stream.

We managed to light a fire near by, and adjourning to this we sat around it with our waterproof sheets over our heads.

One of our Zulus came in from the fight carrying a wounded girl on his back. It was rather a surprising thing that a Zulu should save one of the enemy, so we asked his reason; he informed us that this was his niece who had been in a hut near the line of fire when

* LVL, 151–2; WSCD, 129–30.

a stray bullet had struck her in the stomach and gone clean through her.

We had no doctor with the force so McKean and I took charge of the girl. I think that most white women in the circumstances would have been in a state of collapse or fainting, but not so with this tough Zulu girl. She knelt up when we told her to so that we could plug the holes and bind her up. Her only clothing was a bead girdle and a necklace of black and white beans. So we procured a good big thick mealy sack and, cutting holes for her head and arms to go through, slipped it over her and made her comfortable by the fire; then we boiled up a little soup and after giving it to her we left her in charge of her uncle while we retired to our bedroom under the wagon with a view to getting a little sleep.

Under the wagon one lay on one's side in the mud trying to feel warm. Imagination went a long way, but when your hip got tired and you turned over to the other side you found the fresh mud so cold and wet that you didn't want to repeat the performance. The rain coming down on top of one was wet it was true, but it had one good effect, namely that it washed off a good deal of the mud which was continually being splashed and spurted on to one by the mules picketed round the wagon stumping in the slush. It was a jolly night.

Then after a time the poor girl at the fire near by began moaning. So I got up and went to see how she was getting on. Here she was, stark naked again, with the rain beating down on her and her uncle hunched up with the sack over his shoulders smoking a pipe. I ran at him in fury and landed him one kick before he disappeared into the darkness taking the sack with him.

McKean came and lent a hand in trying to make the girl more

comfortable. We put his mackintosh coat over her and gave her some more soup.

But my help was of little avail, as the poor girl died before morning.

We had to make a very early start, before daybreak, so he and I put her into an ant-bear[1] hole and filled it in as well as we could, and threw a great heap of thorn bushes over it to keep the hyenas away.

> *Politeness does not cost anything, and I hope all Scouts, at any rate, will try to practise it rather more than is usually done. It is all very well to be a 'rough diamond', or to have a good heart beneath a surly exterior, but remember that it is the exterior that people see when they meet you for the first time.*

SRW, 21

The relief of Pretorius*

We relieved old Pretorius all right and found him in his post, fairly fortified, and crowded with a collection of traders with their wives and children and friendly natives from the neighbourhood around. He had stood a heavy attack successfully but lost forty killed and fourteen wounded before he beat it off.

We improved his fortifications and returned to Headquarters, leaving a small garrison to protect him and taking the white women and children with us.

* LVL, 153.

As amateur doctor of the force I had a very busy time of it, dealing with the wounded, some of whose hurts had not been dressed or dealt with in any way since they were received.

One of the white women also was very ill with dysentery; so altogether I served a very practical apprenticeship.

Duty done dolefully is duty half done: done cheerily, its value is doubled.

Tit-Bits, quoted in BPBB (25 September)

*The ballroom staircase**

Different small columns were sent through the country as soon as all organized resistance was at an end, to clear up and collect surrenders and arms. Here and there there were little scraps but as a rule the Usutus gave in readily.

When accompanying one of these reconnaissances for rounding up cattle I came to the edge of a high cliff overgrown with thick bush.

Peering down into the valley below to see what had become of some enemy scouts whom we were following up, my orderly suddenly called out: 'Look out, Sir, behind you.'

I jumped round and there stood a splendid figure of a Zulu warrior, in all the glory of glistening brown skin and the white plumed head-dress from which the Usutu had their nickname of 'Tyokobais'.

* LVL, 155–9.

With his great shield of ox-hide and his bright assegais he made a fine picture. He had popped up from under the brow of the cliff to get me, but finding another with me he did not stop to argue but sprang down into cover again. I could see him and a companion running and scrambling along a sort of track on the face of the bluff. I kept along above them with my pistol ready, and before long they crossed a bit of open rock-face giving me a chance.

But I didn't take it. I wanted to see where they were making for, and very soon they disappeared into what was evidently the mouth of a cave. My particular friend caught his shield in a bush in the course of his flight and rather than be delayed left it there.

So, accompanied by my orderly, I went down the path and got the shield.

Following the path I presently found that in place of a cave there was a deep crevice or gully in the cliff face which ran right down to the plain below.

As I looked down into this a strange sight met my eyes. The gully was packed with the brown faces, with rolling eyes and white teeth, of hundreds of women and children, refugees hiding from us. Down below, nearest to the plain, were crowds of warriors, evidently waiting for an attack from that direction. I had come in at the back door!

I made my Basuto orderly call to the Usutus that fighting was all over now and that no harm would be done to them if they surrendered quietly, and in my heart of hearts I warmly hoped they would. Just then our flanking party turned up moving along the base of the cliff, and this helped them to make up their minds, which had been pretty well joggled up by our unexpected appearance also at the back door. So they called 'Pax'.

Then I made my way down through them. The women seemed to think that this was the beginning of slaughter and began screaming and pushing to get out of my reach. In the struggle a small brown imp fell off a rock on which he had been put so I naturally picked him up and replaced him, giving him something to play with. This had a miraculous effect; the hubbub died down; remarks were passed from mouth to mouth and I was able to squeeze down among them without further trouble.

One of my fellows below, seeing me doing this, shouted:

'What is it like there?' To which I replied: 'Just like the squash at a London ball'; from which bright remark the gully came to be known as the Ballroom Staircase.

There is a motto which says: 'Be good and you will be happy.' My version of it is: 'Be good-humoured and you'll be happy.'

WSCD, 142

NOTE

1 A large African (and South American) anteater.

9. The Ashanti Expedition

In camp life we learn to do without so many things which, while we are in houses, we think are necessary, and find that we can do for ourselves many things where we used to think ourselves helpless.

GG, 68

Using my wits

Shortly afterward* Lord Wolseley sent for me to the War Office and told me he had selected me to go to the West Coast of Africa

* LVL, 161.

to raise and command a native contingent for the Ashanti Expedition.

'Not that it is a Cavalry Service,' he explained, 'but one where you can use your wits.'

The causes of the expedition*

For a hundred years or more the Ashantis had been a thorn in the side of the British Protectorate of the Gold Coast.[1] They were a powerful and fairly bloodthirsty tribe living a hundred miles inland in dense forest country. They not only waylaid all rubber- and ivory-traders coming from the interior to the coast, but also raided the harmless coast tribes whenever they were in want of slaves.

And this was more or less generally the case, slaves were needed in goodly numbers to take the title-role in human-sacrifice performance.

More than one expedition, notably that of Lord Wolseley, had gone to Kumasi, and had made treaties and exacted promises from the King of Ashanti that human sacrifices should cease, and the road be kept open for peaceful trading with the coast.

But the existing king, Prempeh, just like his predecessors, had ignored all such agreements, and things were as bad as ever.

So an expedition, under Sir Francis Scott, was sent up to remedy matters.

* AD–AC, 92–3.

Playing the Game

*A native levy**

On landing at Cape Coast Castle, I set to work. My duty was to raise a contingent of 800 native warriors from among the friendly natives in our own district, who were to act as scouts, and prepare the way for the British force that was going to advance into the country.

Notice was therefore sent to the chiefs of the different tribes close by, telling each to send a company of his best men to join me at Cape Coast Castle on a certain day.

Having got my companies together, the next thing was to put them into uniform.

I gave each a red fez to wear, a flint-lock gun, a belt, and a bag to carry his food in, and a blanket to sleep in at night, and in a very short time my army was ready and equipped for taking the field.

A few of them owned drums, and one or two had horns on which they could blow weird sounds. These horns were made out of elephants' tusks, and the drums were hollowed out of the trunks of the trees, and, with these drummers and trumpeters at the head of the force, we started off gaily on our first day's march into the 'bush' towards the enemy's country.

Scouting is not only fun, but it also requires a lot from you.

SFB, DE, 19

* OWF, 61–2; AD–AC, 61–2; LVL, 161; DP, 56–8.

The Adventures of My Life

*Our task and organization**

We had lots of work to do. We were the scouts of the Army. We had to keep a look-out, and try to find the enemy in case he should be hiding in the woods, ready to open fire on the main body of our force when they came along.

Then, also, we were the pioneers of the Army, which means that we had to cut the path, and where the ground was very boggy to build a road of logs across the bad places; where one of the giant trees had fallen and lay across our road we had to make an inclined path up one side and down the other, so that it did not check the advance of the soldiers.

Here and there the path had to be doubly wide, so that the troops going up and others going down the road could pass one another.

Whenever we came to a stream we had to make a bridge across it, and in the course of our journey we built no less than two hundred of these, out of any kind of material that we could find on the spot.

Out of the thousand men, a great many did not know how to use an axe to cut down trees, and, except one company of about sixty men, none knew how to make knots — not even bad knots. So that, very often, when they had built the bridge of poles and had tied it all together, the whole thing fell to pieces again because the lashings had not been properly tied.

We had no rope with us so we used strong creeping plants, and thin withes or long whippy sticks, which we made still more

* OWF, 66–70; DP, 166–8; SFB, 84, 86 and 95; AD–AC, 62–3; LVL, 162.

pliant or bendable by holding one end under foot and twisting the other round and round with our hands.

Every seven miles or so we cleared a space of ground, chopped down trees, and built large wooden sheds, thatched with leaves, in which the troops could rest for the night when they came to the end of their day's march, and under these sheds we made long tables upon which the men could lie and sleep, well off the damp ground. Store huts were also built for reception of supplies, and forts were made round them for their protection.

And all the time this was being done we had to keep a crowd of scouts and outposts ahead and around us to guard against surprise, and to gain what news they could of our enemies' moves and intentions.

The ultimate organization that was found to be best adapted for all purposes, whether for pioneer work, drill, reconnaissance or outposts, was the division of each tribe into small companies of from twenty to thirty men each. Each tribe was under the orders of its chief, and he, or his orderly, understood English, and acted as the adjutant of his detachment. Each company was under a 'captain', assisted by an under-captain.

The companies were permanently detailed to certain kinds of work; thus, one was charged with the work of building bridges, another with making huts, another with digging the road and draining it where necessary, another with felling timber and log-cutting, and so on; so that every man knew his proper work and, with a few days' practice, became proficient in it. But at first much instruction had to be given in the method of using felling axes, spades, levers, and in knotting ropes – or rather the substitute for rope, the kind of creeper known as 'monkey-rope'.

Each 'captain' was made responsible for tools used by his company (and these had to be checked daily, both before and after work), and also for the presence of all his men during working hours, which, with the exception of two hours' rest for the midday meal, generally lasted from daylight until dusk. It was some time before this idea of responsibility for the working of their men could be instilled into the captains, but once it had been grasped by them, and the system had got into working order, all went smoothly and efficiently, so long as one of our officers was at hand to keep the rate of progress up to the mark.

We had plenty of occupation for our men if only they could be kept to their work. But work was not habitually in their line at all. It was only by treating them cheerily that work could be got out of them. They were quite ready to laugh and sing, but equally ready to sulk and to mutiny, according to the cue you gave them.

Patience, and always patience, was the only way. Our motto was the old West Coast proverb, 'Softly, softly, catchee monkey'; in other words, 'Don't flurry; patience gains the day.'

Games are but steps to learning how to play the bigger game — the game of life.

BSA Microfilms, 00916, *The School of the Copse*, c. 1922.

Health precautions*

The endless marching among trees day after day, and week after week, got on the nerves of a good many of the men, and they became depressed and sick.

* YFBS, 84 (identical in WSCD, 140) and 78; WCH, 144; RTS, 77–8.

Playing the Game

The commander of our corps said to me that he was going to make his men sing choruses while on the march, in order to keep up their spirits. So I replied, 'Then your men will get fever by breathing the germs in through their mouths. It is bad enough to have the men depressed; but even that is better than having them no use through sickness.'

I was one of the very few who came through that expedition without getting it but I believe that one of the causes of my escaping fever was that I always kept my mouth shut and breathed through my nose.

With me I had two shirts; one I wore, the other I carried hanging on my back with the sleeves knotted round my neck. This shirt was drying at the time while the one I was wearing was getting damp. As soon as we halted, if it were only for a few minutes, off came my damp shirt, and on went the dry one. In this way I did not sit still in a wet shirt, catching the breeze and getting a chill, as so many did.

Those men who had lived fatly and well in their ordinary life went down like ninepins. It was the moderate feeders and the active men who survived. Incidentally on that trip one discovered that meat was not a necessary part of one's food. For a long time I lived on nothing but bananas and plantains, and, though one was buried in a deep, dark forest where you seldom saw the light of the sun, and the scent in the atmosphere was like that of an old cabbage garden from vegetation rotting in the swamp, I was never fitter in all my life, and averaged my twenty miles a day marching with a light heart if a thin tummy.

The Adventures of My Life

With the use of spare diet, outdoor exercise, lots of work and laughter, one can, at eighty, be as fit as ever in body, mind and spirit. Even at eighty there is still a vast field for their use in happifying others and for their enjoyment in a world so full of beauties and wonders — and kindnesses.

8oth Birthday Outlook, in *The Scouter*, February 1937

*Advancing on Kumasi**

Now we were within a day's march of the Capital, a hundred and fifty miles from the coast.

Needless to say, these last few miles of our long march through the dense forest, as we advanced to the great denouement, were full of intense excitement for us.

Was the enemy going to fight us or not? We did not know. What we did know from our spies and deserting slaves was that the King had summoned to the capital his ten chiefs and their contingents to go through the fetish ceremonial that was customary before war, and which usually took some fourteen days to complete.

Our object was to rush them before they could complete this. Our orders were that moral force, rather than Maxim guns, was to be used if possible, i.e., quickness and display of strength were likely to be successful.

So my advance force was divided up into three columns, operating by separate paths in such a way as to appear simultaneously, on a fixed day and hour, on three sides of the capital.

* AD–AC, 93–6; DP, 112.

Playing the Game

Warily we went, with scouts creeping and cutting their way through the undergrowth in and on either side of it. Ambuscades were positive disease with our enemy.

We were now on a regular track leading to the town. Here we presently found a whole line of little wooden dolls planted in the ground facing towards the coast. This was a fetish and gentle hint to us to turn about and go the same way otherwise their gods would be exceedingly unkind to us – if not absolutely brutal.

Had we been a normal enemy, and had they not been on the defensive in the matter of human sacrifice, they would not have placed wooden dolls there, but slaves planted alive in the ground up to their necks, and left for the ants to do the rest.

The appearance of victims executed in this way was generally sufficient to deter any enemy from pursuing that path.

It was nearing the hour at which our detachment was due to arrive at the front of Kumasi in co-operation with the two other wings of our column, working from either flank.

Reports were flying around that the enemy meant to oppose us at the gates of Kumasi, to make one stand there, and, if beaten, to blow up the city, and disperse into the bush.

Presently we passed a group of huts, empty at the moment, but evidently of recent occupation: the owners had fled at our coming. Then more huts and openings among the trees, with a high thick jungle of elephant grass all round.

Suddenly there came a weird sound in the air, the throbbing and boom of drums ahead; some of them far away, some of them near at hand. This sounded like business!

In a moment every one seemed to be grinning and sparkled; men hurried their pace; expectation and excitement were in the air.

The enemy drums were calling the alarm. It was exactly as though a swarm of bees in a hive was being disturbed. Evidently our approach, or that of our flanking party, had been observed.

Then some of our leading scouts came running back to tell us that we had reached the place.

Suddenly as we all stood listening there was a marked pause in the drumming, and a change of rhythm or cadence. It was 'drum-talk', the wireless of the woods.

Our men were listening in with all their ears. A moment later my Haussa orderly grumbled out: 'Ah! Him dam blood fella Ashanti say in talking to white fella don' wanter fight, he want sit down and make palaver-talk; my saying him dam blood fella.' And he spat neatly between his teeth to show what he thought of them.

If you can't think of anything nice to say about her, keep your mouth shut.

From a letter to his daughter Betty when at school.

*Entering Kumasi**

Out of the dark, soggy depths of the forest we came, for the first time for weeks, into the open sunshine. There lay before us a clear space like a parade ground, a quarter of a mile wide, and beyond it, on a gentle slope in a hollow, a mass of thatched roofs, stretching away into the jungle beyond.

Kumasi! Just a vast village, nothing imposing about it; no walls

* AD–AC, 96–100; DP, 113–18.

or ramparts, no spires or minarets; yet a place with a long and lurid history of its own; the key to a vast hinterland.

With an eye to due effect, we paraded our force along one side of the parade ground, while on the opposite edge of it the Ashantis were beginning to throng from the town to look as us. We had marshalled ourselves into some sort of order, and after a body of advance scouts came our political officer and staff of two British officers with the Union Jack on a hog-spear. These were followed by some companies of the native levy in their uniform of brown skin (provided by nature) and red skull-caps (provided by the Government). Then a company of the Gold Coast Haussas, headed by a small band of drums and fifes. This force formed up in line facing the town.

We were not leaving things to chance. The drum-talk of peace and goodwill might have been but a blind to disarm suspicion while they sent out surprise packets against our flanks or rear. So, as we formed up on our parade ground, we detached pickets to act as outposts to watch and guard our flanks.

While we were still busy forming up, there appeared from both sides of the town simultaneously connecting parties from our two flanking columns, which meantime had arrived on the tick, in their allotted places.

Kumasi was surrounded.

Had the enemy resisted the entrance of the centre main column, he would have found himself immediately attacked on both flanks simultaneously, and the fight, had there been one, could not have lasted long.

Now the drumming from the town boomed louder and the roar of voices filled the air. Great coloured umbrellas were soon seen dancing and bobbing above the heads of the surging crowds of natives as they poured onto the parade ground. Stool-bearers ran before their masters, followed by whirling dancers with their yellow skirts flying around them. Great drums like beer barrels, decked with human skulls and carried on the heads of the slaves, were booming out their notes, while bands of elephant-tusk horns added to the din. The King and his chiefs were borne on elevated chairs and arranged themselves in a dense line along the edge of the parade ground to see the troops arrive. The umbrellas formed a row of booths beneath which the chiefs sat on their brass-nailed chairs, with their courtiers round them.

A long wait ensued, during which two minor incidents occurred which, small as they were, had their import. The first was when a little party of our force, consisting of three white soldiers, with four natives, came hurriedly across the ground, carrying a reel and winding off the field telegraph.

Thus, within a few minutes of the arrival of the advance force before Kumasi the fact was known all the way down to the coast and thence to England.

We could not help a cheer of admiration for those gallant fellows of the Engineers for their plucky and determined work.

Just after this the white officer with me, by way of whiling away his time, strolled towards a dump of huge cotton trees just behind us. As he did so I noticed a sudden liveliness among the Ashantis. Several of them jumped to their feet and, talking anxiously among themselves, watched his movement, as it were with pricked ears.

Suspecting an ambush, I promptly called him back and ordered a few scouts to go and investigate. In a few moments they were back, grinning broadly, to report that the whole copse was full of dead men. And it was. A nasty sight, but at the same time a useful one for our purpose; it disclosed, without need of further proof, that human sacrifice, though denied by the King, was still too prevalent.

Presently our General and his staff were seen approaching, followed by the main body of the white troops in military array.

The King, under instruction, came forward to salute the General, but on starting to question why the troops had come was told in other words to 'dry up' until the arrival of his Excellency the Governor on the morrow: he would then learn why we were there.

Meantime the troops were billeted at different points round the outskirts of the town.

It is not the abolition of armies that will do away with war, any more than the abolition of police will do away with crime. We have to do away with the cause of war; armies are rather the effect, that is the result of fear and of the fighting spirit. And that is a matter for education.

Jamboree, January 1923

*The blood bowl**

It was a warm, starlight night and we were out in the bush, a small party of ten, acting neither as a fixed outpost to watch a given

* AD–AC, 129–39.

spot, nor as reconnoitring party to search a definite line of country: our business lay betwixt and between the two. It was to hang about in likely places and keep a look-out for any moves on the part of the enemy.

Presently a sound detached itself from the others of the forest. It was like the 'quit-quit-quit' whistle of a frog. Yet not the same, for it was rendered long-short-long as the quail gives it. But quails don't grow in the forest. It was the password of our patrol, sounded by one of the outlying scouts.

Answering the call I crept quietly out in its direction, keeping in the shadows with eyes watching and trying to pierce the gloom, looking a little over, rather than directly at, any suspicious object.

In front of me was a pathway, one of those that we were watching, since it led from the fetish-place of Bantama to Kumasi, and the priests or medicine men of Bantama were the most trusted of King Prempeh's messengers.

An almost whispered call led me on across the road to where among the roots of a great banyan² tree I could just discern two of my scouts squatting. One of these came silently forward and led me by the wrist into the deep shadow of the tree, and there he guided my hand until it touched the rim of a great metal bowl or cauldron. Again he gave the call, and before long more scouts like shadows had grouped themselves round us.

They crowded to the bowl, and their eager whisperings and movements showed that it had a more than common interest for them. Then one of them pointed out to me something among the lower branches of the tree above us. In the darkness I could see nothing, but going closer to the great gnarled tree-trunk he guided my hand as high as I could reach and I touched what quickly proved to be a human jaw-bone hanging there. And then another, and yet more.

It was a fetish tree.

With the coming dawn our watch was ended. I realized that the bowl, a brass one about four feet across and eighteen inches deep, was just of a size to make a glorious tub for me. So with some lianas cut from the nearest trees we slung it on a pole and carried it off in triumph to camp, my ruffians grinning and whispering joyously among themselves.

Our camp was close around the sacred place of fetish buildings of Bantama.

This day we were ordered to open up the vaults among them in which are laid the great Kings of Ashanti. It was known that with each King was buried the treasure which he had accumulated during his life. Thus Bantama was the treasure-house of the nation. And some of this treasure was overdue to us.

The treasure-house was known to be under the charge of some eighty priests or medicine men, and the spells which according to repute they could cast over any would-be looter were quite sufficiently awful to make it decidedly thief-proof.

When we took the place and surrounded it we found it to consist of an unimposing group of thatched sheds and hovels with only one decrepit old boy in charge.

The royal mausoleum was a kind of crypt whose entrance was bricked up. The plaster which sealed this doorway was evidently comparatively fresh, only a few weeks old, whereas the last King who had died had been buried there for some years.

This fact, coupled with the absence of the priests, prepared us to expect disappointment. A few blows of the pick, and the doorway was open. Within were ranged nine brass coffins or rather caskets in line, and on the top of each stood *kuduos*, or cups and bowls containing food for the departed monarchs.

All looked in order. But when the bowls were removed and the lids of the caskets were opened there was nothing but emptiness within.

A few pieces of stiff tape with angular bends in them showed that recently there had been ingots of gold tied together there, but, as we afterwards learned, all of these, together with the bones of the Kings, had been removed a fortnight previous to the landing of the expedition by the guardian priests, who had dispersed into the jungle, each carrying a portion into safe concealment.

They had certainly done their work well and effectively. And we in our turn did ours. After setting fire to all that was burnable in the place we flattened the walls with improvised battering-rams made of saplings.

Thus we made an end of Bantama.

This was not done with any idea of sacrilege or want of respect for any religious convictions of the people, but because for well over a hundred years it had been the great centre for human sacrifice.

On returning to my camp after the destruction of the fetish house I found a crowd of soldiers of the Special Service Corps and the West Yorks Regiment assembled there. They were being addressed by one of their officers. I joined in, to find that my new bath-tub was the centre of interest, and the officer was explaining to his audience that this was the celebrated fetish bowl mentioned by Bowditch, who visited Ashanti in 1817.[3]

The King of the country was accustomed to visit Bantama

every three months to perform his devotions, and on such occasions twenty men were sacrificed by having their heads cut off over the bowl in order to fill it with blood. Eighty men a year was the complement required. But also at the 'Yarn Custom' or Harvest Festival each year a further number were sacrificed. Also it was customary for the King occasionally to 'wash the bones' of his forebears by making further extensive libations of blood.

The blood thus obtained was allowed to coagulate in the bowl and was then cut into portions, sewn up in cloth, and sold as charms to those desiring immunity from witchcraft and other dangers.

As I heard all this my idea of using the bath received a rude shock which was accentuated when I came to look at my possession in broad daylight. It had a suggestive high-water mark of a horrible kind which quite put from me any desire to bathe in it.

But realizing now the identity of my prize I had it packed up without delay in a spare tent. It was then slung on a pole and within an hour was on its way down country in charge of six of my men, consigned to a friend of mine at our base at Cape Coast Castle.

Somehow the natives of the country got wind of its departure. All along its journey of 150 miles groups of them came to see it pass and just to touch it. Even after it had been packed in a crate and safely deposited on board ship, parties of them went off in boats to have a farewell glimpse at it.

One Ashanti explained to me that its loss to them was more than that of their King. 'A King we can replace but never the great Blood Bowl.'

The Adventures of My Life

A great coral island is built up of tiny sea animals blocking themselves together; so also great knowledge in a man is built up by his noticing all sorts of little details and blocking them together in his mind by remembering them.

SFB, OFP, 22

*The voyage home**

Next came the march down to the coast with all the royal and other prisoners. The part taken by the levies in the early portion of this march was not an unimportant one, since to them fell the duty of searching the bush, and of holding all by-roads, to guard against attempts which we had reason to expect would be made to assassinate Prempeh. They found numbers of individual men in the bush, but these always came in asking for news, and were evidently runaway slaves rather than would-be assassins.

On the 22nd January the levy marched out of Kumasi; on the 29th it arrived at Cape Coast Castle, thus completing a march of 150 miles in seven days, which in that climate is not a bad performance.

The last march was partly done in the night, so that I was able to pay off and dismiss my army at daybreak on arrival at Cape Coast Castle.

Then, in order to cadge a good breakfast, I went on board the hospital ship *Coromondel*. They gave me a hearty welcome and as I sat in a deck-chair waiting for breakfast, with all my responsibilities

---

* DP, 176; LVL, 166.

off my shoulders, I quietly fell asleep. I did not wake up till the following day to find myself in bed in a comfortable cabin.

On arrival at the London Docks, a big ship entered the dock just ahead of us and as she did so a band on the wharf struck up 'See the Conquering Hero Comes', and a large posse of generals and staff officers from the War Office formed up on a red carpet to receive her as she moored at the quay.

As our ship was then warped in to the opposite side of the dock the band suddenly ceased playing and the bandsmen, together with generals and staff, were observed scuttling round the dock, hastily leaving the first ship to come round and welcome us. There had been a slight mistake.

The first ship proved to be the transport bringing from South Africa as prisoners, for trial and punishment at home, the officers and men implicated in the Jameson Raid.[4] 'Conquering heroes' and red carpets didn't exactly fit the case!

By character I want it understood that I do not merely think of passive self-restraint and self-discipline: it includes also, beside these, the active desire to do things. It is not merely the 'being' good, but it is the 'doing' good that counts.

HQG, July 1914

The Adventures of My Life

NOTES

1 In 1957 the Gold Coast merged with British Togoland to form the independent state of Ghana (capital Accra).

2 Strictly speaking, a banyan is an East Indian fig tree, from whose almost horizontal branches grow shoots that take roots and become new trunks.

3 'The Kings and the Kings only are buried at Bantama, and the sacred gold is buried with them. Opposite the building in which their bones are deposited is the largest brass pan I have ever seen (for sacrifices) being about five feet in diameter with four small lions on the edge. Here human sacrifices are frequent and customary to "water the graves" of the Kings.' (Extract from *A Mission to Ashanti*, by Bowditch, 1817) [Note by B.-P., AD–AC, 129].

4 The attempted invasion of Transvaal, carried out from 29 December 1895 to 2 January 1896 by 600 British colonists from Rhodesia led by Dr. L. S. Jameson and secretly encouraged by Cecil Rhodes, which ended in failure, was a prologue to the Boer War.

10. The Matabele Campaign

A bad habit is like a bad tooth. Have it out. But the gap must be filled in, not merely for appearance's sake, but for use.

LS, 49

The first Matabele campaign*

After the Ashanti show I was quartered with my Squadron of the 13th Hussars at Belfast.

One day I received a telegram from General Sir Frederick Carrington, to the effect that he was ordered on service to South

* LVL, 169–72.

Africa and was starting in three days' time; if I could join him he would take me as his Chief Staff Officer.

The reason for the sudden call for General Carrington was that the Matabele tribe in South Africa had broken out, and its warriors were murdering the white settlers there.

The Matabele were originally Zulus who under the leadership of 'Msilikatsi, son of Matshobane, had been sent on a raiding expedition by the Zulu King, Tshaka, in 1847.

Their attack having failed they were expected to return, according to custom, and to be disarmed and then to have their necks broken by the women of the tribe. On this occasion they did not see it in the same light, and elected not to return home but to go off, on their own, with unbroken necks, to the north-ward, until they could discover a suitable country to settle in.

This they eventually found in what is now known as Southern Rhodesia.

The second campaign in Matabeleland*

We now come to 1896, when the Matabele had settled down and had been hoping that the British invasion of the country was merely a temporary raid, such as they were in the habit of doing themselves.

Finding that the British intended to remain there, they turned in their dilemma to the 'Mlimo' – their god – whom for generations

* LVL, 172–5.

past they had been wont to consult for advice on national emergencies.

This oracle gave out his instructions in a certain cave in the Matopos, and also in two or three other places in Mashonaland.

On this occasion his advice was that the Matabele warriors should make their way to Bulawayo on a certain night and massacre the white people in the place, and after that should go out and kill the individual white settlers on their farms.

This plan miscarried owing to the impatience of the warriors when making their way to the rendezvous, as they could not resist the temptation of killing some of the farmers as they passed near their homesteads. Several of these men, however, managed to escape and to get away to Bulawayo and to give warning of the impending attack.

The townspeople in Bulawayo formed a strong defensive laager[1] in the Market Square, into which they all congregated for safety against attack. The Matabele coming to the town in the night found it all dark and unnaturally quiet and suspected that this must mean some sort of trap. Therefore they did not venture to enter the place but contented themselves with destroying outlying farms and murdering any stray white people they could come across.

Meantime the settlers organized themselves into fighting units mounted and dismounted, and carried out bold attacks on the enemy when and where they found it possible.

Relief forces were meantime raised amongst the residents in Salisbury in Mashonaland and by Colonel Plumer in Cape Colony, and it was to take command of these forces and of the general situation that General Carrington was now summoned.

The nearest railway station to Bulawayo was at Mafeking – 587 miles away – and the road thither was a heavy sand track, waterless for the greater part of the distance. Ox wagons were the only means for transporting heavy goods and at their usual pace of two miles an hour it was naturally a long job to get supplies of food and ammunition, equipment and hospital stores, up to the front.

As if this were not sufficient handicap rinderpest[2] now broke out and swept the country so that whole teams of oxen died in their tracks and hundreds of wagons were left stranded along the road.

From Mafeking the General, with his Staff, including myself as Chief Staff Officer, proceeded by coach, a regular old 'deadwood' affair, with eight mules, on our long trek.

It took us ten days *and nights* to get there, the most unrestful journey I have ever endured. We picked up fresh mules at the mail stations every fifteen miles or so. The marvel was that, though in the enemy's country, the Matabele never interfered with the traffic on this roadway. The reason which they afterwards gave for this was that they supposed that if they left open a way of retreat the people of Bulawayo would be glad to avail themselves of it and escape out of the country.

It was not in their programme that we should use it the other way.

If a man cannot make his point to keen boys in ten minutes, he ought to be shot!

The Scouter, November 1928 (rep. BPO, 125)

Playing the Game

A close shave

On one occasion* I had a close shave. I went to help two men who were fighting a Matabele at the foot of a tree, but they killed him just as I got there. I was under the tree when something moving over my head caught my attention. It was a gun-barrel taking aim down at me, the firer jammed so close to the tree-stem as to look like part of it. Before I could move he fired. The bullet just ploughed into the ground at my feet, and I saw my friend right above me preparing to have another go at me.

Fortunately his first shot had attracted the attention of some of our marksmen close by, and they killed him before he could do any more harm.

After that I always took good care to look up, as well as down and around, when searching for an enemy.

Scouting in the Matopo Hills†

There were a few fights around Bulawayo and the Matabele eventually retired to their great stronghold in the Matopo Hills.

These hills consisted of a tract of country, broken up into piles of granite boulders, mounting in many places to eighty or one hundred feet in height, full of caves and deep ravines half-hidden in vegetation of cactus, mahobahoba and baobob[3] trees.

The district extended for some fifty miles in length and twenty

* MC, 60; OWF, 49; ATS, 47.
† LVL, 175–6; SIW, 16–18.

in depth and was the most damnable country that could be imagined for fighting over.

Here the enemy hid their cattle and women and took up strong positions for defence, not in one but in half a dozen different places. Though we had many friendly natives and plenty of white volunteers to act as scouts we found the information which they brought back so lacking in military details as to be of little use for working out tactical plans, and in the end the General sent me to reconnoitre the positions, handing over my duties in the office to my far abler assistant, Captain Vyvyan.

These reconnaissances became the joyous adventure of my life even if they were a bit arduous.

In this work I was on several occasions associated with Major Fred Burnham, the American scout.

Scouting played a very prominent part in the preliminaries to major operations, and gave opportunities for the exercise of all the arts and resources of woodcraft, coupled with the excitement incidental to contending against men of special cunning, pluck and cruelty.

This scouting, to be successful, necessitated one's going with the very slenderest escort – frequently with one man only, to look after the horses – and for long distances away from our main body, into the districts occupied by the enemy. Thus, one was thrown entirely on one's own resources, with the stimulating knowledge that if you did not maintain a sufficient alertness of observation and action, you stood a very good chance indeed, not only of failing to gain information which you were desired to seek, but also of getting yourself wiped out, as many a better man had been before, by the ruthless foe.

'Spooring', or tracking, was our main source of guidance and information, and night the cover under which we were able to make our way about the enemy's country with impunity.

The Matopo Hills were some thirty-five miles away from Bulawayo.

My usual method of procedure, after one or two essays, was to ride off with one assistant so as to get half-way there in daylight. The remainder of our journey had to be done in the dark in order to escape observation, our plan being to get to a position before dawn where we could watch unseen the doings and gather if possible the position and strength of the enemy.

In this way the enemy got to know me fairly well; they gave me the name of 'Impeesa' – i.e. 'the Wolf', or, as Jan Grootboom translated it, 'the beast that does not sleep, but sneaks about at night'.[4]

Camp is the boy's Elysium and the Scoutmaster's opportunity. And, moreover, it is Scouting.

HQG, June 1919

*Jan Grootboom**

Jan Grootboom was a Zulu who had had some education and a pretty wide experience, having travelled and mingled with Europeans of the right sort.

Though I knew Zululand I was new to Rhodesia and its

* LVL, 138–41.

people, and I needed therefore a really reliable guide and scouting comrade. When you are choosing a man for a job like this where your life is going to depend on him, and, what is also considerably to the point, where he at times will have to rely on you for his life, the selection is not one that can be lightly made.

But in my case there was no time for having a dress rehearsal or preliminary test with likely men, and I had to take this one on his reputation and his face value. As it happened both appealed to me, and I never had to regret my choice. The character given him in the first instance exactly described him; he proved the bravest man I ever saw.

When at the end of the campaign I left Matabeleland Jan and I parted as real friends.

A tell-tale leaf*

One day I learned a lesson in observation and deduction from Jan.

I was out scouting with him over a wide grassy plain near the Matopo Hills. Suddenly we crossed a track freshly made in grass where the blades of grass were still green and damp, though pressed down – all were bending one way, which showed the direction in which the people had been travelling. After following it for a bit, the track got on to a patch of sand and we then saw that it was the spoor of several women (small feet with straight edge, and short steps) and boys (small feet, curved edge, and longer steps),

* SFB, 159–61 (from ATS, 67–8, identical in GG, 106–7); LVL, 130–31; MC, 100.

walking, not running, towards the hills, about five miles away, where we believed the enemy was hiding.

Then we saw a mahobahoba leaf lying about two yards off the track. There were no trees for miles, but we knew that trees having this kind of leaf grew at a village fifteen miles away. It seemed likely therefore that the women had come from that village, bringing the leaf with them, and had gone to the hills.

On picking up the leaf we found it was damp, and smelled of native beer. The short steps showed that the women were carrying loads. So we guessed that according to the custom they had been carrying pots of native beer on their heads, with the mouths of the pots stopped up with bunches of leaves. One of these leaves had fallen out; and since we found it two yards off the track, it showed that at the time it fell a wind was blowing. There was no wind now, that is, at eleven o'clock, but there had been some about five o'clock.

So we guessed from all these little signs that a party of women and boys had brought beer during the night from the village fifteen miles away, and had taken it to the enemy in the hills, arriving there soon after six o'clock.

The men would probably start to drink the beer at once (as it goes sour in a few hours), and would, by the time we could get there, be getting sleepy and keeping a bad look-out, so we should have a favourable chance of looking at their positions.

We accordingly followed the women's tracks, found the enemy, made our observations, and got away with our information without any difficulty.

And it was chiefly done on the evidence of that one leaf.

The Adventures of My Life

A man without chivalry is no man.

RTS, 108

*Noticing all signs**

I was out with a boy reconnoitring a hill occupied by enemy. In order to get a better view of it, we had to cross a difficult river, which lay between high, steep banks, and consisted of a chain of deep-water reaches and rocks, with only one practicable 'drift', or crossing. It was not a very safe proceeding to commit ourselves to one single line of retreat, but in this case there was no alternative.

So we crossed over, but kept, if possible, a more than usually bright look-out for enemy, while keeping ourselves as well concealed by the bush as we could. As we went, we took special note of guiding marks, to direct us back to our crossing-place should we be obliged to make for it in a hurry.

We went on for about a quarter of a mile beyond the drift, and then, leaving the horses with the boy, I climbed up a *kopje* and got a view of the place.

So far, we had seen no enemies about, but presently, glancing back towards the drift, I saw three buck suddenly appear, coming as hard as they could away from the bush near the river and towards us. Presently they stopped, and, without noticing us, wheeled up and faced the way they had come, ears pricked up. For

* MC, 351–3.

a moment or two they stood, and then, springing round, they dashed past us evidently fully alarmed. We did not wait to see what had startled them, but, clambering down the rocks, I mounted my horse, and we headed back for the drift as fast as we were able, keeping our eyes 'skinned' the while.

We got to the bank all right, and, looking into the gully that formed the river bed, were relieved to find it all clear; but, on looking back, we could now see a number of black heads and shoulders bobbing along among the rocks and bush, evidently hastening down to occupy the drift and to cut us off. Luckily, by acting on the hint given by the buck, we were before them, and were not long in getting across to the open ground on the other bank of the river.

When there is danger before you, don't stop and look at it — the more you look at it the less you will like it — but take the plunge, go boldly in at it, and it won't be half as bad as it looked, when you are once in it.

SFB, DE, 227

*The end of the campaign**

The result of our reconnaissance work was that we were able to locate the different positions held by the enemy and to attack them in detail.

These attacks required unorthodox methods, not cut-and-

* SRW, 20–21; LVL, 176–7 and 180; AA, 142; SMEA, 77; MC, 251.

dried order of tactics, owing to the very unusual terrain on which we had to work.

There was no drawing up of opposing forces in battle-array, or majestic advancing of earth-shaking squadrons to the clash of arms; but you had to approach a *kopje*, or peak of piled-up granite boulders, within which were natural caves and tunnels, and in some of them, springs of water, where not an enemy was visible, but which you knew was honeycombed with caves and crannies secure from shell fire with bolt holes in various directions, and full of watchers fingering guns of every kind and calibre.

You were expected to climb this loopholed pyramid to gain the entrance to its caves, which was somewhere near the top as a rule, and when unsuspectingly you came near enough they would let you have it from the old elephant gun, which fired a bullet as big as a plum.

And if you were lucky enough to escape an elephant bullet from one side or another, or a charge of slugs from a crevice underfoot, you had the privilege of firing a few shots down the drain-like entrance to the cave, and of then lowering yourself quickly after them into the black uncertainty below. Although I never appreciated this form of sport at its proper worth, there were many in our forces who did. It cannot be denied that there was a 'glorious uncertainty' about it, such as could not be surpassed in any other variety of amusement.

And so with some rough fighting we gradually overcame the resistance in the Matopos. In the end the Matabele gave in.

Playing the Game

It is a commonly quoted saying that 'Only those can lead who have first learned to obey'. Yes, but like many truisms it has its limits. I prefer also as a leader the man who has learned to lead.

HQG, June 1918 (rep. BPO, 71–2)

NOTES

1 Afrikaans for a camp, an encampment, especially a temporary one in the open, marked out by an encircling barricade of wagons.

2 A virulent, infectious disease affecting ruminant animals, especially oxen, characterized by fever, dysentery and inflammation of the mucous membranes: also known as *cattle-plague*.

3 The *mahobahoba* is not identifiable. The *baobob* (or *baobab*) is a tall tropical tree (*Adansonia digitata*) with an enormously thick stem, found throughout Africa (and long naturalized in India); its edible fruits are known as 'monkey bread'; the fibres of the bark are used for ropes and cloth.

4 This translation is given in MC, 128. Grootboom was right. In fact, *impeesa*, or *impisi* (a Sindebele word from a Zulu root) does not mean 'wolf' (there are no wolves in Africa), but rather a kind of hyena, the spotted hyena (*Crocuta crocuta*).

11. India Again, with the 5th Dragoon Guards

The difference between a leader and a commander: almost any fool can command, can make people obey orders, if he has adequate power of punishment at his back to support him in case of refusal. It is another thing to lead, to carry men with you in a big job.

LS, 93

Playing the Game

Farewell to the 13th Hussars[*]

I had been awarded a Brevet Lieutenant-Colonelcy for the Ashanti campaign, and a further Brevet of full Colonel for the Matabele campaign, so although I figured as Major in the Regiment, below the Lieutenant-Colonel in Command and the Senior Major, Second in Command, I was actually senior to both of these in rank, which was a bit of an anomaly.

This had not occurred to me until the Colonel sent for me one day and informed me that I was appointed to command the 5th Dragoon Guards. He then explained to me that as a full Colonel it was impossible for me to remain where I was, and so I had to go.

Leaving my old Regiment was perhaps one of the bitterest moments of my life.

I had served in it for twenty-one years, the very best years of my life, and the going away was a big wrench, especially in the actual departure, which was worse than I expected.

I arranged with my servant that I would slip away in the early morning before breakfast; and, so that it should not be noticed, he was to have a cab round at the back door of my quarters and get it loaded up with all my luggage so that I could nip away unseen.

When all was ready I sneaked out of the back door, there to find my cab, with the Regimental Sergeant-Major sitting on the box and conducting the Band which was also in attendance, every

* LVL, 181–3.

man of my Squadron harnessed in on long ropes, and the whole Regiment there to see me out of the barrack gate.

And off we went, the most choky experience I ever had.

My last glimpse of the barracks showed blankets being waved from every window, and all through the slums and streets of Dublin went this mad procession which finally landed me at the station with a farewell cheer.

Ambition to do the right is the only ambition that counts.

RTS, 143 and 168

*Fifth Dragoon Guards**

No sooner had I got home from Ashanti than I was ordered to Matabeleland, and now I was barely settled at home again when I had this order to go out to India.

I made an appeal to be allowed to go on leave, as two fairly arduous campaigns in succession left one a bit played out. But I was told that my services with the 5th were urgently required, and I must go at once, but as soon as I had got matters straight there I could ask for as much leave as I wanted.

So off I went.

I soon found after arrival at Meerut that with the excellent lot of officers and non-commissioned officers I should have no difficulty in having the Regiment in tip-top order, so soon as I got to know them and they me.

* LVL, 183.

Playing the Game

There is no job on earth, that I know of, as delightful as that of Colonel of a Regiment, especially if, as it was with me under Sir Bindon Blood, your General is sympathetic to your fads.

I found in both officers and men a most responsive team of keen soldiers and between us we took up several new lines of training for the development of efficiency. These were both interesting experiments and productive of useful results.

*Manmastership**

Horsemastership was naturally developed as it is primarily the great aim of every Cavalry Regiment; but in addition to this we promoted 'Manmastership' which was occasionally a subject that was lost sight of. Whereas the horse is after all only the instrument for bringing the man into action, it is the man, his fitness, his efficiency and his spirit, that is important.

A man can only be a good horsemaster if he is fond of his horse. He can only be a good soldier if he is fond of soldiering. Similarly an officer can only be a good manmaster if he likes his men.

By manmaster I don't mean a slave driver, but one who, like the horsemaster, has his men in the best condition for fighting. This involves keeping them fit and fed, but not fed up, and he must give them the spirit that keeps them cheery, keen and loyal.

Any fool can give commands, but to be a successful *leader* a man must be a manmaster.

* LVL, 184–5.

Knowing the value in my own case of having had responsibility thrust upon me as a young officer by my Colonel, I carried out that principle to the full with the young officers of the Regiment. By organizing the men in small squads responsibility was devolved on to the junior non-commissioned officers, as being the backbone of discipline and efficiency.

When I was a Squadron commander I had made it a practice, though it was strictly contrary to the regulations, to see every man in my Squadron privately and alone in my room. I set him at his ease by giving him something to smoke or letting him have tea with me; and, in ordinary conversation, I got him to tell me what induced him to join the Service, what his past life had been, what were his ambitions, who were his people, and so on. In this way one got into close friendly touch with each individual and by inviting their confidences one secured their confidence.

It is still a neglected item in education that the boy should be taught that his rights as a citizen should in the first place be earned by serious performance of his civic duties and responsibilities. It should be an unwritten but a none the less acknowledged law that a man only has rights when he has earned them, and he earns them not merely by fighting the impulse to become a waster or a criminal, but by energetically and conscientiously playing his part as a good citizen. In a word, he must play in his place and play the game for the community if he wants to wear the colours of his team.

HQG, July 1914

Playing the Game

Regimental scouts*

I started a system of organizing and training scouts in the Regiment, which eventually came to be adopted for the Army generally.

I obtained leave from Army Headquarters for those men who had taken the trouble to go through the training to wear on their arm a distinguishing badge as scouts. For this I chose the *Fleur-de-Lys*, which marks the North point on the compass, as the scout is the man who can show the way like a compass needle.

Lord Haldane informed me later that this scheme of scouts had been adopted for the Army generally and that to encourage it men who had passed their tests as scouts would receive two pence a day extra pay. I assured him that two pence a year, in the shape of a badge to wear, would do the trick at less expense. Men will do a lot for a badge – vain creatures that we are.

'A Scout is loyal', and he does not show it by flag-waving and shouting. Any ass can do that.

BSA Microfilms, 00928, re: *The Coronation*

Realistic manoeuvres†

Our Scout work was done as much by night as by day. In order to give the men practice I obtained permission for them to take part

* LVL, 187–9.
† IM, 272–5; LVL, 188.

in the Army manoeuvres at Attock. They had to go dismounted, as these manoeuvres were entirely among the mountains. The Pathan companies of Indian regiments were let loose in the mountains to act as an enemy against us, pursuing their own natural tactics for mountain fighting. They adopted their own national dress, and once they were up in the hills they behaved exactly as on active service against an invader. On one occasion I went up with them to see how they carried out their tactics, and it was a most interesting experience. At one time it even became exciting, for after popping away with their rifles and blank cartridge on columns of regular troops in the valley below, they began to get more bloodthirsty as they saw their fire made no impression on the enemy.

The troops began slowly but surely to climb the heights which they were holding. Behind them were some of their native tom-tom drummers, and these began drumming louder and louder and more furiously, yelling their war songs and gradually exciting the whole of the firing line, till, forgetting that it was not real war, and that they were not free Pathans, they began to lever up great boulders and to roll them down the mountain-side on the advancing troops. As the Ghoorkas came pressing on up the slopes against them, one great hook-nosed giant near me, with his eyes gleaming and his teeth glistening in a grin of rage, hurled a great rock down at the advancing riflemen. It bounced from point to point, and finally glanced off the head of a little Ghoorka, cutting open his scalp.

The Ghoorka's action was typical of his kind. Up till then he had been cheerfully panting up the mountain-side, kneeling to fire when told, and advancing with the rest in good order. Now this was all over. He stood for a moment and looked up with the blood running down his forehead, and with a grin of anger on his face; and while both hands were searching at his belt he seemed to say: 'That lets you out, you swine!' Then having found his *kookri* – the great curved knife – he put it between his teeth and proceeded to scramble up the rocks with such a speed as brought him very quickly to the crest. There was a rush of Pathans together to meet him, all throwing down their rifles and drawing their knives. In another few moments there would have been mincemeat, but one Pathan officer fortunately kept his head. Thrusting his own men back he ordered the Ghoorka, as an officer, to halt, about face, and retire. Then he seized a huge rock himself and hurled it at his own drummer, who still was tom-tomming and shrieking war-cries at the top of his voice. In that way he silenced him and closed the incident.

Drill will never make a citizen, that is fairly obvious.

HQG, January 1914 (rep. BPO, 45)

On the first day my scouts were rather astonished to find that operations ceased at nightfall, and the General in Command was equally surprised when they told him that night was just their time for getting on with the job. Up till then he had thought it was the time to rest his men, but on their suggestion he thought it a good thing to give them some night operations and afterwards expressed himself as astonished and pleased at the reconnaissance work done by the scouts and the good information they were able to supply. He was also struck with their independence in carrying all they needed in a rucksack on their backs and cooking their own meals when and where they required them.

Naturally every scout had to be able to swim rivers with his horse.

I did not allow a man* to take up scouting unless he was capable both as a horseman, marksman, and swimmer. In this latter particular a man was merely questioned as to his capabilities, but the time arrived when we actually put him to the test. On one occasion in the course of our work we had to swim a big canal, and one of the scouts in swimming over was apparently playing the fool, diving down and bobbing up again, making most fearful grimaces, which drew roars of laughter from his assembled comrades, until it suddenly struck them that he was actually in distress, when some of them promptly went to his rescue and brought him ashore.

When we had given him artificial respiration and he had recovered, we asked him whether he had learned to swim. He said 'No', but as everybody else seemed able to swim he had supposed that he could too, so he went in with the rest and found that he couldn't!

Every man ought to be able to swim. Mentally, it gives the boy a new sense of self-confidence and pluck; morally, it gives him the power of helping others in distress and puts a responsibility upon him of actually risking his life at any moment for others; and physically, it is a grand exercise for developing wind and limb.

HQG, February 1914

* IM, 109–10; PYOC, 126–7.

Playing the Game

*The taking of the Sanghao Pass**

What adds to the zest of soldiering in India is the fact that there are always rows going on on one part or other of the North-West Frontier.

Shortly after my return to Meerut I got a telegram on the 4th of January from Sir Bindon Blood, saying: 'We are having a pheasant shoot on the 7th. Hope you will join us.'

I read between the lines and started off then and there for Nowshera, the nearest station to Mardan and Dargai.

I eventually caught up with the General and his column at Sanghao. He had been assigned the task of invading the country of the Bunerwals with his division.

Soon after dawn next morning the whole of our force was on the move to attack the pass, which was only a mile distant from the camp. The ground consisted of a deep valley with a high steep ridge of about two thousand feet on each side of it. The near ridge was occupied by us, the far one by the enemy, at a distance of about 1,200 yards. The pass was merely a footpath, very steep and stony, leading over the ridge held by the enemy. There we could see Bunerwals mustering under their standards, of which there were thirty-nine, and taking their places for defending the position. These standards were tall narrow triangular flags about twelve feet high, with tufts of black fur at the head of the flag-pole. At every favourable point they had built stone breast-works or *sangars*, which their riflemen now occupied, while their swordsmen took up positions out of fire behind the ridge, to await the time when

* AD–AC, 140–44; IM, 211–17; LVL, 191–3.

our attack came near enough for them to make an effective charge with the cold steel.

But they were nonplussed by the form which the attack took: instead of advancing at once to the assault as they expected him to do, Sir Bindon Blood opened fire with two batteries of mountain artillery and one of field artillery, and for over two hours these kept up a continual hail of shells on the *sangars*. So soon as they had demolished one they turned their aim onto the next in the line, making excellent practice all the time; and they gradually and systematically blew down all the breastworks.

The enemy, considering how little they were able to do in reply, behaved with great pluck and coolness. They continually endeavoured to rebuild their walls as fast as they were knocked down. You would see a number of them in a *sangar*. Directly the flash of a gun appeared down, they all went out of sight, then, a moment later, as the shell passed over them or stuck into their wall, up came all their heads again, and they went on calmly building as before.

Here and there a man got up on a rock and waved his sword and harangued his pals or yelled at us, while others in the *sangars* stood up and reloaded their long muzzle-loading jezails.

They fired a few shots at us now and then, but the distance was too great for them: nevertheless we found it best not to stand in too much of a group near the General.

In the meantime our infantry were forming in the valley below, ready to clamber up the face of the position to take it by storm; while a battalion scaled the mountain away to the west of the enemy to take them in flank.

As the attack began to develop the enemy tried to resist it with musketry and by rolling great rocks down the mountain-side. These latter were the worst kind of missile, as one of them in its career might crash through half a company at a time.

It was fascinating to watch one of these rocks rolling over and over, faster and faster, knocking chips off other rocks as it bounded from them in its mad descent, then taking a clear leap over a cliff of a hundred feet or so and splashing down among the stones of a water-course, going faster till it was flying through the air, then plunging out of sight into a ravine, to reappear a second later, tearing on lower down, banging from one side to the other of the *nullah* till it disappeared out of sight in the thick bush of the basin below us.

The troops, having experienced these rock-rolling games in previous fights, always kept well out of ravines, but this served the enemy's ends all the same because, by so doing, the troops necessarily exposed themselves all the more to the rifle fire. But on this occasion the enemy did not get a fair chance with their rifles, as our guns and our long-distance infantry fire did not leave the enemy alone for a second.

Under such an unrelenting storm of shell the enemy could do nothing; their defences were knocked to pieces, they themselves were losing heavily, and presently they realised that we were taking them in flank as well as in front. Many of their leaders had fallen, and others had begun to think that it was time to exercise discretion rather than valour, and to make their best way home.

Thus gradually a retirement began. The standards were all kept flying at their different stations to make it appear as though the whole force were there, but in reality the retreat had begun before our infantry had come within reach of the defenders. And when our flanking force made good its attack, followed directly afterwards by the final rush of the main body on the front, the enemy's retreat became a rapid flight, and the position was ours.

> *The only true and sound foundation for peace in the world is the development of broader-minded, unselfish character in the peoples themselves, whereby they may form a united community in their own country and at the same time be sympathetic and friendly neighbours to others.*
>
> *Jamboree, July 1935*

The bravest man I ever saw*

While the artillery were in the midst of pounding the *sangars* we noticed three men, in one *sangar*, armed only with swords, who disdained to take cover when the shots came near them, but coolly stood up, waving their curved glittering blades. They were evidently encouraging their fellow-tribesmen to make a counterattack on the British troops, who were now clambering up the face of the position.

In the midst of their harangue a well-aimed shell smashed down the wall that had so far protected the trio, and for the moment we thought that they too must have fallen. But out of the smoke and dust of the explosion the three leapt forth untouched. Then, instead of making for other shelter, they came running rapidly down the mountain-side as if to attack their would-be

* AD–AC, 144–7; IM, 217–22; LVL, 194–6.

attackers. After coming a few yards one of them turned off on a side path, which led up the hill again and over the crest, and he soon disappeared out of sight. As he did so the second man also turned and made his way after him.

But the third came steadily on. There was something very much to be admired in the bold, determined way in which he advanced alone, without a single friend to help him, to attack a whole force of enemies. With all the coolness and agility of a trained mountaineer he came springing down the rock hill-side, his loose flowing robes flying in the wind, and his curved sword glittering in the sunlight as he waved it above his head.

At first it seemed as if he were making for a big rock to roll down, but he passed it. Coming to a bit of a precipice, he stopped a moment to find a way of descent; then, after carefully creeping down, once more he took up his running, leaping pace.

Looking at him through glasses, I could see little spits of dust flicked up by bullets aimed at him, now above, now below, or to one side: closely, but never hitting him, nor causing him to falter for an instant.

Suddenly he stumbles and nearly falls, but he is up again in a moment: he is hit, evidently in the leg, for, tearing off a bit of his *pugaree*, he hastily binds up his thigh above the knee. Now, having felt the sting of lead, he will surely retire or hide by a friendly rock — but no; having tied up his leg, he came on again just as though he had merely stopped to tie up a shoe-lace in an ordinary way.

I noticed, however, that he kicked off his sandals at this moment: whether it was that they did not give him sufficient foothold, or that he felt that he was about to tread on holy ground — in death — I know not, but he now increased his pace. It was evident that he meant to die at the enemy's hands. Such an act, in his belief, gave him certain entry into Heaven; but if, in being killed, he could compass the death of an infidel, his entry would be enhanced by higher honours; and for this reason he was now rushing down through a spray of bullets to try to cut down one man ere he fell himself.

It was a grand and pathetic sight to see his rush; one only felt a longing to stop the merciless shots that were being aimed at him. Some of our men in front of him did cease firing at him, whether out of admiration or under orders I don't know. It seemed a race between him and his fate. Would he live to reach our line, from which he was now but a hundred and fifty yards distant?

No — suddenly he pitches heavily forward onto his face, rolls over a couple of times and lies motionless. His fate has met him. He is dead.

Shortly after, I passed him where he lay: a fine bearded man in the prime of life. A few minutes before so very full of vitality and frenzy, now inert, and never again to be excited.

His face was very calm and solemn, almost as though he were looking away beyond our range of earthly vision, and could see before him the pleasures of eternal peace which he had won for himself by fighting this one short battle, in which earthly attractions and fear of death were deliberately set aside at the supposed call of his god.

I was glad to see that one of our men, on coming to the spot, laid him straight, took the dead man's waistcloth and reverently covered him with it. It was a little act that showed a large heart and a respect for an enemy who had died for his faith — differ though it might from his own. It was a lesson, in its way, to many of us who are perhaps better educated, but less broad-minded than this simple soldier.

> *Jesus Christ came into the world to tell us that our duty was to serve God by doing two things:*
> 1. *To love God.*
> 2. *To love our neighbour: that is, to be friendly and helpful to our fellow creatures.*
>
> *So you see, our duty is quite simple.*
>
> ATM, 191

*The call of Kashmir**

There are times in every man's life when his whole being cries out for a steady spell of doing nothing in particular, at least nothing that matters. Nowhere is this so acutely felt as in India. A feeling of staleness comes over you, and instinctively you look round for an antidote. If the call of the wild then makes itself heard the right thing is to yield to it and obey, for to many that is the one effective antidote for staleness. It is to me.

I had been thinking a good deal of Kashmir in the summer of 1898, and, curiously enough, soon afterwards I was prostrated by an attack of this strange disease. I decided to take a trip to Kashmir, to loaf in the lowlands, with the object of getting a month's complete laziness and change of climate – and I got it.

* IM, 288.

The Adventures of My Life

*Each can imbibe for himself, under the general encouragement of the teacher,
the wonders and beauties of the universe around him, and thus develop an
outlook of wider interests together with some realization of the Creator and
the spiritual side of life.*

SYM, 64

Between a wizard and a panel doctor*

When I was in Kashmir, some natives brought to me a young man.
They said he had fallen off a high bank. He was in great pain, and
his friends and relatives were already considering him as good as
dead.

On examination, I found no bones broken, but his right shoulder out of joint at the socket. So I told them to lay him flat on his
back, and I began to take off my right shoe, or rather the grass
sandal that I was wearing.

Some of the bystanders, seeing me do this, said: 'Oh! he is
going to pray,' and immediately began unfastening my other sandal for me.

But I wasn't going to pray, and took only my right sandal off.

Then I sat down alongside the patient, facing towards his head,
my right leg against his right side, so that my heel came into the
armpit of the injured shoulder. I got one of his friends to sit on
the other side of him to hold him down.

Then I caught hold of his wrist with both hands and gave a

---

* SFB, 219–20; IM, 338–42; YKE, 38–9.

long, steady pull at his arm, using my heel as a lever, till the shoulder suddenly clicked into its place again. Then he fainted.

His mother howled, and said that I had made a nice mess of the job, and had killed him. Then there came a discussion as to whether he was not dead: then they began to get excited and not to like me any more.

But I grinned and put on my shoe, and told her that I would now bring him to life quite sound and well – which I proceeded to do by sprinkling a little water over his face. He gradually came to his senses and found that his arm was practically all right. Afterwards I gave him some Jacob's oil to rub on the shoulder.

His own astonishment and theirs was very great, and within half an hour my tent was full of fruit and chickens and eggs as thankful offerings.

'Come on', rather than 'Go on', when you want a job done.

Wade, 56

12. The South African War

Camping is the joyous part of a Scout's life.

SFB, DE, 9

Mission to South Africa*

I was at home in London, just back from India in June 1899, enjoying what I considered my well-earned leave, when, lunching at the Naval and Military Club, a new bomb was hurled at me.

George Gough, ADC to Lord Wolseley, sitting at a table near

* LVL, 198–9.

by, suddenly came across and said: 'I thought you were in India. I have just cabled to you to come home as the Commander-in-Chief wants to see you.'

With such coolness as I could command I said: 'Well, here I am'; and after lunch we went down together to the War Office and I was once more shown into Lord Wolseley's room.

He had a knack of trying to spring surprises on you and was all the better pleased if you were not bowled out by them. I think it was his way of judging a man's character, and I took care accordingly not to be caught out if I could help it.

On this occasion he said: 'I want you to go to South Africa.'

With the air of a well-trained butler I said: 'Yes, sir.'

'Well, can you go on Saturday next?' (This was Monday.)

'No, sir.'

'Why not?'

Knowing well the sailings of the South African steamers, I replied: 'There's no ship on Saturday, but I can go on Friday.'

He burst out laughing and then proceeded to tell me that there was danger of war with the Boers, he wanted me to go and quietly raise two battalions of Mounted Rifles and organize the Police Forces on the North-West Frontier of Cape Colony, in readiness should trouble arise.

He had already appointed my Staff, Lord Edward Cecil, Grenadier Guards, to be my Chief Staff Officer, and Major Hanbury-Tracy, Royal Horse Guards, to be Staff Officer.

He then asked me what my address would be before sailing, and I said that if he didn't want me in London I should be at Henley for the boat races.

'What about kit?'

'I have got all that is necessary, and South Africa is a civilized country.'

He then took me in to see Lord Lansdowne, Secretary of State for War, who accorded me the high-sounding title of 'Commander-in-Chief, North-West Frontier Forces'.

Having had my instructions I had by that evening formulated in my own mind my plan of campaign.

> When a Wolf Cub hears the words 'Nature study' his first thought is about
> school collections of dried leaves, but real Nature study means a great deal
> more than this; it means knowing about everything that is not made by man,
> but is created by God.
>
> The Wolf Cub, October 1920

Staff Officers and preparations*

My orders were to raise two battalions of Mounted Rifles, to mount, equip, train and supply them, with the least possible delay and the least possible display.

For this purpose Colonel Plumer and Colonel Hore, with several Imperial officers, would be sent out to join me, and I should have to make up the remainder of the establishment of officers from likely men in the colony.

Also, I was to take charge of and organize the Police of Rhodesia and Bechuanaland as part of my force.

But I was to make as little show as possible of these prepar-

* LVL, 199–200.

ations for fear of precipitating war by arousing the animosity of the Boers.

*The plan of the campaign**

The duty of my force was to hold the frontier on the west of the Transvaal from Vryburg in Cape Colony to Bulawayo in Rhodesia, a distance of some 650 miles, with two Regiments of Mounted Rifles (if we could raise them) and about four hundred Police, but no regular troops at all.

The railway ran most of the way close to the border of the Transvaal, and a great portion of the country was practically desert inhabited by native tribes.

I realized that to distribute men all along the border would be futile, so Colonel Plumer took the duty of raising his Regiment in Rhodesia, while Colonel Hore organized his at Ramatlabama, sixteen miles north of Mafeking.

The reason for this was that Ramatlabama was in Imperial territory, in the Bechuanaland Protectorate, whereas Mafeking was in Cape Colony, and the Cape Government, being in sympathy with the Boers, would not allow us to raise troops in that territory.

Incidentally this proved a help to our scheme of producing a moral effect on our enemy, since Ramatlabama was to the Boers a dread spot, because it was there that Dr. Jameson had three years previously organized his Raid on Johannesburg.

Thus the forming of a mounted column in this same spot

* LVL, 201-3.

naturally foreboded our making another rush from this place to capture Pretoria and the President.

At least that is what President Kruger evidently thought, judging from his frequent telegrams to his border Commandants in which he repeatedly urged them to watch Ramatlabama.

Ramatlabama was nothing more than a name, a small railway siding; there was no town there.

Mafeking, on the other hand, had railway workshops, sidings, and goods sheds; so it was here that I collected from Cape Town our stores of food, equipment, etc.

When eventually Colonel Hore had organized his Regiment at Ramatlabama I got permission from the Cape Government to place an armed guard in Mafeking to protect these stores; but as the strength of that guard was not stipulated I moved the whole Regiment into the place without delay.

At the same time Plumer's newly raised Rhodesia Regiment, together with the British South African Police in Rhodesia, took post at Tuli on the border at the ford of the Crocodile River where the main road of the Transvaal entered Rhodesia.

Thus, at the end of September we held two important strategical points both of which attracted considerable forces of Boers for a longish period during the early months of the war. They attracted more attention from the Boers owing to the fact that both forces were mounted and therefore palpably intended for active aggression and not merely for passive defence.

In this way we endeavoured to carry out, as fully as possible, our instructions, which were:

1. To draw Boer forces away from the coasts during the landing of British troops.

2. To protect British subjects in Rhodesia, Bechuanaland and Mafeking.

3. To maintain British prestige among the Bechuana, Matabele and other native tribes in those parts.

Ultimately we might link up our forces and form a column for attacking the Transvaal from the north-west, in co-operation with the troops coming from the south.

That was the general idea, but in the meantime – in order not to precipitate war – we had to enlist our men unostentatiously in different parts of Cape Colony, Natal and Rhodesia, equip them, obtain remounts, and train these as well as the men, collect our supplies and transports, and all this within a space of three months with very little help from the General or from the local Government.

It must be remembered that the ordinary training of a soldier, even with everything ready found, usually takes at least twelve months. So it meant in our case intensive and energetic work on the part of all. The marvel is that, although we only started in July, we had our force ready for service and in the field when war was declared by the Boers on the 11th October 1899.

Military training and discipline are exactly the opposite of what we inculcate in the Scout Movement.

Jamboree, October 1925

The Adventures of My Life

*The defence of Mafeking**

Mafeking was a small town of some two thousand white inhabitants which stood in the British territory, close alongside the border of the Boers' country, the Transvaal. It is about nine hundred miles from Capetown, far away up in the north-west of Cape Colony, on the railway which goes on northward to Rhodesia.

Mafeking was a very ordinary-looking place. Just a simple tin-roofed town of small houses in rectangular streets, plumped down upon the open veldt close to the Molopo stream, and half a mile from the native town – better known as the *stadt* – consisting of red-clay circular huts with thatched roofs, housing about seven thousand natives. All around is open, undulating, yellow grass prairie.

Enough and more than enough has been written about the so-called siege of Mafeking in books and the papers of the time. As an actual feat of arms it was a very minor operation; it was in reality an investment – of a rather domestic kind at that. And it was largely a piece of bluff, but bluff which was justified by the special circumstances and which in the end succeeded in its object.

At the same time the objects of our holding on in Mafeking have if anything been under-estimated. It is now in fact known that twenty thousand Boers were to rise in Cape Colony alone on the receipt of the news that Mafeking had fallen.

The besieged consisted of a thousand men, newly organized and armed, six hundred white women and children, and seven thousand natives. We retained there at first some 8,000 Boers

* SMEA, 25–30 and 33–4; AA, 134–6; LVL, 203–4 and 211.

under Cronje and later smaller numbers under Snyman, from October 1899 till 17th May 1900.

For the first month of the siege General Cronje commanded the Boer investing force. After he went south to Kimberley General Snyman was in command, and, occasionally in his absence, General Dantje Botha.

Snyman was a cowardly creature who shelled the hospital, convent and women's laager, but had not the pluck to lead an attack. His own men had a low opinion of him, and he was reduced to 'private' after his failure. Dantje Botha was, on the other hand, a fine type of the old Boer: a dour, stolid man who, though he had been friendly with Englishmen before the war (being a good sportsman and an owner of racehorses) took up his country's cause with a whole heart, and went through the campaign to the bitter end, though he could easily have obtained good terms for surrendering after the relief of Mafeking.

That Cronje and his men were so tied was however due, I think, not so much to our defence as to the unwillingness of the Boer to be shot in getting possession of an unimportant little town which did not appeal to him. Kruger refused permission to Cronje to storm Mafeking if it were likely to cost more than fifty burghers.[1]

From this [see map opposite] it will be seen that we made a circle of small detached defence-works completely round the town and native *stadt*, which were held by our seven hundred enlisted men, while an inner ring round the town itself was manned by the three hundred townsmen. The perimeter of our outer line of defence was at first over five miles, but we gradually pushed back the investing enemy at various points till it was extended to over eight miles — an absurdly large allowance for so small a force under ordinary circumstances, but one which we found necessary to keep the town out of close rifle range.

We acted as much as possible on the principle that aggression is the soul of defence, and delivered kicks at the enemy whenever we could with our small numbers find opportunity; and these, together with various ruses for shaking the Boers' confidence in themselves, had the effect of toning down any ardour they may have had for attack.

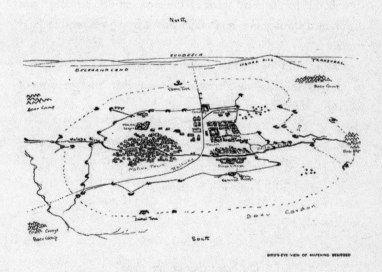

BIRD'S-EYE VIEW OF MAFEKING BESIEGED

The sketch-map gives a bird's-eye view of Mafeking and its defences and attacked positions.

Playing the Game

Very much of the praise that was showered on Mafeking for holding large forces of the Boers up in the north-west at a time when they were needed in the south and for reassuring the native tribes of the frontier, was really due to Colonel Plumer and his Rhodesian column co-operating with us outside the place. If any proof were needed it is to be found in Kruger's captured telegrams to his commandants before Mafeking, in which his anxiety was shown by continual injunctions to 'Watch Plumer at all costs,' and his repeated bleating of 'Where is Plumer?'

But that it should have resulted successfully in the end was entirely due to the good spirit of the men and officers which was maintained throughout, and under pretty trying circumstances at times.

Cronje, who for the first month commanded the Boers against us, did us the honour afterwards to say that 'the garrison of Mafeking are not men, they are devils'.

Remember that St Paul said that God was 'the God of Hope'. Hope gives you pluck and comfort at a bad time, and your hopefulness will comfort others round you and nerve them to stick out.

YKE, 69

The beginning of the siege*

I was lucky enough to see the first Boer artillery appear on the scene, as well as the first shot fired in the siege of Mafeking.

* SMEA, 35–6; LVL, 204.

The Adventures of My Life

After the enemy had cut the line north and south of us on the 11th of October, I was looking to Signal Hill, a rise about six miles to the NE where we usually had a look-out post of Cape Police. I wanted to see whether they were making any signals yet of an enemy in sight. To my surprise no one was on the hill, but while I looked two or three figures came in view from the far side, and, after an interval of a few minutes, three little groups of men and horses at equal distance appeared on the sky-line. They were guns coming into action. A puff of smoke, a distant bang, and a cloud of dust 200 yards away from the town showed that the bombardment had begun; but the Boer gunners soon found that the range was too great, and they moved to a nearer position and were thus enabled to throw their shells into the town.

The first shell fell very short, and while I was watching these from a corner of the street, a girl came bicycling past me. I said: 'Young lady, you had better go home and get under cover. The Boers are beginning to shell us.'

She said: 'Oh, are those shells? May I stay and look at them?'

But I packed her off home. She would soon learn to know quite enough about shells, when they got the range of the town. But her fearless spirit was typical of that which distinguished all the women of Mafeking.

Choosing a wife is a most delicate and difficult job and fellows are too apt to fall in love with a pretty face and not to look too closely into the character behind it. It is the character which makes all the difference in after years.

Letter to a young man asking advice on marriage, quoted in BPBB

Playing the Game

*My look-out tower and Headquarters**

My look-out tower was on the top of a house in the Market Square. I spent many happy hours there – in fact, most of my time by day. There was a writing-desk on top, and a speaking-tube which communicated with the underground telephone exchange below. From here I was able not only to see every one of our own defence works but also all the works of the Boers, and could observe what went on in their main camps.

Close to the tower on the same roof was my 'pepperbox' refuge made of sandbags, into which I could retire when bullets came too thickly.

Our bomb-proof headquarters and telephone exchange was a queer dark hole in which an officer was always on duty, and most of the staff passed many weary hours there.

The earthen roof was covered with a tarpaulin to prevent it getting soaked and over-heavy in the tropical rains that fell: the front door was protected from bullets by some bales of hay. We flew a tiny Union Jack on weekdays to give as little mark as possible for the Boer fire, but we flaunted a big one on Sundays, when there was no firing.

In the early days of the siege we also had here the bell which rang out the warning to the town when our look-out men saw the enemy loading and aiming their big gun. Small hand-bells

---

* SMEA, 42–4.

signalled when she was fired and gave people twenty-two seconds in which to gain shelter.

> *Life would pall if it were all sugar; salt is bitter if taken by itself, but when tasted as part of the dish, it savours the meat. Difficulties are the salt of life.*

RTS, 15

Fort Ayr*

Our extreme Western fort was called Fort Ayr, originally so named because it had to be made detached from the remainder of the defences, *en l'air.* The reason for our making it so was that there was a small ridge which the Boers one day showed signs of occupying by a number of artillery officers visiting it. Through our glasses we observed a spot on the ridge where a *meerkat*[2] was sitting up which showed to us that at least one portion of the ground was soft and not rock, otherwise the *meerkat* would have no burrow.

Taking the compass-bearing of the *meerkat* we moved there at night, found soft ground, and dug a fort before morning. When the Boers came with the view of occupying the ridge they found us already in position, and had to make their work some 800 yards further back.

A curious little episode happened at this fort one Sunday when the garrisons of both works were sitting about looking at each other. A man in our fort accidentally fired the Maxim, and the

* SMEA, 64.

Boers at once sought cover and prepared to retort to what they considered an act of treachery. Lt. Greenfield, commanding the fort, considered that he was to blame, and walked straight out to the Boers without a white flag to apologize. Fortunately they were sporting enough not to open fire on him and accepted his explanation over a mutual exchange of cigarettes and newspapers.

This fort of the Boers we styled Standard and Diggers' Fort, because the garrison were generally willing to exchange copies of the 'Standard and Diggers' News'[3] for cigarettes, especially when there were any accounts of British disasters in the paper; when they declined to part, we always took it as a negative sign that our army had gained a success somewhere.

> *Efficiency is all very well, but inside there must be something more, there must be courage and pluck and the determination to do your duty no matter what risk or danger it means to yourself.*
>
> PYOC, 130

A home-made gun*

Our men started to manufacture a gun out of such material as they could find in the town.

They got a steam-pipe out of an engine, and then heated up a lot of bars of iron like the rods of iron railings, and twisted them while red hot round and round this steam-pipe, and hammered them tight until they made a complete iron casing to it, and then

* YFBS, 151–3; SMEA, 58.

they put on a second layer to make it doubly strong. That made the barrel of our gun, the steam-pipe being the bore. Then they made wooden models of a big ring with a big knob at each side to form the 'trunnions' of the gun, by which it is supported on the gun-carriage.

By means of these wooden models they were able to make a 'mould' — that is, the exact shape of the trunnions and ring — out of damp sand. Into this mould they poured molten bronze, and then made a metal trunnion ring, which they slipped on to the barrel while still hot, and then quickly cooled it so that it was shrunk on quite tight.

But the barrel was still open at both ends, so a big block of metal called the 'breech' was made in the same way in a mould and shrunk on to one end, and our gun was complete.

After that they merely had to bore a tiny hole near the breech through the barrel into the 'bore' through which the charge could be lit, and also they had to add the sights and to mount the gun on a carriage (which was really part of the carriage of a threshing-machine), and then we had a first-rate gun. They called it 'The Wolf', because that was my nick-name.

Major Panzera was the commander of our artillery, and he superintended the making of the gun, which was carried out by the men at the railway repairing shops.

But then a gun is not much use without ammunition, and shells don't grow on every bush, nor do you pick up gun-powder wherever you walk. All these things had to be made, and out of the very limited supply of material which we had in the place.

Of course, for the shells we had again to make moulds of sand of exactly the right size to fit the bore of the gun, and to pour molten iron into the moulds to make the shells. They were made hollow, in order to hold a bursting charge of powder, and a hole was left by which they were afterwards filled with the charge, and in which a cord was inserted, which, after catching fire in the flame of the discharge of the gun, would burn while the shell was flying through the air till it reached the charge in the shell, and so burst the whole thing among the enemy.

It all sounds very easy and simple, but to get hard metal sufficiently hot to run it into moulds you want something more than an ordinary fire, and we had to make a kind of special 'blast-furnace' for the purpose. Here again our men made their 'bricks without straw'. They got an iron house-cistern and filled it with firebrick, which they got out of the furnace of a locomotive. Then they introduced 'forced draught' – that is, they pumped air into the furnace, as a blacksmith does at his little fire, but on a big scale – by means of a fan driven by an engine through a hose-pipe. In this way they got sufficient heat to melt the metal.

Then we had to make gunpowder to fire the gun with, and this we did by making charcoal from charred willow wood, and mixing in saltpetre (which was used in that part of the country for washing the sheep) and other ingredients, till they made a very fair powder.

It was a great day when we first fired the gun. She was loaded and set ready for firing, and then the gun's men and onlookers lay down under cover in case she should prefer to burst rather than send out the shell. But she didn't burst; she seemed to know what was wanted of her, and banged out the shell with a tremendous burst of smoke and flame!

It was a grand success, and considerably astonished the Boers, who thought that we must have had a new gun sent up to us unknown to themselves. But we never trusted the 'Wolf' so far as to stand up to her when firing her, and it was lucky we didn't, for one day she not only sent the shell flying on its way to the front, but she also sent her own breech flying backward, luckily without damaging anybody.

But after that we not only shrunk the breech on again, but we clamped it there with iron bands passed round it and hooked on to the trunnion ring, so that it could not blow off. After this it did useful service in the defence of the place.

'Ask a policeman' is the well-known formula for dealing with any ordinary dilemma in every-day life. Similarly, when you are in doubt as to what is the best way to deal with the boy in training him, it will save you time, worry, thought and eyesight if, instead of studying volumes of psychology, you consult the better authority on the subject — that is, the boy himself.

HQG, October 1922

*The Mafeking Cadet Corps**

When we found we were to be attacked at Mafeking, we ordered our garrison — some 700 trained men, police and volunteers — to the points they were to protect. Then we armed the townsmen, of whom there were some 300. Some of them were old frontiersmen,

* SFB, 9–10; LVL, 274; SMEA, 63; PYOC, 140–41.

and quite equal to the occasion. But many of them were young shopmen, clerks and others, who had never handled a rifle before.

Altogether, then, we only had about a thousand men to defend the place, which was about five miles round and contained 600 white women and children and about 7,000 natives.

Every man was of value, and as the weeks passed by and many were killed and wounded, the duties of fighting and keeping watch at night became harder for the rest.

It was then that Lord Edward Cecil, the chief staff officer, gathered together the boys of Mafeking and made them into a cadet corps. He put them in uniform and drilled them. And a jolly smart and useful lot they were. Previously, we had used a large number of men for carrying orders and messages, keeping look-out and acting as orderlies and so on. These duties were now handed over to the boy cadets and the men were released to strengthen the firing-line.

The cadets, under their sergeant-major, a boy named Good-year, did good work with the greatest pluck, even under fire, and well deserved the medals they got at the end of the war.

Many of them rode bicycles, and we were thus able to establish a post by which people could send letters to their friends in the different forts, or about the town, without going out under fire themselves. For these letters we made postage stamps which had on them a picture of a cadet bicycle orderly.

I said to one of these boys on one occasion, when he came in through a rather heavy fire:

'You will get hit one of these days riding about like that when shells are flying round.'

'I pedal so quickly, sir, they'll never catch me!' he replied.

These boys didn't seem to mind the bullets one bit. They were always ready to carry out orders, though it meant risking their lives every time.

> *Why is a boy's psychology like a violin string? Because it needs tuning to the right pitch and can then give forth real music.*

HQG, August 1922 (rep. BPO, 104)[4]

*Money**

As money was a necessity for paying wages and for stocks commandeered we took over the cash in the Standard Bank, but also found it necessary to issue paper money of our own, because anybody who possessed or obtained money took good care to bury it, not knowing what the next night or day might bring forth.

I therefore drew a design for one-pound bank-notes and printed minor ones for two shillings and one shilling.

Banknote-making does not unfortunately come in our Army curriculum either in practice or theory: in fact, at our ruling rates of pay junior officers hardly know what a banknote is, even by sight.

We tried various dodges – drew a design on copper, bit it out with acid all right, but could not get sufficient pressure to print it well though we tried it through a mangle.

The design for the one-pound note I drew on a boxwood

* LVL, 209–10; SMEA, 44–6.

block, made from a croquet mallet cut in half, but this again, owing to improvised tools, was not satisfactory from the artistic point of view, so we used that as a ten-shilling note and I drew another design which was photographed for the pound note.

These could all be exchanged for cash if presented within six months of the end of the siege. But none of them were presented, since people kept them or sold them as interesting mementoes.

Thus the Government scored at least six thousand pounds and for two years afterwards were calling on me for an explanation of what they supposed was faulty book-keeping which showed us so much to the credit. Sentiment didn't enter into their calculations.

A man with hobbies never has time to waste.

RTS, 46

Stamps*

It was only fair that people who sent letters should bear part of the cost. For this purpose shilling stamps were issued. In order to obtain stamps we bought up the stock at the post-office, and printed across them their new siege value.

Then it became also necessary to start a postal service inside Mafeking by means of which people could communicate with their friends stationed in different parts of the defence. For this service it became necessary to manufacture stamps of our own.

* SMEA, 46–7; HQG, June 1915; LVL, 210–11.

The Adventures of My Life

Some time after the siege I received from some postal authority in England an objection to the stamps we had made for ourselves in Mafeking, saying for one thing they were not legal tender, and for another that they were of no use to collectors as a genuine issue of stamps.

I felt inclined to reply that I did not care very much for either reason, because they had done their work. That these should have become of value to collectors in spite of official objection I did not foresee. If I had I should have kept some myself.

The stamps were devised by the Chief Staff Officer and Postmaster, who put their heads together, and then had them printed. One day they produced the stamps, penny ones, bearing a picture of one of our cadet cyclist dispatch riders, and this became the regulation stamp for internal postage; but in addition to this, apparently as a little surprise for me, they printed a sheet of stamps with my portrait on them as a memento of the siege.

As they were entirely for local and temporary use it was not a matter of any importance, but later I heard that it was considered a piece of gross *lèse-majesté* on my part, if not of treason, to print my own head on the stamps, and that the Queen was very annoyed with me! Well, if she was, Her Majesty did not show it but on the contrary sent me most gracious and appreciative messages both during and after the siege, and personally directed my promotion to Major-General. It is amusing to see how rumour gets about.

Remember, you are you. You have your own life to live, and if you want to be successful, if you want to be happy, it is you who have to gain it for yourself. Nobody else can do it for you.

RTS, 2**

Playing the Game

*Messages to Mafeking**

When we sent letters out from Mafeking during the siege, we gave them to natives who were able to creep out between the Boer outposts. Once through the line of sentries, the Boers mistook the natives for their own and took no further notice of them. They carried the messages in this way: the letters were written on thin paper and half a dozen or more were crumpled up tightly into a little ball, then rolled up into a piece of lead paper, such as tea is packed in. The native scout would carry a number of these little balls in his hand, or hanging round his neck loosely on strings. If he saw himself in danger of being captured by an enemy, he would notice landmarks round about him and drop all the balls on the ground, where they looked like small stones. Then he would walk boldly on until accosted by the enemy, who, if he searched him, would find nothing.

The messenger would wait around for perhaps a day or two, until the coast was clear, then come back to the spot where the landmarks told him the letters were lying.

During the siege I had two letters from Cecil Rhodes in Kimberley; they were rather to the effect that I should appeal for more troops to be sent to help Mafeking, but I was not able myself to see any reason or necessity for this.

* SMEA, 67–8; LVL, 211; SFB, 73–4; ATS, 118–21; MAAS, 71–3.

The Adventures of My Life

*Lively nights**

I was always expecting a night attack, and in order to discourage this we started searchlights in every fort, that is to say we made one searchlight with a big cowl made of biscuit tins on top of a pole which we stood on the ground and turned gently round in the direction required.

Apropos of disturbing the enemy at night I had a joyous little dodge of my own. I had a big megaphone made out of tin, with which I could proceed to one of our advance trenches in the night, and play a ventriloquist stunt upon the enemy, as I found that one's voice carried quite easily twelve hundred yards, and I would command an imaginary attacking party, giving in the voice of the officer orders to advance very silently.

Trenches and grenades†

Another bright invention which necessity mothered upon us was -- bombs.

These we made out of old meat or jam tins filled with dynamite or powder with a fuse attached, and we hurled them into the Boers' trenches. They soon replied with more artistically made hand grenades. But they did not like ours and they withdrew their advanced trench a few yards, and there we stuck for a fortnight at sixty-eight yards apart.

* LVL, 205–6.
† LVL, 207; QTW, 54–5; SMEA, 58–9.

Playing the Game

To Sergeant Page, who had done sea fishing from the docks at East London,[5] it occurred to 'cast' bombs from the end of a fishing rod, which he did with great effect, and a range of nearly a hundred yards.

*A Boer ruse**

At one time, during the siege of Mafeking we had a fortnight of close contact between ourselves and the Boers' trenches, at sixty-eight yards apart. We finally made a determined effort to get into their works, mainly by cutting our way into the communication trench which led from their advanced work back to their base.

In the middle of our effort, at about three a.m., we heard the Boers making a considerable noise, calling to each other to retire, and we could see them making their way through their communication trench, evidently vacating their front line.

My men were wild with joy and eager to rush in to take possession, but I stopped them.

Observation. Why should the enemy be leaving noisily, when one would expect them to creep away quietly?

Deduction. There was something suspicious and caution was necessary.

So we sent forward two trusty scouts to discover what was up. They got into the communication trench and were feeling their way along it towards the main work just vacated, when they found that the wall of the trench was wet to the touch, and presently they

* LVL, 132–3.

discovered that a wire ran along inside the wall in the trench and was just recently plastered over with mud, evidently to hide it.

We cut the wire, and then followed it up into the main trench, where it led to a beautifully laid mine of two hundred pounds of nitro-glycerine, which would have blown us sky-high had we gone in as a body.

Not content with discovering this we got hold of the end of the wire, and reeled it, nearly a hundred yards of good copper wire with which we were now able to lay mines, using the nitro-glycerine in smaller proportions.

Our men gave three cheers for the Queen, while our friends at the other hand were trying to touch off their mine and cursing their luck at its very greatly delayed action.

> *Ill-luck is a cowardly fellow. He will get you if you show fear or believe in him. If you turn on him, kick him and tread him down, he will dissolve away into nothing.*

> LS, 29

*The food problem**

As time went on naturally we began to get anxious about our food supply; everybody was strictly rationed and my wretched Staff had to live on a lower ration than the men, as we were then able to judge how little was necessary for keeping us going, and at the

* LVL, 208–9.

same time the men could not complain that the officers were living on the fat of the land while they were starving.

Incidentally we learned to economize very rigidly in the matter of food and also to devise food substitutes.

When a horse was killed his mane and tail were cut off and sent to the hospital for stuffing mattresses and pillows. His shoes went to the foundry for making shells. His skin, after having the hair scalded off, was boiled with his head and feet for many hours, chopped up small, and with the addition of a little saltpetre was served out as 'brawn'.

His flesh was taken from the bones and minced in a great mincing machine and from his inside were made skins into which the meat was crammed and each man received a sausage as his ration.

The bones were then boiled into a rich soup, which was dealt out at the different soup kitchens; and they were afterwards pounded up into powder with which to adulterate the flour. So there was not much of that horse that was wasted.

Our flour was made from the horses' oats, pounded and winnowed. But with all our appliances we never succeeded in getting completely rid of the husks. We managed thus, however, to issue to every man daily a big biscuit of oatmeal.

The husks of the oats were put to soak in large tubs of water for a number of hours, at the end of which the scum formed by the husks was scraped off and given as food to the hospital chickens, while the residue formed a paste closely akin to that used by bill-stickers. This was called sowens,[6] a sour kind of mess, but very healthy and filling.

Amongst other things we supplied for the invalids in hospital a special blancmange which was made from the *Poudre de Riz* commandeered from the hairdressers' and chemists' shops.

Locusts in Mafeking*

Locusts are brutes and deserve no pity.

Once, however, while we were besieged in Mafeking, we were glad to see them. A big swarm settled in the place though there was not much for them to eat there; but there was still less for us, so we all sallied out with empty sacks and beat them to death. Then we collected their remains, dried them in the sun, pounded them up and made our dinners off them.

Sunday entertainments†

On the Recreation Ground, we used to have our Sunday Carnivals. As you may remember the Boers did not fire on Sundays, and we therefore kept that day as the Sabbath up till noon, and treated it as Saturday in the afternoon, when we gave everybody as big a dose of cheerfulness as we could manage, to carry them through the next week's shelling.

On one occasion we had a babyshow of babies born during the siege.

* MSK, 50–2; SMEA, 61.
† SMEA, 51.

Playing the Game

A good dose of laughing is to me like a bath for the brain.

RTS, 83

Eloff's attack*

I received a letter from the Boer Commandant, Sarel Eloff, one day, in which he said that he and his friends proposed coming into Mafeking shortly to play cricket with us.

To which I replied: 'My side is in at present and yours is in the field. You must bowl us out before your side can come in.'

Not long afterwards he made his effort to do so.

It was on the Western side that the Boers made their great attack on May 12. It began by a heavy long-range fire from the East side at 4 a.m. One of the bullets (an explosive one) fell under my bed, having come over the wall of biscuit boxes with which I was protected, which showed that it must have been fired at a great elevation and therefore at a great distance. Heavy fire was maintained from the same direction, which soon showed that it was merely a demonstration, and we telephoned therefore to the defences on the opposite side to warn them to be on the look-out for something more serious in their direction. About half-past four the Western defences telephoned that a party of about 300 Boers had made their way up the river-bed and had got into the native *stadt*.

I ordered the Western defenders then to close in on the river-bed so as to prevent any supports from coming in after the leading body, and sent a reserve squadron down to assist them.

* SMEA, 65–6; LVL, 211–13.

They succeeded in driving off about 500 of the enemy without difficulty and then applied themselves to preventing the advance party from getting back. These Boers in the meantime had pushed their way through the native town, setting fire to part of it, and had rushed the old police fort in the centre and had made prisoners of the regimental staff of the Protectorate Regiment in it, viz. 3 officers and 15 men, who in the darkness mistook them for friends.

The Boers had in passing through the native town got split up into three parties, and when it became light we were able to surround and attack them one at a time. The first party surrendered, the second were driven out with loss by three squadrons of the Protectorate Regiment under Major Godley, and the third in the police fort, after holding out all day and making a vain attempt to break out, surrendered.

During the day while the struggle was going on in the *stadt* the enemy outside made a demonstration as if about to attack and kept up a shell fire on the place, but without much effect.

We captured 108 prisoners, among whom was Commandant Eloff, Kruger's grandson, and several German and French officers; we also found 10 killed and 19 wounded Boers, and their ambulance picked up 30 more killed and wounded. Our losses were only 4 killed, 10 wounded.

Our men, although weak from want of food and exercise, worked with splendid pluck and energy for the fourteen hours of fighting, and instances of personal bravery were particularly numerous.

During the action barrows with such refreshments as horse soup and other delicacies went round to the men who were fighting, and one of these good fellows on passing me after the fight was over said he would like a fight like that every day if it were going to bring such an increase of his rations.

> *The academic training has taught to generation after generation their national history with all its victories in war, too often dishonestly omitting its defeats, and maligning its enemies while extolling its piracies. The desirable course seems to be to change all this and to teach the rising generation the peaceful triumphs of their country and to think in terms of Peace towards other countries.*

Jamboree, January 1923

*A brave orderly**

While the firing was going on between our men and the Boers, my orderly[7] was seen to ride out into the open going towards the Boer position. He waved a white handkerchief to show them that he was coming on a peaceful mission, but they fired at him all the same. Still he continued to advance, although bullets whistled past him or spat up the dust near him.

My orderly pressed on until suddenly his horse collapsed and fell, shot. The orderly regained his feet and instead of lying behind the horse or shamming death, as he might have done, he got up and went forward on foot. Still forward, mark you, towards the enemy who were firing at him. And, though it was only one soli-

* ATM, 57–8.

tary man coming towards them, they continued to fire on him, till at last he reeled and fell, wounded.

Two of our men rushed out from their cover near by and dragged him hurriedly behind a building which gave him protection. But he was mortally wounded, and as he sobbed out his life he said to his rescuers: 'Tell the colonel that I tried to carry his message to the Boers, but they shot me before I could get there'.

I had given him no message to take and to this day it is a mystery what message he was taking or who had given it to him to take. But what we do know is that the gallant fellow received from someone what he understood to be an order to go out to the enemy, and he went.

'My country before myself' should be your aim.

SFB, DE, 15

*The relief**

A week after our repulse of Eloff's attack Mafeking was finally relieved.

It was from the Western front that our relief took place.

On May 16 and 17 the Boers around us were seen to be sending parties round to the west. We had complete information now by runners and by carrier-pigeons of the approach of a relief column from the South to join hands with Plumer, who was too

* SMEA, 69–71; LVL, 213.

weak in numbers to effect anything himself, but was standing not thirty miles away ready to help us.

On the afternoon of May 17 the sound of guns to the westward told us that our relief was coming. Some of us climbed up on to the high engine-sheds of the railway works for a better view.

We could see the dust and smoke of the bursting shells in the distance, and even mounted men hurrying about from point to point.

At last came the flick-flick of a heliograph through the haze – to which we promptly sent acknowledgement.

Then we got the following:

FROM x COLONEL x MAHON x HOW x ARE x YOU x GETTING x ON x.

Then there was a pause of a long time. Again the flicker went on.

WE x ARE x FIGHTING x HARD x BUT x GETTING x ON x WE x ARE x D x F x H x (Diamond Fields Horse) AND x . . .

And that was the end of it; evidently the enemy interfered with their position.

However, it was good enough for us. With a small party of men who had volunteered themselves as fit to march five miles (though we soon found that several could not do it) and a gun, we moved out to the front of Fort Ayr and made a diversion against the rear of the Boers who were barring the advance of the Relief Force. This was late in the evening.

The Boers cleared away from being between two fires, and in the night the relief force came in, much to our surprise, as we thought they would not attempt it till daylight.

Karri Davies,[8] with three or four men, turned up in the darkness first, bringing me a box of Queen's chocolate and the welcome news that the relief was practically accomplished.

So I went to bed.

A few minutes later I was awakened to find my brother in the Scots Guards[9] was there. He had come up as Intelligence Officer of the Relief Column.

Then I walked out, and near Fort Ayr found a whole crowd of men coming along in the darkness. It was the Relief at last!

And in a few minutes Mahon, Plumer, Frankie Rhodes, Maurice Gifford and a host of unexpected friends were foregathering over a cup of cocoa in the old Police Barracks, where a few days before Eloff had been in temporary possession.

And early next morning to our surprise we found the enemy on the east side of the place still in their positions. They did not seem to realize that the relief force had got in.

They were quickly undeceived when we pushed out against them and rushed them out of their headquarter laager into a rapid retreat to the Transvaal.

We got one of their small guns and a flag which they used to flaunt on an exceedingly high pole in front of the town; and, best of all, we got 'Boy' McLaren,[10] who had been kept a prisoner in their hospital with a shattered thigh and two wounds from bullets fired into him as he lay helpless on the ground after a fight just outside Mafeking.

Playing the Game

We received then from the Queen a message of which nearly every man kept a copy. This was what she wrote with her own hand, at her dinner-table, on receipt of the news:

I AND MY WHOLE EMPIRE GREATLY REJOICE AT THE RELIEF OF MAFEKING AFTER THE SPLENDID DEFENCE MADE BY YOU THROUGH ALL THESE MONTHS.

I HEARTILY CONGRATULATE YOU AND ALL UNDER YOU, MILITARY AND CIVIL, BRITISH AND NATIVE, FOR THE HEROISM AND DEVOTION YOU HAVE SHOWN. – V. R. AND I.

I have always maintained that if the right spirit is there, it can knock the 'im' out of the word 'impossible'.

LVL, 235

Campaigning in Northern Transvaal*

After we got out of Mafeking my column, reinforced by fine contingents of Australians and Canadians, pushed into the Transvaal through the districts of Zeerust and Rustenburg, and eventually joined hands with Lord Roberts' main army at Pretoria.

Once I had to hold three of the passes through a mountain range against the Boer forces which wanted to get through them. Their Commandant, de Wet, sent me a note written in Afrikaans,[11] in which he said that I must surrender to him, and if I did not do

* LVL, 213; ATS, 137; MAAS, 69–70; AA, 128–9.

so before the next morning he would come through with his force and take my men prisoners.

I wanted to see whether de Wet was really there or had only sent a note to pretend that he was present at that spot, when probably he was preparing a surprise for us in some other unexpected place. So I replied to his note and sent him a letter by his messenger (who had come to us under a white flag of truce), and in it I said I was not good at reading Afrikaans, and so could not make out from his letter whether he wanted us to surrender or whether he wanted to surrender to us. I soon got his reply, signed by himself, explaining that we must surrender, which assured me that he was actually there.

However, we did *not* surrender, and finding that he could not get through, de Wet went away himself next morning, while his force retired in another direction. We followed it up in pursuit and surprised it two days later at Warmbad, capturing a number of prisoners.

A comic touch was given on this occasion. A number of Boers were captured by the Australians in the act of bathing. The 'Diggers', being in rags themselves, eagerly commandeered their prisoners' clothing, and garbed in frock coats and Boer hats brought back their captives clad in towels.

Smartness in uniform and correctness in detail may seem a small matter, but has its value in the development of self-respect and means an immense deal to the reputation of the Movement among outsiders who judge by what they see.

Aids, WB, 43

Playing the Game

NOTES

1 *Harper's Magazine*, May 1900, p. 827. [Note by the Author.]

2 A South African name for the *suricate*, a small, four-toed burrowing mammal of Southern Africa, related to the mongoose and also tamed as a pet.

3 An English-language Boer newspaper published in Johannesburg.

4 One of B.-P.'s 'shaving paper notes'.

5 A port on the south-eastern coast of South Africa.

6 Strictly speaking, this Scottish word indicates a kind of porridge made from fermented oat husks.

7 The orderly was Arthur Hazlerigg, the son of a Leicestershire baronet. It seems that he was given a wrong order by a drunken officer (perhaps Ronnie Moncrieffe). While he was trying to reach the police fort conquered by Eloff he was shot in the groin and his agony lasted, in fact, several hours.

8 A very popular figure among the British of South Africa, 'Karri' Davies had spent over a year in a Boer gaol for taking part in the Jameson Raid. In the Boer War he entered besieged Ladysmith with the advance units of the British relief forces. At the relief of Mafeking he belonged to the Mahon column as Deputy Commander of the Imperial Light Horses.

9 Baden Baden-Powell, B.-P.'s companion in Russia.

10 Kenneth McLaren (known as 'The Boy' for his boyish look) was probably B.-P.'s closest friend. He had been with him since the first period in India with the 13th Hussars, where he was his sporting and hunting mate. In the Boer War he had been wounded and taken prisoner in a clash while serving in the Plumer column. B.-P. tried in vain to organize an exchange of prisoners by writing to Boer commander Snyman. Freed as mentioned in the text, 'The Boy' was pronounced invalid and sent back to England. Later he went with B.-P. to the first Scout camp at Brownsea Island and served as The Scout Association's first Secretary-General. He died in 1924.

11 Here and below: original text, *Dutch*.

13. The South
African Constabulary

*A first step should be to develop the spirit of goodwill and toleration, trust
and justice, in place of envy, hatred and malice.*

Jamboree, October 1939

Planning a police force*

'I want you to see me without delay regarding formation of Police
Force for Transvaal, Orange River Colony, and Swaziland.'

* LVL, 215–16.

Playing the Game

Such was, on the 29th of August, 1900, the telegram from Lord Roberts at Belfast (Transvaal), just as I had taken over command at Nylstrom of a force of all arms with which I was to operate in the Northern districts.

Accordingly 'without delay' I handed over my newly acquired command to Colonel Plumer, who at the time commanded its Rhodesian contingent.

On my way to Belfast I roughed out on a half-sheet of paper my ideas for a police force, whose strength was computed according to the area, population, white and native, mining centres, and cities involved. These met with Lord Roberts' approval.

A few days later I was on my way down country to see Lord Milner, the High Commissioner, at Cape Town, since the Police as a civil force would be under his direction.

It was a long railway journey in those days of blown-up bridges, all-night stoppage, broken lines and 'deviations'; but I utilized the time in planning out my scheme in fuller detail on several sheets of paper, with estimates of personnel, ranks, equipment, food, horses, transport, training, distribution, duties, finance, medical staff, housing, etc., etc.

For passing the time on a long journey try planning a police force; it beats jig-saws and crossword puzzles.

*Reception at Cape Town**

On the journey down country I met with a wonderful experience. At several places where the train stopped there were large lines of

* LVL; 216–18.

communication camps, and the men crowded around the train to cheer. At one place they swarmed into the carriage itself to shake hands.

The day before I was due to reach Cape Town I got wind of an unnerving ordeal which I should have to go through. The Mayor and Corporation were going to meet me at the station. In order to avoid this I telegraphed on to Government House, where I was to report myself, that I was unfortunately delayed and might not arrive until a day or two later.

This, I knew, would be passed on to the Mayor, who would then postpone the reception till at least the following day, and meantime I should slip in unnoticed and 'un-received.'

So, when my train drew into Cape Town station, I happily rolled up all my small kit, ready to walk to Government House, with an eager eye to bath and breakfast. But – goodness, what was this? The platform was a swaying mass of humanity, overflowing on to the roofs of neighbouring trains, all cheering and waving.

I have but a confused memory of what followed. I believe that a tiny space was cleared in which the Mayor was able to greet me with a short speech, and then I was bundled off, on the heads of a roaring mass, out of the station into the sunlight of Adderley Street. I do remember that two excellent fellows seized hold of my breeches pockets on either side to prevent my money from falling out, and in this way I was marched – more or less upside down – through Cape Town, all the way to Government House. There I was carried past the bewildered sentry and was at last deposited with a flop in the hall.

The butler, hastily summoned from his pantry, appeared on the scene to find a dishevelled, dirty, khaki-clad figure standing there, with a roaring mob outside the door. He, naturally, looked upon me for the time as a truculent leader of a revolution.

But a British butler is nothing if he cannot be dignified, even in the worst crisis, so he sternly demanded what I wanted. I was at a loss. I realized that I was not expected there until the following day and that Government House had not passed on my message to the Town. All I could think of to blurt out at the moment was: 'Could I have a bath, please?'

Our method of training is to educate from within rather than to instruct from without; to offer games and activities which, while being attractive to the boy, will seriously educate him morally, mentally and physically.

WCH, 158 and GG, 190

Difficulties of organization*

On the 22nd of October, 1900, the Constabulary came officially into being, but previous to that date we had already collected a scratch staff and a number of officers and men from various units in the field, and we also took over the small local police contingents which had been organized as a temporary measure.

The original undertaking with Lord Roberts in September, 1900, was to have a force of ten thousand mounted men prepared by the middle of 1901 to take over the police duties of the country.

* LVE, 218–21.

Meantime I had to do the best I could with such officers as I could pick up.

Beyond food and equipment the Army found themselves unable to supply our needs in clothing, men, horses, transport, etc. We were further told not to get these from sources of Army supply since they were already working at full power.

Consequently it devolved upon us to arrange our own recruiting and the transport from overseas of men and horses, and to a large extent their equipment, and to organize our own medical staff and hospitals.

Then, as time went on and the war did not come to an end as had been expected, our objective was changed, and from being police we had to prepare ourselves in training and organization to be a fighting force in the field — a very different pair of shoes.

Foiled in my efforts to get officers from the Army I turned to the depot camp at Stellenbosch. This was a sort of purgatory in which officers were placed who had been responsible for any 'regrettable incident' in the campaign, and there were a good many of them corralled there.

But I reckoned that any man makes a mistake some time or other in his career. As Napoleon said: 'The man who never made a mistake never made anything.' These men had made their mistakes and were therefore all the more likely not to do so in the future, so I took them. I don't remember having to regret taking them in any single instance.

So soon as the Force became known applications flowed in for commissions in numbers that were difficult to deal with. Some three thousand were received where only three hundred officers were required. Literally hundreds of mothers plied me with letters recommending their sons, many getting influential friends to back them. It was a whole-time job for one of my officers to open, acknowledge and burn these letters.

The work of organizing with a scratch staff, and under agreement to produce and train a large and efficient force of mounted men for either military or police work, within eight months, was undoubtedly a tough job; at the same time it was a most interesting and joyous one, seeing that the force was to be entirely self-contained, with its own auxiliary branches for its feeding supply, housing, medical treatment, payment, transport, remount, criminal investigation, and this in a far-off country in the midst of a difficult campaign going on around one.

We were asked to have our force complete and in the field, if possible, by June, 1901. Well, we raked in men and officers wherever we could get them, all over the Empire; stock-riders from Australia, farmers from New Zealand, North-West constables and cowboys from Canada, planters from India and Ceylon, RI constables from Ireland, and yeomen from England.

In addition to these British contingents we enlisted some six hundred friendly Boers and two thousand native Zulus for police work. A fairly mixed lot, but all of first class quality.

To take yourself too seriously as a young man is the first step to becoming a prig. A sense of humour will pull you through this danger, as well as through many a bad time.

RTS, 168

The Adventures of My Life

*Quick training for the men**

We established a central training depot and headquarters in a dynamite factory at Modderfontein, situated between Johannesburg and Pretoria, and here we started training our men in batches as they arrived, by our patent short-cut method.

No other form of training, certainly not that then usual in the Army, could possibly have attained the results in the short time in which we got them. It was done by putting it to the men to train themselves to a very large extent, and the spirit in which they responded, and the results which followed, were a real eye-opener to most of us.

Decentralized responsibility was the secret. To every man, from Divisional Commandant down to the last corporal in charge of a group, responsibility was given and praise or blame dispensed according to the results of his work.

Discipline was bred from within instead of being imposed from without. It is true that our method of training was criticized by many military disciplinarians, especially as I had said that I did not want old soldiers on the Constabulary. I wanted intelligent young fellows who could use their wits and who had not been drilled into being soulless machines only able to act under direct orders.

* LVL, 221–2.

Playing the Game

Uniform[*]

I designed a uniform for the men, based on my experience of work in different climates, of an economical type and one which differed in appearance from that of the Army. Since officers and men had to be continuously on duty and therefore always in uniform, it was essential that this should be not merely smart but also comfortable to wear.

We therefore adopted khaki coats with roll collars and khaki shirts and collars with neckties, instead of the military stand-up stock collars. Our innovation was afterwards adopted by the Army.

The facings of the uniform were green, with yellow piping, the national colours of the Transvaal and the Orange Free State respectively.

For headgear we wore Stetson hats with flat brims which distinguished them from the hats worn by the Army with soft brims looped up at the side. These hats, which were imported from America, were known in the trade as 'Boss of the Plains' or 'B.P.' pattern, which brought about the mistaken notion that they had something to do with me.

In order to make the greater distinction from the Army headgear, the Constabulary hats were fitted with a feather cockade, termed in the trade 'Jay's Wings'. Although they were nothing more than chickens' feathers dyed green for the purpose, I received angry protests from bird lovers in England for massacring the race of jays.

[*] LVL, 225–8.

The Adventures of My Life

In March, 1901, a train bringing the supply of our SAC hats was wrecked by the Boers. Fearing that they would adopt these hats for their own uses for purposes of disguise I had a notice printed in Afrikaans[1] and posted about the country, giving warning to all and sundry that anyone found wearing these hats unlawfully would be liable to be shot.

Although we had hundreds of instances of Boers wearing British soldiers' equipment, we never found one wearing a Constabulary hat.

Besides planning what the men should have as their uniform, it also fell to me to design the uniform for our nurses; and for a man, and a bachelor at that, to attempt to dictate what ladies should wear was a pretty bold start on my part.

I quite expected mutiny, since, among other things, I departed from the universal custom of nurses wearing voluminous cloaks over their uniform dress and gave them instead khaki serge greatcoats rather like those worn by the officers. To my surprise these were so popular that the ladies on taking their discharge (which they had to do on getting married – and they were always getting married) universally asked to purchase them.

Also their uniform proved popular, comprising as it did a brown holland[2] dress with a green shoulder cape with yellow piping, a white headkerchief for indoor duty, and a cowboy hat like those of the officers for outdoors.

I see a tendency to go about hatless when in uniform. Well, I know, if you have shingled hair or a fluffy quiff it must be very tempting to show it. At

*the same time it is rather swanking over the other poor chaps who can't show
as fine a crop. And, moreover, it is not uniform.*

Jamboree, April 1929

Spirit triumphs over the impossible*

I have always maintained that if the right spirit is there it can
knock the 'im' out of the word 'impossible', and this certainly
proved itself true in the early days of the SAC.

The spirit of the officers and men was indomitable. For the
most part ill-fed, ill-clothed and living in such shelter as they
could improvise, they carried on. At one time I found a detachment performing their work of trench digging in continuous
heavy rain, dressed in nature's garb in order to keep their only suit
of clothes dry.

So in spite of all these difficulties by June, 1901, the Constabulary
was 8,000 strong, out of its ultimate establishment of 10,000,
mounted, equipped, trained, and doing effective work in the field.

Our new responsibilities†

The end of our soldiering came on the 7th June, when peace was
made with the Boers at Vereeniging.

* LVL, 235–6.
† LVL, 239–42.

The SAC were at once released from their duties as soldiers, to take up those of civil police.

The pacification of our late enemies was undoubtedly a most important task and no easy one.

Indeed, I went so far as to suggest that some of the Boer leaders, notably Botha, Smuts, Delarey and de Wet, might be offered commissions in the Force, the idea being that they would thereby feel that they were not losing caste among their people, and would be the more loyal to the new regime and less inclined to accept the tempting offers which were being made to them by unscrupulous sensation-mongers at home to come and deliver lectures in Europe.

From old acquaintance* I had a liking and a great admiration for the average Boer. When I had been on a joint Commission of Boer and British delegates to Swaziland in 1889, I got to know and understand them, and to recognize the many sterling qualities which, especially among the older generation, they possess.

He had a certain dignity about him which would resent any familiarity. At the same time any sign on our part of humouring him would be taken as weakness, and he would presume upon it. So we had to be mighty tactful and exhibit a fine sense of justice and duty, coupled with human understanding.

Well, it was naturally obvious to everybody that such was the right line to take, but to put it into actual practice through our troopers, acting individually each on his own beat, was a bit of a problem.

In giving out my orders to the force for their new duties I

* LVL, 240; SMEA, 19.

quoted the well-known speech of Abe Lincoln at the conclusion of the Civil War in America, since his words aptly met the present situation:

'With malice towards none, with charity for all, with firmness in the right, as God gives us to see the right, let us finish the work that we are in; to bind up the nation's wounds, to care for him who shall have borne the battle, and for his widow and his orphans, to do all which may achieve and cherish a just and lasting peace among ourselves and with all nations.'

The men rose nobly to the occasion and, carefully instructed by their officers, they shed their war hatred and assumed their role of good-humoured peacemakers with a great adaptability.

War is a man-made infliction upon himself, bringing nothing but human misery in its train. It is therefore up to man to devise the remedy, and to restore to himself the blessing of peace with its prosperity and happiness for all.

A first step should be to develop the spirit of goodwill and toleration, trust and justice, in place of envy, hatred and malice.

Jamboree, October 1939

'Be Prepared'*

The South African Constabulary had adopted as their motto, on the selection of the men themselves, the words, 'Be Prepared.'

'Be prepared for what?'

* LS, 43. ·

'For any old thing,' was the reply.

And certainly it applied with them, for a South African constable was called upon at any time alternately to train a horse, vaccinate a baby, build his own barrack, expound the law for a Boer farmer and his tenant, exterminate locusts, settle native disputes, peg out mining claims, act as fireman, soldier, or first-aid doctor, etc.

And whichever it was he did it well; but it was simply through carrying out the principle of 'being prepared'.

Lone journeys for the most backward*

When commanding the Constabulary I was given the duty of escorting Joseph Chamberlain on his tour through the country. At one point of our journey we saw a solitary trooper of the force riding across the veldt. Mr Chamberlain asked me what would be this man's duty. I replied that as a rule the men were sent out in pairs on long patrols of two to three hundred miles; but if a man was not sufficiently intelligent or self-reliant he was sent alone on long journeys in order to cultivate and develop his common-sense, intelligence and self-reliance. On signalling the man to us on this occasion a few questions showed that he was going through such form of self-education.

He had been ordered on a three hundred mile ride to pick up information at various spots, but with strict orders that he was not to have the help of any other constable.

* QTW, 59–60; Aids, 34–5; IM, 29.

Remember that a statesman *is different from a politician. A politician is a man who merely thinks of helping his party in Parliament, whether it is Liberal or Labour, or Unionist or Socialist and so on. But a statesman is the man who thinks most of helping his* country; *he is far above the small party questions.*

YFBS, 190

I leave the SAC*

My own connection with the force came to a sudden end early in 1903.

I received the announcement that I had been appointed Inspector-General of Cavalry for Great Britain and Ireland.

Here was a promotion which I had never expected, especially as I was already employed on active work in South Africa.

I at once put myself in the hands of Lord Milner, since I was serving under him, as to whether I should accept the step or not.

He replied very generously showing that the appointment was, as he termed it, 'the Blue Riband' of the Cavalry, and as the SAC was now in good working order I might accept it with a clear conscience.

With many feelings of elation and regret I accepted accordingly. I made a farewell round of my Divisions and eventually handed over my command of the Constabulary to Colonel Nicholson.

* LVL, 246–7.

The Adventures of My Life

Usefulness is the rent that we pay for living on the earth.

Date unknown. Quoted in Wade, 57

It was with huge misgiving* that I faced the ordeal of taking up this 'Blue Riband' of the Cavalry service, implying as it did responsibility for the efficiency of the regular Cavalry and the Yeomanry in Great Britain and Ireland, and of the Cavalry in Egypt and South Africa.

A pretty large order!

My first step in taking over my duties was to educate *myself* as far as possible in up-to-date Cavalry methods. With this intent I visited personally, first the Cavalry Schools of France, Germany, Austria, Belgium, Italy and America; and secondly the Cavalry manoeuvres in France, Germany and Italy, in order to see the results of their training actually in the field and in large masses.

A Scout's cunning†

I remember being caught out when inspecting the scouts of a certain Cavalry regiment. I stood on a central knoll and sent the scouts out each in a different direction to creep unseen towards me and then to watch all that I did and note it down. Meantime I should keep a look-out and should set a mark against each man whom I detected watching or moving. At the end of the exercise I called them all in, examined their reports, and then deducted

* LVL, 248.
† QTW, 70–71.

marks from those whom I had spotted. One man had done an excellent report, but I told him that with much regret I had seen him about five times peering at me through the bushes; he ought to have used more cunning. Then he explained that he had found a countryman near where he was hiding, so he had told him to look very cautiously and he would see me do some very funny tricks, but he must not let himself be seen or I should probably not perform. It was the decoy whom I had seen. I had no reason to blame the scout for want of cunning!

The end of my term[*]

On the 5th of May, 1907, my term as Inspector-General of Cavalry came to an end. A number of my Cavalry comrades generously gave me a farewell dinner.

I was tremendously taken by this unexpected expression of their goodwill, accompanied as it was by numerous letters expressing approbation for the steps that we had been taking for bringing the Cavalry up-to-date.

Now that it is too late for me to be demobbed I don't mind confessing that personally I was entirely unfitted both physically and intellectually, for the position of IG of Cavalry. Physically because I had long had a loose leg as a result of a shooting accident in Afghanistan, and more recently I had broken the cartilage and ligaments of the other knee so that both legs were like bits of string, and I could not supply, as I ought, an example of hard rid-

[*] LVL, 259–60.

ing horsemanship. Intellectually I was deficient because I had not been through the Staff College and my knowledge of strategy and military history was limited to common sense and admiration of Oliver Cromwell's methods.

NOTES

1 Original text: *Dutch*.

2 A linen or cotton fabric, sometimes glazed, used for women's or children's clothing, upholstery, etc.; originally so called because it was first made in Holland; called *brown holland* when unbleached.

14. With the Terries

What a difference it makes when you work for love of the thing.

RTS, 80

The completion of my term* as Inspector-General of Cavalry was not the final act of my service, though it left me as a Lieutenant-General at the top of the Cavalry tree, a position which in my wildest dreams I had never visualized (nor indeed desired).

I was now placed on half-pay. The custom was that one remained on half-pay for four years, and if by that time no further appointment was found for you, you retired on the pension authorized for your rank.

* LVL, 261–3.

At this time Lord Haldane was Secretary of State for War, and he was considering the question of developing our military reserves by the organization of Territorial Officers' Training Corps. He invited me to stay with him at Cloan to talk over these matters, and while I was there he asked me whether I would care to take command of Territorial Division, and to try out any ideas I might have for the better training of this branch.

This would not count as regular employment for me since the command was only that of a Major-General and I was a Lieutenant-General. But since it offered work, and work of an interesting kind, I readily accepted the offer, and knowing something of the German plans I realized the urgent need for making our reserves efficient for service in the field and not merely on paper.

I was appointed to command the Northumbrian Division which included Northumberland, Durham and North and East Yorkshire. Here I found splendid men to work with, more particularly those who came from the mining districts. They were pretty rough, but hearty sportsmen and brave fellows.

We had had as our adversaries in the Boer War men who had never had a day's drill in their lives and yet were effective in the field against our trained troops through their individual intelligence, pluck, and will to succeed.

So it was on this line that I tried to develop our training in my Division. I had a motor-car made to my own pattern which was at once a bedroom and an office, and I continually toured my division, getting into personal touch with every unit and studying the local conditions under which it had to work. I organized week-end 'battles', at which attendance was voluntary, but which drew better attendance than the average ordered parade.

> *A motor-car is a wonderful contraption of machinery, with its valves, cylinders, electric connections and complicated gears all assembled and neatly fitted to act on each other, but useless as a mobile agent without the addition of the right spirit.*
>
> From the foreword to Lord Hampton, *Scouting Sketches*, London,
>
> Pearson, 1925

Warning of the Great War*

I got into hot water once over a talk to my Staff about the possibilities of a German invasion.[1]

The Germans had agreed that the most suitable opportunity for the invasion of England would be afforded by the Bank Holiday in August of any year in which we were least prepared. I decreed the Bank Holiday as a suitable occasion for practising the mobilization of our units, and in order to explain this and the German plan, gave an address to my officers.[2]

A report of this lecture leaked into the papers, and this led to a demand for my dismissal from certain members in the House of Commons, but, what was far more important, it drew upon me some irate anonymous letters from Germany,[3] and also news from private friends over there that my appointment to that particular

* LVL, 263–4; MAAS, 53–7.

district as Lieutenant-General (in place of the usual Major-General) had caused considerable comment in military circles.

So we had hit the spot.

When I was held up as a miscreant in Parliament in this way I took the night train to London and explained to Lord Haldane that my speech that had been reported was only a private one to my officers, and should have never appeared in the press, and that I wanted to apologize for the fuss that it had caused in the House. To my surprise he replied that he was delighted and that it was a good thing that people's eyes should be opened to the fact that there was a danger from Germany.

> *If peace and happiness are to be brought about in the world it will not be through force of arms. Rather it must be through a spirit of brotherhood coupled with the recognition of the rights of others.*
>
> *Jamboree, July 1929*

King Edward and my retirement[*]

By about this time the outbreak of Scouting, on a suggestion which I had made, had produced such a crop of Scouts all over the country that the demands upon my time and energies grew to such an extent that I had to consider whether I was justified in continuing my soldiering or whether to take up this new growth and organize it.

King Edward had invited me to Balmoral, and there he talked

[*] LVL, 264.

over the question of the Scouts with me at great length, and though it was all in embryo he showed a strong belief in its possibilities and urged me to go on with it. So later, when the question rose in my mind as to whether I could do both works adequately, it came to the ears of the King that I was contemplating retiring from the Army, and he at once sent word to ask whether this was the case, saying he considered that it would be unwise of me to leave the service when, as he expressed it, I had just got my footing on the ladder.

But the next day, having thought it over more fully, he agreed that seeing the possibilities that lay before the Scout movement, and the need for its organization it would after all be right on my part to resign from the Army and devote myself to this work.

Here are some of the things that Scouting is not:

- *it is not a charity organization for people in society to run for the benefit of the poor children;*
- *it is not a school having a definite curriculum and standards of examination;*
- *it is not a brigade of officers and privates for drilling manliness into boys and girls;*
- *it is not a show where surface results are gained through payment in merit badges, medals, etc.*

These all come from without, whereas the Scout training all comes from within.

Aids (1919), 13

The Adventures of My Life

*The end of my life number one**

On my sending in my request to retire from the Army there arose the question of my pension. To my horror I was told that the Royal Warrant did not allow of a pension for one of my age.

My promotion had been so rapid that I was a Lieutenant-General at fifty, whereas the Warrant did not allow for anybody holding that rank under sixty-two.

Arrangements, however, were eventually made for my pension.

It was a big wrench to take this last step out of the Service that I had loved so well, though at the same time I did not mind taking my foot off the ladder, for I had no wish to do any further climbing up it. I was not built for a General. I liked being a regimental officer in personal touch with my men.

It was no small consolation to receive from the Secretary of State for War the letter which he sent me, expressing his kindly regret in losing me from the Army, in which he added: '. . . But I feel that the Organization of your Boy Scouts has so important a bearing on the future that probably the greatest service you can render to the country is to devote yourself to it.'

And so ended my Life Number One.

*It's no use standing still. It is one thing or the other, either progress or relax.
Let us progress — and with a smile on.*

Aids, WB, 21

---

* LVL, 267–8.

NOTES

1 In 1905 or 1906 a gang of German-American forgers who had set up a 'spy-bureau' in Belgium managed to sell B.-P. a false 'German invasion plan' of England, based on a landing in central England. The plan is described in detail in MAAS, 53–7. The same plan was sold to General J. S. Ewart, Director of Military Operations of the British Army, and to novelist William LeQueux, who made it into a novel published in 1906 (*The Invasion of 1910*). The whole story is told in A. J. A. Morris, *The Scaremongers*, London 1984, 156–7. B.-P. continued to believe in the existence of such a plan, even though no trace of it was found when the German General Staff documents were published in the period between the two World Wars.

2 B.-P.'s lecture to his officers took place in Newcastle on 2 May 1908.

3 One such letter as reported by B.-P. reads: 'You are but a brown-paper general, and if you think that by your foolish talk you are to frighten us from coming, you are not right' (MAAS, 57).

15. Life Number Two –
the Boy Scouts and Girl Guides

The Scout / Guide Law

1. *A Scout's / Guide's honour is to be trusted.*

2. *A Scout / Guide is loyal (*).*

3. *A Scout's / Guide's duty is to be useful and to help others.*

4. *A Scout / Guide is a friend to all and a brother / sister to every other Scout / Guide, no matter to what social class the other belongs.[1]*

5. *A Scout / Guide is courteous.*

6. *A Scout / Guide is a friend to animals.*

7. *A Scout / Guide obeys orders – of his / her Patrol Leader or Scoutmaster / Guider,[2] without question.*

8. *A Scout / Guide smiles and whistles / sings under all circumstances.[3]*

9. *A Scout/Guide is thrifty.*

10. *A Scout/Guide is/keeps herself clean/pure in thought, word and deed.*[4]

(*) *[for Scouts]: to the King, and to his officers,*[5] *and to his country, and to his employers; [for Guides]: to God and the King, to her parents and Guider, to her friends and fellow-workers, and to those over and under her at school or at work.*

SFB, OFP (4th), and GG, 65–7

I now started* on my second life in this world.

I had definitely left the Army in 1910 and the Scout movement had started itself and was finding its feet far and wide.

This, though it promised to be the biggest job of my life, was at the same time the easiest since everybody connected with it met me more than half-way with their keenness.

In 1912 all was going smoothly and well when out of the blue an entirely new kind of bomb suddenly caught me in the midriff!

Double harness†

It was in this way. During my first life I had had my time fairly fully occupied, with little leisure for thinking of such extraneous matters as marriage; indeed, I had been railed by my best friend, 'Ginger' Gordon,[6] 15th Hussars, on being a confirmed old bachelor; and when I said that I had no desire to get married and I felt

* LVL, 269.
† LVL, 269–71.

sure that nobody would desire to marry me, he looked at me quizzically for a space and then remarked, with the laugh of one who knew: 'You'll get it in the neck one day when you least expect it, old boy!'

And I did.

In the course of following up the science of tracking I had practised the art of deducing people's character from their footprints and gait. Native trackers the world over read the character as well as the actions or intentions of the foot-printer, e.g. toes turned out imply a liar, outside heel depression means adventurous, and so on.

In this research I came to the conclusion, for instance, that about forty-six per cent of women were very adventurous with one leg and hesitant on the other, i.e. liable to act on impulse.

So when I came to an exception it caught my attention.

One such I noted where a girl – a total stranger to me and whose face I had not seen – trod in a way that showed her to be possessed of honesty of purpose and common sense as well as of the spirit of adventure. I happened to notice that she had a spaniel with her.

This was while I was still in the Army and I was going into Knightsbridge Barracks at the time. I thought no more of it.

Two years later, on board my ship for the West Indies,[7] I recognized the same gait in a fellow-passenger. When introduced I charged her with living in London. Wrong. My sleuthing was at fault; she lived in Dorsetshire!

'But have you not a brown and white spaniel?'

'Yes.' (Surprise registered.)

'Were you never in London? Near Knightsbridge Barracks?'

'Yes, two years ago.'

So we married — and lived happily ever after.

Thus began my second life, and with it the Scouts and the Guides.

I generally do a little tracking every day, because it is only by constant prac-
tice that a fellow can learn tracking or keep his eye in when he has learnt it.

YKE, 34

*Origin of Scouts and Guides**

The amount of notoriety thrust upon me by the want of per-spective in the reviews of the Boer War gave me some anxious thought. It was all so unexpected, unearned, and unsought.

Could there be some higher purpose underlying it? Was it a call to me? Could it be utilized to some good end? If so in what way could I act up to it? Such were the questions which thrust them-selves upon me.

They began to answer themselves for me by letters which poured in to me while I was still in South Africa in 1901–3, from boys and girls in different parts of the Empire. I had somehow personally caught their interest and was, without seeking for it, in touch with them.

I have been asked: 'How did the Scouts start?'

* LVL, 271; *The Parents' Review*, April 1923.

Well, I believe it was largely due to — whom shall we say? — a Field Marshal's governess.

It was this way: Brigadier-General Allenby,[8] as he was at that time, was riding to his home after a field day, when from the branches of a tree overhead, his little son called to him, 'Father, you are shot: I am in ambush, and you have passed under me without seeing me. Remember, you should always look upwards, as well as around you'.

So the General looked upward and saw, not only his small son above him, but also, near the top of the tree, the new governess, lately imported from Miss Charlotte Mason's Training College at Ambleside.

Her explanation of the situation was that a vital point in up-to-date education was the inculcation of observation and deduction, and that the practical steps to this were given in the little handbook for soldiers, *Aids to Scouting*. The present incident was merely one among the various field stunts from that book, which might be put into practice by her pupil and herself.

Taken as a warning, I daresay the governess' explanation opened the General's eyes pretty widely, if only in regard to his own future security against ambuscades and false alarms.

But it certainly opened mine to the fact that there could be an educative value underlying the principles of scout training; and since it had been thought worthy of utilization by such an authority as Miss Charlotte Mason, the founder of the House of Education for training women teachers, I realized that there might be something in it.

Playing the Game

A good many young men find at twenty-two that they know practically all that there is to know and they want other people to know that they know it.

When they get to thirty-two they find that they have still got one or two things to learn; at forty-two they are learning hard. (I am still doing so at seventy-three.)

RTS, 147

The application of Scout training to citizen training*

In 1904, as a result of these straws (including the important lesson of the Mafeking Cadets), I sketched out some ideas for training boys somewhat on the lines of the scouts in the Army.

In 1905, I was invited by Sir William Smith to inspect his Corps of 'Boys' Brigade' at Glasgow on the twenty-first anniversary of their existence.

When I saw this splendid gathering of some six thousand boys, and heard how widespread was the movement, it opened my eyes to yet another trait among boys, namely, that they would come eagerly in their thousands of their own accord to be trained where the training had its attraction for them. Also that hundreds of adults were willing to sacrifice time and energy in the service of training these boys.

When Sir William told me that he had no less than fifty-four thousand lads in the Brigade, I congratulated him on the magnificent result of his work; but as second thoughts occurred to me I could not help adding that considering the number of

* LVL, 274–6.

boys available in the country there ought, in the space of twenty years, to be ten times that number in the ranks, if the programme offered them were sufficiently varied and tempting.

He asked how I would add to its attraction, and I told him how scouting had proved its popularity with young men in the Cavalry, and that something of the kind might prove equally attractive to these younger boys, while its aim might easily be diverted from war to peace, since the inculcation of character, health and manliness was its basis, and these qualities were as much needed in a citizen as in a soldier.

He cordially agreed with my idea and suggested that I should write a book for boys on the lines of *Aids to Scouting*.

So in the few spare moments from my work as IG of Cavalry, I set to work to formulate my idea, for here seemed to be the work waiting to my hand for which that damnable notoriety I had incurred could now be usefully employed.

We are simply out to help the boys to become happy, healthy, prosperous citizens, and we want the trust and friendship of their parents in doing so.

From a circular letter to the parents of new Cubs,
written in the 1920s. In SAA

The first camp at Brownsea Island*

Before bringing out the proposed book I made full experiment of the scheme by holding a camp for trial of its programme.

* B.-P.'s report (in Reynolds 1942, 143–4); LVL, 276.

Playing the Game

Mrs Van Raalte invited me to use her island, Brownsea, in Poole Harbour,[9] for this purpose, as I was anxious to get a camping ground away from outsiders, press reporters, etc., where I could try out the experiment without interruption.

There I tried it out with boys of every class and kind mixed up together.

The troop of boys was divided up into Patrols of five, the senior boy in each being Patrol Leader. This organization was the secret of our success. Each Patrol Leader was given full responsibility for the behaviour of his Patrol at all times, in camp and in the field. The Patrol was the unit for work or play, and each patrol was camped in a separate spot. The boys were put 'on their honour' to carry out orders. Responsibility and competitive rivalry were thus at once established, and a good standard of development was ensured throughout the troop from day to day. The troop was trained progressively in the subjects of scouting. Every night one Patrol went on duty as night picket – that is, drew rations of flour, meat, vegetables, tea, etc., and went out to some indicated spot to bivouac for the night. Each boy had his greatcoat and blankets, cooking pot and matches. On arrival at the spot, fires were lit and suppers cooked, after which sentries were posted and bivouac formed. The picket was scouted by Patrol Leaders of other Patrols and myself, at some time before eleven p.m., after which the sentries were withdrawn and the picket settled down for the night.

We found the best way of imparting theoretical instruction was to give it out in short instalments with ample illustrative examples when sitting round the camp fire or otherwise resting, and with demonstrations in the practice hour before breakfast. A formal lecture is apt to bore the boys.

The practice was then carried out in competitions and schemes.

For example, take one detail of the subject, 'Observation' – namely, tracking.

1. At the camp fire overnight we would tell the boys some interesting instance of the value of being able to track.
2. Next morning we would teach them to read tracks by making foot-marks at different places, and showing how to read them and to deduce their meaning.
3. In the afternoon we would have a game, such as 'deerstalking', in which one boy went off as the 'deer', with half a dozen tennis balls in his bag. Twenty minutes later four 'hunters' went off after him, following his track, each armed with a tennis ball. The deer, after going a mile or two, would hide and endeavour to ambush his hunters, and so get them within range; each hunter struck with his tennis ball was counted gored to death; if, on the other hand, the deer was hit by three of their balls he was killed.

This was our principle for teaching most of the items.

Discipline was very satisfactory indeed. A 'court of honour' was instituted to try any offenders against discipline, but it was never needed. In the first place the boys were put 'on their honour' to do their best; in the second place, the senior boys were made responsible for the behaviour of the boys forming their patrol. And this worked perfectly well.

Playing the Game

The experiment met my anticipations, and I published *Scouting for Boys*.

> *The average Scout life of a boy is a comparatively short one, and it is good for each generation of Scouts to see at least one big rally, since it enables the boy to realize his membership of a really great brotherhood, and at the same time brings him into personal acquaintance with brother Scouts of other districts and other countries.*
>
> The Scouter, September 1932 (rep. BPO, 151)

*The Girl Guides**

Rapid as has been the rise of the Scout Movement, and surprising as has been the measure of its adoption by foreign countries, the Girl Guide Movement has surpassed it in both these particulars.

'We are the Girl Scouts,' was the announcement made with a certain air of confident self-assertion by a pert little person of some eleven years at the first Rally of the Scouts. This was at the Crystal Palace in 1909.

She was the spokeswoman of a small group of girls dressed as nearly as possible in imitation of their brothers, the Scouts.

The presence and the quite evident keenness of these girls opened one's eyes to the fact that here lay an opening for a further application of the Scout method of character-training and self-development.

* LVL, 302–4.

At that time, women were only just coming into their own in the work of the world. Character development was actually more needed by them than by their brothers since they had had less opportunity of forming it in their comparatively more secluded life.

One had long realized that girls generally preferred to read boys' literature, that stories of Wild West dramas appealed to them far more than those about heroines in academies for young ladies.

Now the girls were coming forward of their own volition to get the same adventure as their brothers.

This has since become the usual thing, but it was a big innovation in 1909.

With such spirit, however, meeting one half-way, it was not a difficult task to devise a scheme similar in principle to that of the Scouts while differing in detail to meet the requirements of the girl's life.

Miss Mason had to some extent foreseen this when she adopted as a text-book for the instruction of women teachers a little book called *Aids to Scouting*, which I had written for young soldiers. She found in it something educative, so after my encounter with these self-assertive 'Girl Scouts' I was not without hope in suggesting a sister movement to that of the Scouts. To this we gave the name 'Girl Guides'.

The term 'Guides' was intended to give an idea of romance and adventure while it indicated also their future responsibilities for directing their menfolk and bringing up their children on right lines.

The general aim of its training was similar to that of the

Scouts, generally to develop character and health and sense of service to others, while in particular it would give girls practical instruction in home-making, mother-craft, etc.

The Guides, like the Scouts, were organized in small Companies not exceeding thirty-two in number so that each individual temperament could be studied and educated. Then the girls were grouped progressively according to age, as Brownies, Guides, and Rangers.

In the first two or three years little could be done in the way of organizing the Guides since one was fairly snowed under by the phenomenal growth of the Scout Movement; but in the hands of a committee of energetic ladies things then began to take shape and before long the Movement had its own headquarters, its uniform, and its handbook and rules as a chartered association.

Very gradually, like a snowball, Scouting and Guiding grew into an international movement, and like a snowball, if you go on pushing it, it will one day become so big that it cannot be pushed any further, and that will mean that every girl and boy in the world, who is keen to do so, will have a chance to become a Scout or a Guide. I want you to help me to go on pushing the snowball.

Quoted in Beaumont, 49

The Rovers*

After the War, in 1919, we made a start with the senior branch of the Movement for Scouts over 17½, whom we called Rovers. This

* LVL, 291–2.

branch gradually took shape under the direction of Colonel Ulick de Burgh, and promised to meet a great need. I therefore wrote a book called *Rovering to Success*, in which I said, much as I have done at the beginning of this book:

> *It always seems to me so odd that when a man dies he takes out with him all the knowledge that he has acquired in his lifetime while sowing his wild oats or winning his successes. He leaves his sons or younger brothers to go through all the work of learning it over again from their own experience.*
>
> *Why can't he pass it on so that they start with his amount of knowledge to the good to begin with, and so get on to a higher stage of efficiency and sense right away?*

That book has brought me as great a return, if not a greater than *Scouting for Boys*, seeing that it has induced a very large number of young men to write to me personally and privately seeking further advice.

These letters I have treated entirely in confidence and have answered them myself to the best of my ability. It has been an eye-opener to realize how great is the need for some such advice for the adolescent lad, when so very many of them explained that they had been left in ignorance and were shy of asking their parents or pastors, but having read the book had come to me for sympathy.

> *Scouting aims to teach the boys how to live, not merely how to make a living.*[10]

SFB, 1940 preface

Playing the Game

*Gilwell**

In 1919, Mr de Bois Maclaren presented to our Association the estate of Gilwell Park, adjoining Epping Forest. His idea was to provide a camping ground within easy reach of London for the poorer class of boy, but, seeing that there were suitable buildings on the estate he consented to my suggestion that we should make it also the Training School for Scoutmasters, which I looked upon as an all important step in the development of the Movement.

Captain Frank Gidney was appointed Camp Chief in charge of the training, and no better selection could have been made.

It is mainly thanks to this school and its curriculum that our methods have become thoroughly understood and practised not only throughout the United Kingdom but in all the countries in the world, since foreign nations have sent their representatives to be trained at Gilwell and to go back to their own countries as organizers of the same system there.

The First World Jamboree at Olympia†

After the War a great meeting of Scouts from all countries was organized in London to bring the nations together through Scouting and to signalize the peace.

It was something bigger than a Rally so we called it a

* LVL, 292.
† LVL, 293–4, B.-P.'s account (in Reynolds 1942, 204–5).

Jamboree. I have often been asked: 'Why call it by that name?' And my reply has been: 'What else could you call it?'

This took place in Olympia and lasted for ten days. Some twelve thousand boys were present, representative groups coming from a large number of foreign countries for the occasion.

The show proved popular beyond our expectations. Not having foreseen this our accommodation for the public was too limited and we lost money, but at the same time gained a reputation.

On the final day representatives of all the foreign countries met and elected me to be Chief Scout of the World. To enunciate this, a vast rally of Scouts from dozens of different countries was assembled in the arena at Olympia, before an equally vast concourse of interested spectators. Displays were given by the boys and it wound up with a processional pageant, carefully planned and worked on by a group of enthusiastic Scouters, mostly American, and adept at this sort of thing. It was calculated to rouse the patriotic fervour of the veriest louse among the onlookers.

The crowd is too often an ass: it doesn't think for itself, nor does it bother to look at both sides of a question.

RTS, 39–40

*Kandersteg**

In 1923 our International Bureau obtained possession of a large chalet at Kandersteg in Switzerland, which was made into a

* LVL, 296.

hostel for Scouts of all nations. There they could lodge in large or small numbers for biking and mountaineering in the district. It is in lovely surroundings and a convenient centre for Europe. It has never ceased to attract Scouts from all countries at all times of the year, and the boys of the different nations come together there in the friendliest spirit of comradeship.

Mortimer Schiff, one of the leading lights of the Boy Scouts of America, shortly before his death added to the amenities of the place by presenting a neighbouring piece of ground capable of camping about two thousand boys.

This has given tremendous encouragement to the development of international Scouting.

The Jamboree at Arrowe Park*

1929 saw the biggest event in our Scout history since the inauguration of the Movement, when we opened a camp for 30,000 Scouts of all nations at Arrowe Park, near Birkenhead. This was to mark the coming-of-age of the Movement.

The summer of 1929 had been an exceptionally long period of sunshine and drought to the actual day of the opening of the camp, when the rain came down in sheets and continued to do so for the three following days.

But, though it should have ruined the occasion, it didn't. The boys rose superbly to it and seemed to enjoy the misadventure and the mud. It certainly put them to the highest test of camp-craft

* LVL, 299–301.

and one soon realized that they had all been trained on the right lines, viz., of open air camp-life.

There was no sickness, no grumbling, and international friendships were developed on every side to a remarkable degree among the thousands represented there.

The Prince of Wales attended it as the representative of His Majesty the King and announced that the King had been pleased to raise me to the Peerage[11] as a mark of His Majesty's approval of the Movement and its aims.

This fresh honour was overwhelming and for a time I could not make up my mind to accept it. I vainly pleaded that it was not I but the thousands of Leaders who had by their devoted work made the Movement what it was.

This was immediately followed by the presentation from the boys themselves of a motor-car and camping caravan, and a portrait of myself by Jagger;[12] and last, but not least, a pair of braces.

The reason for this last was that these presents were the result of a general subscription throughout the Movement of one penny per boy. It was got up quite secretly by Denmark. In order to find out what sort of present I would like they approached my wife and asked her to find out, without letting me into it, what I most wanted.

She accordingly asked me one day what I would like most if a present were offered to me. I thanked her blandly, but replied that I was not in want of anything.

'But,' she said, 'think again – you surely would like something.'

I reflected for a moment and remarked: 'Yes, my braces are getting past work – if you would like to give me a new pair I should be thankful.'

So the braces were presented in due course – as also a motor-car and etceteras.

What a wonderful gift, coming from a million and a half of youngsters of all countries! And given, as one had reason to know, with wholehearted enthusiasm and loyalty to an Idea. It made one feel very humble, very inadequate to the vast possibility revealed of bringing about peace and goodwill among men of the oncoming generation in the world.

At the last parade on the conclusion of that wonderful fortnight the boys of the different nationalities were all mixed up together and formed into an immense wheel – a great circle with files of Scouts in lines radiating from centre to rim like so many spokes. My part, at the hub of the wheel, was to bury an axe – the axe of war and ill-will – and then to hand out to the leading boy of each spoke a golden arrow – the sign of peace and goodwill – to be passed from one to another till it reached the head of each national contingent, to be taken by him back to his own country so that the message of the Jamboree should be conveyed to all nations and there developed.

I gave a short exhortation in which I urged them to carry this symbol of Peace and Fellowship into all the world, each individual Scout being an ambassador of love and friendship to those around him.

Of course, when one is trying to be sublime the ridiculous is sure to arise.[13] I gave my address to the whole circle, but the boy standing directly opposite me and who got therefore the main force of my remarks, looked preternaturally unmoved by them. I assumed that he must be a foreigner ignorant of English. I found that he was the one boy out of the 30,000 who was deaf and dumb! Just my luck!

> *The question has been put to me from time to time: 'Is a Jamboree a good thing for the boy, or for the Movement or for the country or for international relations?' Personally I have my own answer, but always before making any decision of that kind I consult the authority that I think of as the best — and that is the boy himself.*

> Address at the International Conference in The Hague,
> 1937, in SAA

Playing the Game

NOTES

1 In later years: 'no matter to what country, class or creed the other belongs'.

2 In later years 'his/her parents' were added.

3 Later: 'under all difficulties'.

4 The tenth Law was added in 1911.

5 In later years 'his Scouter, his parents' replace 'his officers'.

6 Major James Redmond Patrick ('Ginger') Gordon served as B.-P.'s deputy in the Ashanti campaign in 1895. He died in 1910. Calling him his 'best friend' is clearly an overstatement on the part of B.-P., since Gordon – a womanizer and a spendthrift – had a totally different lifestyle from his.

7 In January 1912, on board the *Arcadian*.

8 Edmund Henry Hynman, first Viscount Allenby (1861–1936), was Commander-in-Chief of the British Expeditionary Force in Egypt in the latter part of the First World War. His son Michael (mentioned in the episode) fell on the Western front. The governess was Katherine Loveday.

9 A bay on the south coast of England, not far from Bournemouth, well-known to B.-P. (see above, Chapter 3).

10 This sentence was inspired by an article ('Factory Troops') by the Scout Secretary for Birmingham, Sam Harrison, on the January 1919 issue of the HQG (see Aids, 1919 edn, 50).

11 After consultation with the International Committee B.-P. took for himself the name 'Lord Baden-Powell of Gilwell' to underline his connection with the Scout Movement.

12 The original and well-known portrait can be found today in the Chief Scout's Office at Gilwell Park, London, while a copy hangs also in the World Scout Committee Room in Geneva.

13 'It is only a step from the sublime to the ridiculous': a remark attributed to Napoleon following the retreat from Moscow, 1812.

16. Looking Back*

The worst agony of death, at the moment when the sands are running out and minutes are precious, is the feeling that so many hours of life have been wasted on things that did not matter.

GG, 183

When one has passed the 75th milestone and has got to that stage of life when you think twice before deciding whether it is now worthwhile to order a new evening coat, it is allowable for one to look back along the road one has travelled.

The great thing that strikes you on looking back is how

* LVL, 311–16 (entire chapter).

quickly you have come — how very brief is the span of life on this earth. The warning that one would give, therefore, is that it is well not to fritter it away on things that don't count in the end; nor on the other hand is it good to take life too seriously as some seem to do. Make it a *happy* life while you have it. *That is where success is possible to every man.*

Varied are the ideas of what constitutes 'success', e.g. money, position, power, achievement, honours, and the like. But these are not open to every man, nor do they bring what is real success, namely, happiness.

Happiness is open to all, since, when you boil it down, it merely consists of contentment with what you have got and doing what you can for other people.

Tips

Looking back on my own life, I have in my time bumped up against a stupendous lot of good luck. I have, for instance, had the luck to live in the most interesting evolutionary epoch in the world's history, with its rapid development of motor-cars, aeroplanes, wireless, Tutankhamen,[1] the Great War and World convulsion, and so on.

Then, too, I have met with a remarkable amount of kindness everywhere, not only from friends but from strangers as well. Also, I have had the luck to live two distinct lives: one as a soldier and a bachelor, the second as a pacifist and paterfamilias; both having the common attribute of Scouting, and both intensely happy.

That doesn't mean that I have not had difficulties and trials to face, but these have been the salt that savoured the feast.

For these I have found that a smile and a stick will carry you through all right, and in ninety-nine cases out of a hundred it is the smile that does the trick.

'Softly, softly, catchee monkey,' is the West African rendering of a very valuable precept. An awful lot of men fail through lack of patient persistence.

I have been master of no attainment but I have been Jack of many, and have thus enjoyed every variety of the good things that the world has to offer.

Have you ever thought of it, that the duration of the grown-up life of a man of seventy amounts to 291,000 waking hours?

Most men sleep for eight hours when seven are sufficient.

The man who sleeps for seven hours gains an additional *three years* and over, of waking life.

I have found it a good plan to give oneself, in imagination, three years still to live. You then feel that you have got to get things done within that time, whether they are making big dreams come true, or winning happiness. Time must not be frittered away.

I have often urged my young friends, when faced with an adversary, to 'play polo' with him; i.e., not to go at him bald-headed but to ride side by side with him and gradually edge him off your track. Never lose your temper with him. If you are in the right there is no need to, if you are in the wrong you can't afford to.

In a difficult situation one never-failing guide is to ask yourself: 'What would Christ have done?' Then do it, as nearly as you can.

Playing the Game

Religion seems a very simple thing:
1st: Love and serve God.
2nd: Love and serve your neighbour.

SFB, DE, 231 (developed from SFB,
OFP (22nd)), and GG, 71

Looking back, two bright spots among many which at once instinctively spring to mind are:

— in Life Number 1 the rough time among good companions on the sun-baked veldt in the Matabele campaign;

— and in Life Number 2, a little warm hand dragging me down till her two arms can reach round my neck, when with a soft moist kiss she whispers: 'Just one more good-night story, Daddy.'

God has given you a body — no, He has lent it to you — to make the best use of; not to soak it in drink, not to make it limp and weak with debauchery, but to take care of, to strengthen and build up into a really fine figure of a man and a father of children.

You can do this if you like. It is up to you. And what a splendid adventure it can be.

RTS, 120

NOTES

1 A pharaoh of the eighteenth Dynasty who reigned from 1358 to 1349 B.C. The discovery of his tomb by an English mission in 1922 stands as one of the great archaeological discoveries of all times, owing to the abundance, variety and quality of the grave furniture and other objects.

Part II

The Scout Method

The Scoutmaster guides the boy in the spirit of an older brother.

The Scout Leader

As a preliminary word of comfort to intending Scout Leaders, I should like to contradict the usual misconception that, to be a successful Scout Leader, a man must be a know-all. Not a bit of it. He has simply to be a boy-man, that is:

(i) He must have the boy spirit in him; and must be able to place himself on a right plane with his boys as a first step.

(ii) He must realize the needs, outlooks and desires of the different ages of boy life.

(iii) He must deal with the individual boy rather than with the mass.

(iv) He then needs to promote a corporate spirit among his individuals to gain the best results.

With regard to the **first** point, the Scout Leader has to be neither schoolmaster nor commanding officer, nor pastor, nor instructor. All that is needed is the capacity to enjoy the out-of-doors, to enter into the boys' ambitions, and to find other men who will give them instruction in the desired directions, whether it be signalling or drawing, nature study or pioneering.

Playing the Game

He has got to put himself on the level of the older brother, that is, to see things from the boy's point of view, and to lead and guide and give enthusiasm in the right direction. Like the true older brother he has to realize the traditions of the family and see that they are preserved, even if considerable firmness is required. That is all. The Movement is a jolly fraternity, all the jollier because in the game of Scouting you are doing a big thing for others, you are combating the breeding of selfishness.

Regarding the **second** point, the various handbooks[1] cover the successive phases of adolescent life.

Thirdly, the business of the Scout Leader – and a very interesting one it is – is to draw out each boy and find out what is in him, and then to catch hold of the good and develop it to the exclusion of the bad. There is 5 per cent of good even in the worst character. The sport is to find it, and then to develop it on to an 80 or 90 per cent basis. This is education instead of instruction of the young mind.

Fourth. In the Scout training the Patrol or gang system gives the corporate expression of the individual training, which brings into practice all that the boy has been taught.

The Patrol System has also a great character-training value if it is used aright. It leads each boy to see that he has some individual responsibility for the good of his Patrol. It leads each Patrol to see that it has definite responsibility for the good of the Troop. Through it the Scout Leader is able to pass on not only his instruction but his ideas as to the moral outlook of his Scouts. Through it the Scouts themselves gradually learn that they have considerable say in what their Troop does. It is the Patrol System that makes the Troop, and all Scouting for that matter, a real co-operative effort.

Many people think that 'pleasure' is the same thing as 'happiness'. That's where they take the wrong turning.

RTS, 18

The Scout Leader's Duty

Success in training the boy largely depends upon the Scout Leader's own *personal example*. It is easy to become the hero as well as the elder brother of the boy. We are apt, as we grow up, to forget what a store of hero worship is in the boy.

The Scout Leader who is a hero to his boys holds a powerful lever to their development, but at the same time brings a great responsibility on himself. They are quick enough to see the smallest characteristic about him, whether it be a virtue or a vice. His mannerisms become theirs, the amount of courtesy he shows, his irritations, his sunny happiness, or his impatient glower, his willing self-discipline or his occasional moral lapses: all are not only noticed, but adopted by his followers.

Therefore, to get them to carry out the Scout Law and all that underlies it, the Scout Leader himself should scrupulously carry out its professions in every detail of his life. With scarcely a word of instruction his boys will follow him.

The Scout Leader's job is like golf, or scything, or fly-fishing. If you 'press' you won't get there, at least not with anything like the extent you do by a light-hearted effortless swing. But you have got to swing. It's no use standing still. It is one thing or the other, either progress or relax. Let us progress, and with a smile on.

Paddle your own canoe.[2]

The Scout Leader's Reward

A man dared to tell me once that he was the happiest man in the world! I had to tell him of one who was still happier: myself.

You need not suppose that either of us in attaining this happiness had never any difficulties to contend with. Just the opposite.

It is the satisfaction of having successfully faced difficulties and borne pinpricks that gives completeness to the pleasure of having overcome them.

Don't expect your life to be a bed of roses; there would be no fun in it if it were.

So, in dealing with the Scouts, you are bound to meet with disappointments and setbacks. Be patient: more people ruin their work or careers through want of patience than do so through drink or other vices. You will have to bear patiently with irritating criticisms and red tape bonds to some extent but your reward will come.

The satisfaction which comes of having tried to do one's duty at the cost of self-denial, and of having developed characters in the boys which will give them a different status for life, brings such a reward as cannot well be set down in writing. The fact of having worked to prevent the recurrence of those evils which, if allowed to run on, would soon be rotting our youth, gives a man the solid comfort that he has done something, at any rate, for his country, however humble may be his position.

This is the spirit with which Scout Leaders and Commissioners work in the Scout Movement.

The credit for the organization and the spread of the Scout Movement is due to this army of voluntary workers. Here we have remarkable – if silent – evidence of the fine patriotic spirit that lies beneath the surface of most nations. These men give up their time and energies, and in many cases their money as well, to the work of organizing the training of boys, without any idea of reward or praise for what they are doing. They do it for the love of their country and their kind.

It is said that you can tell a man's character from the way he wears his hat.

GG, III

THE BOY

Playing the Game

The first step towards success in training your boy is to know something about boys in general and then about this boy in particular.

It is well to recall, so far as possible, what your ideas were when a boy yourself and you can then much better understand his feelings and desires.

The following qualities in the boy have to be taken into consideration:

Humour It must be remembered that a boy is naturally full of humour; it may be on the shallow side, but he can always appreciate a joke and see the funny side of things. And this at once gives the worker with boys a pleasant and bright side to his work and enables him to become the cheery companion, instead of the taskmaster, if he only joins in the fun of it.

Courage. The average boy generally manages to have pluck as well. He is not by nature a grumbler, though later on he may become one, when his self-respect has died out of him and when he has been much in the company of 'grumblers'.[3]

Confidence. A boy is generally supremely confident in his own powers. Therefore, he dislikes being treated as a child and being told to do things or how to do them. He would much rather try for himself, even though it may lead him into blunders, but it is just by making mistakes that a boy gains experience and makes his character.

Sharpness. A boy is generally as sharp as a needle. It is easy to train him in matters appertaining to observation and noticing things and deducing their meaning.

The Scout Method

Love of excitement. The town boy is generally more unsettled than his country brothers by the excitements of the town, whether they are 'a passing fire engine, or a good fight between two of his neighbours'. He cannot stick at a job for more than a month or two because he wants change.

Responsiveness. When a boy finds somebody who takes an interest in him he responds and follows where he is led, and it is here that hero-worship comes in as a great force for helping the Scout Leader.

Loyalty. This is a feature in a boy's character that must inspire boundless hope. Boys are usually loyal friends to each other, and thus friendliness comes almost naturally to a boy. It is the one duty that he understands. He may appear selfish outwardly, but, as a general rule, he is very willing under the surface to be helpful to others, and that is where our Scout training finds good soil to work upon.

Remember that the boy, on joining, wants to begin Scouting right away; so don't dull his keenness by too much preliminary explanation at first. Meet his wants by games and Scouting practices, and instil elementary detail bit by bit afterwards as you go along.

A Lady Cubmaster was teaching a Cub Natural History, and asked him: 'What is a rabbit covered with — is it hair, or wool, or fur, or what?' The Cub replied: 'Good gracious, Akela, haven't you ever seen a rabbit?'

BBA, 108

Playing the Game

Environment and Temptations

As I have said, the first step to success is to know your boy, but the second step is to know his home. It is only when you know what his environment is when he is away from the Scouts that you can really tell what influences to bring to bear upon him.

Where the sympathy and support of the boy's parents are secured, where the parents have been brought into a mutual partnership with a fuller interest in the working of the Troop and the aim of the Movement, the task of the Scout Leader becomes proportionately lighter.

Occasionally, in the home, there may be evil influences to overcome. In addition there are other temptations to the lad, which the instructor of the boy must be ready to contend with. But, if he is forewarned, he can probably devise his methods so that the temptations fail to exercise an evil influence on his lads; and in that way their character is developed on the best lines.

One of the powerful temptations is that of motion pictures.

Motion pictures have undoubtedly an enormous attraction for boys, and some people are constantly cudgelling their brains how to stop it. But it is one of these things which would be very difficult to stop even if it were altogether desirable. The point, rather, is how to utilize films to the best advantage for our ends. On the principle of meeting any difficulty by siding with it and edging it in one's own direction, we should endeavour to see what there is of value in motion pictures and should then utilize them for the purpose of training the boy. No doubt it can be a powerful instrument for evil by suggestion, if not properly supervised. But, as it can be a power for evil, so it can just as well be made a power for good. There are excellent films now on natural history and nature study, which give a child a far better idea of the processes of nature than its own observation can do, and certainly far better than any amount of lessons on the subject. History can be taught through the eye. There are dramas of the pathetic or heroic kind, and others of genuine fun, humour and laughter. Many of them bring what is bad into condemnation and ridicule. There is no doubt that this teaching through the eye can be adapted so as to have a wonderfully good effect through the children's own inclination and interest in the 'cinema palace'. We have to remember too that motion pictures have the same influence on the schools which are now turning them to good account. In Scouting we cannot do this to the same extent, but we can utilize them as a spur to our own endeavours. We have to make our Scouting sufficiently attractive to attract the boy, no matter what other counter-attractions there may be.

Juvenile smoking and its detriment to health; **gambling** and all the dishonesty that it brings in its train; the evils of **drink**; of **loafing** with girls; **uncleanness**, etc., can only be corrected by the Scout Leader who knows the usual environment of his lads.

It cannot be done by forbidding or punishment, but by substituting something at least equally attractive but good in its effects.

Juvenile crime is not naturally born in the boy, but is largely due either to the spirit of adventure that is in him, to his own stupidity, or to his lack of discipline, according to the nature of the individual.

Natural **lying** is another very prevalent fault amongst lads; and, unfortunately, a prevailing disease all over the world. You meet it particularly amongst uncivilized tribes, as well as in the civilized countries. Truth speaking, and its consequent elevation of a man into being a reliable authority, makes all the difference in his character and in the character of the nation. Therefore, it is incumbent upon us to do all we can to raise the tone of honour and truth speaking amongst the lads.

> *I have known lots of men who ruined their career through drink, through deceit, through wine and through women; but I have known more who have done so through want of patience.*

The Scouter, August 1929 (rep. BPO, 128)

Troop Headquarters and Camp

The main antidote to a bad environment is naturally the substitution of a good one, and this is best done through the Troop Headquarters and the Scout Camp. By Headquarters I do not mean half an hour's drill once a week in a big schoolroom lent for the occasion – which has so often appeared to be the aim of those dealing with boys – but a real place which the boys feel is their own, even though it may be a cellar or an attic; some place to which they can resort every evening, if need be, and find congenial work and amusement, plenty of varied activity and a bright and happy atmosphere. If a Scout Leader can only arrange this, he will have done a very good work in providing the right environment for some of his lads which will be the best antidote for the poison that otherwise would creep into their minds and characters.

Then the Camp (and this should be as frequent as possibly can be managed) is a still further and even more potent antidote than the

Headquarters. The open and breezy atmosphere and the comradeship of continued association under canvas, in the field, and round the camp fire, breathes the very best of spirit amongst the lads, and gives the Scout Leader a far better opportunity than any other of getting hold of his boys and of impressing his personality upon them.

What the Scout Leader does, his boys will do. The Scout Leader is reflected in his Scouts. From the self-sacrifice and patriotism of their Scout Leader, Scouts inherit the practice of voluntary self-sacrifice and patriotic service.

'Do your best' is the Cub's motto.

WCH, 22

OBJECT AND METHOD OF CUB TRAINING

Object

Playing the Game

Our object in taking up the training of the Cubs is not merely to devise a pleasant pastime for the Cubmasters or for the boys, but to improve the efficiency of our future citizens.

The past training of these has not proved adequate for the requirements of today, and if the training is not good enough for today, much less is it good enough for tomorrow, and it is to tomorrow that we must look forward.

Character is acknowledged to be of greater importance than mere book instruction for citizen efficiency. And yet no practical scheme exists for its inclusion in education to even an equivalent extent.

Physical health and how to develop it should be as much a part of education as scholarly scientific or technical attainments.

Our training of the Cubs therefore is directed to these two main ends. It is done at the most important time of their lives, when they are most mouldable both in body and in mind to receive the right directions. With a foundation laid thus early we may hope that the subsequent structure may be all the more satisfactory, especially since it forms part of a progressive system to be continued and maintained during the period of his Boy Scout training.

The Cub Pack is designed to be a Junior Branch of the Scout Movement in order to meet the eagerness of a large number of small boys who want to be Scouts and who are as yet too young. It doesn't do to put them to the same tasks and tests as the older boys, especially in the company of the older boys, as they are likely to overdo themselves in the effort to keep up to the mark. At the same time the older boys on their part do not care to mix with 'kids' in their pursuits. It is for every reason better to keep the two apart.

Cub training is different from but a step towards that of the Scouts. No boy's character is firmly set at eleven or twelve years of age, and Cubmasters must realize that unless the work of the Pack really leads to that of the Troop they are, to a large extent, failing their boys. It is *possible* for a boy to lose, in a very short time, much of the good he has gained by being a Cub if the work is not carried on until he is old enough to choose good from evil.

A normal Cub Pack is not a separate organization, but part of a Scout Group. The Cubmaster should work in close co-operation with the Scout Leaders, the Scouts and the Rovers. He should make it plain to every new boy and to every new boy's parents that the Pack is only an 'ante-room' to the Scouts, and he should always keep the ideal of a 'better Scout' before the Cubs. At the head of the Group there is the Group Scoutmaster, who exercises general supervision over all sections of the Group but delegates the detailed responsibility for the management of each section to the Scout Leader in charge of it. The Cubmaster is thus responsible to the Group Scoutmaster for the conduct and management of the Pack. He will be a member of the Group Council, consisting of all the warranted Scout Leaders of the Group, whose task is to direct the general policy of the Group as a whole.

The Cub Law and Promise are naturally simpler than those of the Scout – it would not be right to ask the younger boys to undertake duties and promises which they could neither grasp nor carry out. Cubmasters should of course teach their boys in a simple and practical manner and in consultation with their Chaplain what is meant by their Promise of 'Duty to God' and should give what other religious and moral instruction they think necessary to prepare the Cub for becoming a good Scout.

To a considerable extent a boy gains the right spirit through right action, whereas the man's action is inspired by the spirit. So we encourage in the Cub, and continue in the Scout, the practice of doing good turns, and thus through action the spirit of helpfulness becomes developed in him; ultimately, as a Rover and a man, he is inspired by the spirit to undertake sacrifice and service.

Paper read at York Conference, in *Jamboree*, July 1928

Method

Our method of training is to educate from within rather than to instruct from without; to offer games and activities which, while being attractive to the small boy, will seriously educate him morally, mentally and physically.

Our aim, as Fisher wrote, is to promote 'not so much the acquisition of knowledge as the desire and capacity for acquiring knowledge.'

In other words, the Cubmaster's job is to enthuse the boy in the right direction. By acting on this principle he will save himself considerable trouble in reaching his goal and in producing a smart Pack of keen and capable boys. It is the means by which the modern schoolmaster scores over his more old-fashioned brother, since he develops a boy to be efficient rather than scholarly, to have character rather than erudition – and that is what counts towards success in life.

The Scout Method

By efficiency I don't mean mere money-making skill, but a general intelligence and capability to live a free, prosperous and happy life.

To preach 'don't' is to incite the doing of wrong. Rather infuse the right spirit; as powder is to the shot so is spirit to action. Direct moral instruction – like drill – produces a pleasing veneer, but unless there is properly seasoned character below this will not stand wear.

Lord Morley has said: 'It is well known to the wise, but an everlasting puzzle to the foolish, that direct inculcation of morals should invariably prove so powerless an instrument, so futile a method.' Wise old Plato long ago gave us the right lead in education, and one which only now is beginning to be followed, when he said that there was innate good in every child, and the aim of education should be to develop these natural 'instincts of virtue' through suitable practices. Here is no mention of reading, writing and 'rithmetic as essentials, but of enlarging the natural instincts, i.e. character by practices, not merely by precepts.

The average boy (if there is such a thing as an average boy) does not want to sit down and passively receive theoretical instruction. He wants to be up and actually doing things in practice, and this is a good lever to work upon if only the teacher will recognize it as the instrument ready to his hand.

Your first step then, is to study the boy himself; to recognize his likes and dislikes, his good qualities and his bad, and to direct his training on these.

Playing the Game

The Attitude of the Cubmaster

There are two fundamental points to be considered in dealing with the Cubs. The first is that the only man who can hope for real success as a trainer of Cubs is the one who can be their 'elder brother'. The 'commanding officer' is no good, and the 'schoolmaster' is doomed to failure (though probably in neither case would the man recognize it himself, or admit it). This fact is being proved daily by the successful results obtained by our Cubmasters, many of whom, of course, are ladies.

By the term 'elder brother' I mean one who can place himself on terms of comradeship with his boys, entering into their games and laughter himself, thereby winning their confidence and putting himself into that position which is essential for teaching, namely where, by his own example, he leads them in the right direction instead of being a finger-post, often too high above their heads, merely pointing the way.

But do not misunderstand me and imagine that I ask the Cubmaster to be 'soft' and 'namby-pamby'. Far otherwise; comradeship necessitates firmness and straightness if it is to be of lasting value.

> If you look at a real wolf, he wears a big grin on his mouth. So, too, the boy-Cub should always be smiling. Even if you don't feel like smiling — and sometimes you may feel more like crying — remember that Cubs never cry. In fact, Cubs always smile, and if they are in difficulty, in pain, in trouble, or in danger, they always grin and bear it.
>
> WCH, 43–4

The Scout Method

The Make-up of the Cub

The second item to recognize, although it is of first *importance*, is that the boy of eight to ten is in every way quite different from the boy of eleven to fifteen. I don't mean that the change comes about with a bang in the tenth year, but the younger boy is growing relatively, in mind and body, more rapidly than the older one, and the transition gradually comes about approximately at those ages in the average boy.

Boyhood's Phases:

6 to 8 – Dramatic instinct and make-believe.

8 to 11 – Self-assertive individuality and rivalry.

11 to 15 – Hero-worship and cooperative loyalty.

It may be taken for granted that boys of Cub age have the following propensities, namely – to lie, to be selfish, to be cruel and to be bombastic or pharisaical; but it must be at once recognized that these attributes are not born of malicious design, they are rather the natural outcome of the peculiar attitude of mind at that age. It has to be recognized that while the elder boy – he of Scout age – is full of hero-worship and eagerness to work in a gang under a good leader and in competition with other gangs, especially in chivalrous service, the younger boy, just emerging from the chrysalis of childhood, is more of an individual, feeling his feet, as it were, more self-centred, for the first time finding himself able to do things, anxious to do things himself and to make things, and the moment that he achieves a step of any kind he is prone to 'show off'.

He is only just out of the age of toys and is still very much in the land of make-believe. He is eager to have, but not to give. He is at the most mouldable period of his *life*.

Thus there are many seeds of evil beginning to sprout into pliant tendrils ready to trail off in wrong directions, but easily taken in hand and trained aright.

The question which troubles many of us is, how can this best be done? It is evident that the Cubmaster must be quick to recognize the evil points where they show themselves. The very usual process on the part of parents who have forgotten their childhood is at once to repress such propensities in the rare cases where they have been smart enough to recognize them; but repression is the very worst possible line to take. It is the cutting of shoots which makes them branch out into more devious growths; it tends to make the boy lie more cunningly, to secrete his selfishness and to put a better gloss on his hypocrisy.

Little boys are apt to bombast and hence to lie without any really vicious intent, but it is well to cure this habit in its early stages lest worse befall. To cure lying it is well, when you nail a lie, not to abuse the boy for it, but merely to show that you are not taken in by it. Contempt will conquer some boys, and ridicule is pretty certain to cure others. Whenever he tries to lie again, some mild chaff to show him that the first lie is not forgotten will probably have a very wholesome effect. But, on the other hand, you have to be at pains to show that past misdeeds are not continually remembered against him, but that you trust him and have faith in him to conquer these signs of weakness.

Selflessness can be taught in a practical way by getting boys to give things away to others.

A youngster cannot naturally keep still for ten minutes – much less for hours as is sometimes expected of him in school. We have to remember that he is suffering from the 'growing itch', both mentally and physically. The best cure is to change the subject, let him out for a run, or for a war dance.

For his athletics do not be content to let him merely run about doing things, but help him with advice and, if you are not too fat, with example, how:

To run	To vault
To jump	To bowl
To throw	To catch, etc.

These are really better for him physically and mentally than even Swedish Drill, as they are direct preparation for practical work in games, etc., while they are equally good in developing his organs and muscles by natural process.

Play is the first great educator – that is as true of animals as of men.

And so it is with our Cubs. We teach them small things in play which will eventually *fit* them for doing big things in earnest.

The great principle for dealing with the Cub Pack, and one by which the youngsters can be attracted and their failings remedied, is by making the Cubs into a happy family – not a family but a *happy* family. Boys want noise: let them have it. When they play let them play heartily, if the Cubmaster has the sense to organize his programme that way.

Laughter essential. We have advocated in the Scout training the development of the Scout smile as a necessary adjunct; with the Cubs the smile should be a laugh. Laughter counteracts most of the evils of the very young and makes for cheery companionship and open-mindedness. *The boy who laughs much lies little.*

Playing the Game

Laugh while you work.

Motto suggested for Guiders,
in GG, explanation (same idea, RTS, 235)

How to Run a Pack

Having considered the make-up of the younger boy and the spirit in which to deal with him – and this is a step of first importance towards success in training him – let me offer a *few* suggestions on the organization and training of a Pack.

Be content to begin with only a few boys. One is too often tempted to make a start with a large Pack. To do so is to make a mistake. You want first of all to establish the right tone on a small scale; to have a handful of yeast to leaven the lump when you get it.

Even then do not go for too big a Pack. I have found by experience that eighteen is as many as I can deal with in giving individual training. Allowing for your being much more capable, I suggest that twenty-four is as large a Pack as any man can adequately train. Of course you can easily *drill* a hundred and twenty-four, but that is not *training* them.

Organisation

The Six System. Scout Troops are divided into Patrols – Cub Packs into Sixes. A Six consists of six boys under the charge of a Sixer, who is helped by a Second. These leaders should only be given actual responsibility in leading and in teaching under the Cubmaster's direct supervision. A Sixer is *not* a 'junior Patrol Leader' and should not be looked upon as capable of taking charge of or of training his Six.

Cubmasters are advised to run a Sixers' Council and a Sixers' Instruction Meeting. A Sixers' Council consists of the Cubmaster, the Assistant Cubmaster, the Sixers, and sometimes the Seconds. It is a body which holds regular but very informal meetings at which the plans of the Pack are discussed, and the Cubmaster has an opportunity of correcting, or praising, and of advising his leaders.

The Instruction Meeting generally follows immediately after the Sixers' Council meeting – the two taking about three-quarters of an hour in all.

At this, old work is revised and new work done. Most Cubs having very short and faulty memories, a Cubmaster who wants to have good helpers – because that is what Sixers really are – must give them some such time to themselves.

Meetings. Meet as often as you can on fixed days and at fixed hours. Punctuality on the part of the boys should be a test not so much of their obedience as their eagerness to be there for fear of missing a good thing. Punctuality on your own part is even more necessary. Have your programme of doings prepared beforehand. There must be no pausing to think what you will do next, and the boys should learn anything but idling.

Have no onlookers or boys awaiting their turn. Every Cub should be busy all the time, at work or play. Remember the young mind at that age cannot stick at a thing for long. Frequent change with variety and contrast should distinguish your programme. Play is the most important thing in life to a boy, so have plenty of games.

Insist on smartness in little things – by praise and not by punishment – in such details of dress as neatness of scarves, and especially alertness of carriage and readiness in saluting.

Keep right away from any form of military drill. 'Forming fours' except when playing O'Grady, should be 'taboo' at a Pack Meeting. The circle is the Cub formation – not the rank, and you can get a circle easily enough if your Cubs understand the call 'Pack! Pack! Pack!'

Meetings should start and end with the Grand Howl.

Ceremonies. The two most important Cub ceremonies are the investiture and the Going Up. These should *never* be performed in any haphazard fashion. A Cubmaster can make any small Pack variations that may appeal to him and to his Cubs, provided that the main outline is adhered to, and that every care is taken to keep the ceremonies within the understanding of the Cubs. Over-elaboration generally means fidgeting. Simplicity and solemnity should be the keynotes of all Cub ceremonies.

Parents. A great help to success is to be in touch with the parents of your Cubs, to consult them for ideas, and most especially to interest them by explaining your reason for the different steps you are taking. You should visit them at least once a year, invite them to Pack functions and camps and get their help with the boys' Cub work at home.

Records. Every Pack should have its own properly kept Register – showing the Cub history of each member – and a simple Log Book will be interesting reading in the future. Each Sixer can have his own Six Book in which to enter the attendance and the sub-scriptions of his Six, but one of the Old Wolves will need to keep an eye on it for him.

Accounts. Cubmasters must see that Pack Accounts are kept and, where boys' subscriptions are concerned, the boys have the right to inspect the accounts. It is as well to put someone definitely in charge of this side of Pack organization, and to co-ordinate matters with the other sections of the Group. If any outside sub-scriptions are received, a Committee must be formed – probably in conjunction with the Group – to deal with these.

> *I heard of a Cub who, when asked what good turn he had done that day, confessed he had not been able to do one, largely because he thought he was too small. Well, he was talking nonsense, because nobody is too small to do a small good turn, even if it is only to smile at other people and so make them feel happier.*
>
> AA, 34

Training

Story-telling. The Cubmaster can command rapt attention at any time by telling his Cubs a story, and through it he can convey the lesson he wants to inculcate. It is a gilding to the pill which never fails – if the teller is any good at all.

The story must be told in an easy, unstilted way and with some dramatic accompaniment – the high voice of the old woman, the whining voice of the jackal, the snarling voice of the tiger, hand action to illustrate the creeping of the snake, or the fists of the

Playing the Game

fighter shot out. But be careful not to overdo this so that the Cubs rivet their attention on your actions instead of your words. Above all, don't let the run of the story be interrupted when all are agog to hear the climax – no questions to or from the audience – carry them along with you to the big sigh of excited repletion at the end. Occasionally it may be a good plan even to *read* a good yarn. If this is properly done, the Cubs can be got to appreciate the value of good books. Telling a yarn is, however, always better than reading one.

Play-acting. Another valuable and ever-popular form of character education is that of dressing-up and play-acting.

Sometimes this is useful in connection with the stories told. I need scarcely try to count up the various points of development which underlie it, such as self-expression, concentration of mind, voice development, imagination, pathos, humour, poise, discipline, historical or moral instruction, loss of self-consciousness, and so on. The Cubmaster will recognize these for himself the moment that he realizes what a mine of help acting provides for him, and how the Cubs, being at a dramatic and make-believe age, will meet his efforts halfway. Charades and impromptu plays are just as good in their way as more highly designed and rehearsed shows.

Games. It should be understood that in this direction lies a great means to success, especially if games can be thought of in relation to their moral and physical benefits to the boys and grouped accordingly on some such principles as those shown below.

Discipline and co-operation: Team games, Basket Ball, Football, Hockey, Rounders.

Concentration of mind and effort: Ball-catching, Marbles, Stepping stones, Skipping.

Observation: Kim's Game, Leaf-hunting, Thimble-hunting, Tracking.

Construction: Kite-flying, Model aeroplanes, Six models.

Eyesight: Far and Near, Patterns, How many? etc.

Handicraft: Knots, Paper-gliders, Combination pictures (for screens, scrap-books), Homecraft.

Physical: Climbing, Hop, step and jump, Ball throwing, Somersaults, Relay races of all kinds.

When used with such ends in view games are, as education for young boys, equal to hours spent in schooling.

Cub Camp. This is a most valuable opportunity in the study of Cubs, for in a few days you will learn more about them than in many months of ordinary meetings, and you can influence them in matters of character, cleanliness and health in such a way as may form lasting habits.

It must not be forgotten, however, that Camp is one of the most serious responsibilities that a Cubmaster can undertake. It is no light thing to take young children from their homes and to make yourself entirely responsible for them for the time they are with you.

Camp is not essential for Cubs as it is for Scouts and it is far better not to attempt camp at all unless you have all the facilities and experience which are necessary. In any case it is advisable only to take part of the Pack – the older and more responsible boys. Camp should not last too long. It is an enormous strain on those in a position of responsibility, and by carrying it on too long you may even dull the keenness of the boys. A week is the outside period, and a long weekend, say from Friday night to Tuesday or Wednesday morning, is quite sufficient. Again, it is not advisable to take Cubs too far from home. A short distance is a big enough adventure for them and if you are far from their homes you may be faced by really serious difficulties in case of illness or any kind of accident.

There should be at least one adult for every six Cubs in camp, excluding the Scouter in charge. A minimum of three adults is always desirable. In this way one Old Wolf can take the general responsibility, another can attend to the cooking and the third will see to the amusement of the Cubs.

Remember you are making yourself responsible for the safety, comfort and health of your Cubs and that you must not let them suffer by reason of your inexperience. Learn how things ought to be done; plan everything beforehand; arrange every detail; leave nothing to chance; and as *far* as is humanly possible provide against accident or emergency. A good camp *may* be of lasting value to your Cubs. A bad one *will* be a lasting reproach to you, your Pack and probably the whole Movement. It is better to train your boys by methods possibly less attractive and slower than to risk this.

Finally, don't attempt to run a camp until you have had some experience and understanding of the difficulties and responsibilities. You must have the necessary knowledge and practical experience before you take your own boys.

If God made the boy a creature of extreme and restless energy, with an inquisitive and eager mind, a sensitive little heart, and a romantic imagi-

nation, it is up to you [Cub Leaders] to make full use of these instead of crushing them.

The Secret of True Education: The Principle,
Wolf Cub Pamphlet, undated, SAA

Summing up

The idea is through:
- *Handicrafts*, to develop application, constructiveness, etc.
- *Nature study*, to develop observation, religion, kindness to animals.
- *Games*, to develop laughter, good nature and comradeship.
- *Athletics*, to utilize individual emulation for physical development.
- *Team Games*, to develop unselfishness, discipline, *esprit de corps*.

The scheme which I have suggested has purposely been left sketchy in many of its details. It is merely an outline on which a Cubmaster can build his own course of training. The essential is that the aim and spirit as here indicated should be thoroughly grasped. I do not want Cubmasters to feel themselves otherwise fettered by traditions, rules and syllabuses. Their own experience and imagination, their own boyishness and sympathy with boy nature, will be their best guide.

A point is not to introduce the Boy Scout training directly into that of the Cubs. It is not adapted to them, and it would tend to rob the Cub of his ambition ultimately to be promoted to the higher grade of Scout.

*[The Grand Howl] means that you will do your best with both hands —
not merely one like most boys, who only use their right hand. Your best will
be twice as good as the ordinary boy's best. 'Do your best' is the Cub's motto.*

WCH, 22

SCOUTING

Scouting is Simple

Scouting is a game for boys, under the leadership of boys, in
which elder brothers can give their younger brothers healthy environment and encourage them to healthy activities such as will help
them to develop **citizenship**.

Its strongest appeal is through Nature study and woodcraft. It
deals with the individual, not with the company. It raises intellectual as well as purely physical or purely moral qualities.

To an outsider Scouting must at first sight appear to be a very complex matter, and many a man is probably put off from becoming a Scout Leader because of the enormous number and variety of things that he thinks he would have to know in order to teach his boys. But it need not be so, if the man will only realize the following points:

1. The aim of Scouting is quite a simple one.
2. The Scout Leader gives to the boy the ambition and desire to learn for himself by suggesting to him activities which attract him, and which he pursues till he, by experience, does them aright.[4]
3. The Scout Leader works through his Patrol Leaders.

The Aim of Scouting

The aim of the Scout training is to **improve the standard of our future citizenhood**, especially in **Character** and **Health**; to replace Self with Service, to make the lads individually efficient, morally and physically, with the object of using that efficiency for service for their fellow-men.

Citizenship has been defined briefly as 'active loyalty to the community'. In a free country it is easy, and not unusual, to consider oneself a good citizen by being a law-abiding man, doing your work and expressing your choice in politics, sports, or activities, 'leaving it to George' to worry about the nation's welfare. This is passive citizenship. But **passive** citizenship is not enough to uphold in the world the virtues of freedom, justice, and honour. Only **active** citizenship will do.

Playing the Game

The Four Branches of Scout Training

To accomplish the aim of training for active citizenship, we take up the following four branches which are essential in building up good citizens, and we inculcate them from within instead of from without:

Character. Which we teach through: the Patrol System, the Scout Law, Scout lore, woodcraft, responsibility of the Patrol Leader, team games and the resourcefulness involved in camp work. This includes the realization of God the Creator through His works; the appreciation of beauty in Nature; and through the love of plants or animals with which outdoor life has made one familiar.

Health and strength. Through games, exercises, and knowledge of personal hygiene and diet.

Handcraft and skill. Occasionally through indoor activities, but more especially through pioneering, bridge-building, camp expedients, self-expression through the arts, which all tend to make efficient workmen.

Service to others. The carrying into daily life of the *practice* of religion by 'good turns', dealing with quite small good actions as well as with community service, accidents, life-saving.

Scouting is a jolly game in the out of doors, where boy-men and boys can go adventuring together as older and younger brothers, picking up health and happiness, handicraft and helpfulness.

The Scout Method

Nine out of ten boys begin smoking largely out of bravado.

RTS, 69

Personally I am none the worse for being a non-smoker.

The Scouter, October 1931

The Activities of Scouting

By the term 'Scouting' is meant the work and attributes of back-woodsmen, explorers, hunters, seamen, airmen, pioneers and fron-tiersmen.

In giving the elements of these to boys we supply a system of games and practices which meets their desires and instincts, and is at the same time educative.

From the boys' point of view Scouting puts them into frater-nity gangs which are their natural organization, whether for games, mischief or loafing; it gives them a smart dress and equipment; it appeals to their imagination and romance; and it engages them in an active, open-air life.

From the parents' point of view it gives physical health and development; it teaches energy, resourcefulness and handicrafts; it puts into the lad discipline, pluck, chivalry and patriotism; in a word, it develops 'character', which is more essential than anything else to a lad for making his way in life.

The Scout training attracts boys of all classes, high and low, rich and poor, and even catches the physically defective, deaf mutes and blind. It inspires the *desire* to learn. The principle on which Scouting works is that the boy's ideas are studied, and he is encouraged to **educate himself** instead of being *instructed*.

Moreover, we encourage personal responsibility in the boy for his own physical development and health: and we trust in his honour and expect him to do a Good Turn to someone every day.

Where the Scout Leader is himself a bit of a boy, and can see it all from the boy's point of view, he can, if he is imaginative, invent new activities, with frequent variations, to meet the boys' thirst for novelty. Note the theatres. If they find that a play does not appeal to the public, they don't go on hammering away with it in the hope that it will in the end do so; they take it off and put on some new attraction.

Boys can see adventure in a dirty old duck-puddle, and if the Scout Leader is a boy-man he can see it too. It does not require great expense or apparatus to devise new ideas; the boys themselves can often help with suggestions.

A further way of discovering activities that will appeal to the boys is for the Scout Leader to save his brains by using his ears.

If you make listening and observation your particular occupation, you will gain much more information from your boys than you can put into them by your own talk.

Also, when visiting the parents, don't go with the idea of impressing on them the value of Scouting so much as to glean from them what are their ideas of training their boys and what they expect of Scouting or where they find it deficient.

Generally speaking, when short of ideas don't impose on your Scouts activities which you think they ought to like; but find out from them by listening or by questioning which activities appeal most to them, and then see how far you can get these going: that is, if they are likely to be beneficial to the boys.

Where a Troop resounds with jolly laughter, and enjoys success in competitions, and the fresh excitements of new adventures, there won't be any loss of members through boredom.

For myself I sleep out of doors in winter as well as in summer. I only feel tired or seedy when I have been indoors a lot. I only catch cold when I sleep in a room.

RTS, 115

The Scout Spirit

The underlying feature is the spirit of the Movement, and the key that unlocks this spirit is the romance of Woodcraft and Nature Lore.

Where is there a boy, or for the matter of that a grown-up man, even in these materialistic times to whom the call of the wild and the open road does not appeal?

Maybe it is a primitive instinct: anyway, it is there. With that key a great door may be unlocked, if it is only to admit fresh air and sunshine into lives that were otherwise grey.

But generally it can do more than this.

The heroes of the wild, the frontiersmen and explorers, the rovers of the sea, the airmen of the clouds are Pied Pipers to the boy.

Where they lead the boys will follow, and these will dance

to their tune when it sings the song of manliness and pluck, of adventure and high endeavour, of efficiency and skill, of cheerful sacrifice of self for others.

There's meat in this for the boy; there's soul in it.

His unit is the natural gang of the boy, led by its own boy leader.

He may be one of a herd, but he has his own entity. He gets to know the joy of life through the out-of-doors.

Then there is a spiritual side.

Through sips of Nature Lore imbibed in woodland hikes the puny soul grows up and looks around. The outdoors is *par excellence* the school for observation and for realizing the wonders of a wondrous universe.

It opens to the mind appreciation of the beautiful that lies before it day by day. It reveals to the city youngster that the stars are there beyond the city chimney pots, and the sunset clouds are gleaming in their glory far above the roof of the 'cinema' theatre.

The study of nature brings into a harmonious whole the question of the infinite, the historic, and the microscopic as part of the Great Creator's work. And in these, sex and reproduction play an honoured part.

Scoutcraft is a means through which the veriest hooligan can he brought to higher thought and to the elements of faith in God; and, coupled with the Scout's obligation to do a Good Turn every day, it gives the base of Duty to God and to Neighbour on which the parent or pastor can build with greater care the form of belief that is desired.

It is the spirit within, not the veneer without that does it.

The Scout Method

And the spirit is there in every boy when you get him, only it has to be discovered and brought to light.

The **Scout Promise** to carry out, *on his honour*, as far as in him lies, and the **Scout Law** is our binding disciplinary force, and with ninety-nine out of a hundred it pays. The boy is not governed by DON'T, but is led on by DO. The Scout Law is devised as a guide to his actions rather than as repressive of his faults. It merely states what is good form and expected of a Scout.

A Scout will go to church on Sunday, but he will keep in touch with God just as much every day of the week by thanking God for every bit of enjoyment he gets or for every success that he makes in his work or play, and by asking God's help and guidance in his work and when he is troubled.

The Scout, 13 January, 1934

The Patrol System

The Patrol System is the one essential feature in which Scout training differs from that of all other organizations, and where the System is properly applied, it is absolutely bound to bring success. It cannot help itself!

The formation of the boys into Patrols of from six to eight and training them as separate units each under its own responsible leader is the key to a good Troop.

The Patrol is the unit of Scouting always, whether for work or for play, for discipline or for duty.

An invaluable step in character training is to put responsibility on to the individual. This is immediately gained in appointing a Patrol Leader to *responsible* command of his Patrol. It is up to him to take hold of and to develop the qualities of each boy in his Patrol. It sounds a big order, but in practice it works.

Values of the Patrol System

It is important that the Scout Leader recognize the extraordinary value which he can get out of the Patrol System. It is the best guarantee for permanent vitality and success for the Troop. It takes a great deal of minor routine work off the shoulders of the Scout Leader.

But first and foremost: **The Patrol is the character school for the individual.** To the Patrol Leader it gives practice in Responsibility and in the qualities of Leadership. To the Scouts it gives subordination of self to the interests of the whole, the elements of self-denial and self-control involved in the team spirit of co-operation and good comradeship.

The best progress is made in those Troops where power and responsibility are really put into the hands of the Patrol Leaders. This it the secret of success in Scout Training.

But to get first-class results from this system you have to give the boy leaders real freehanded responsibility; if you only give partial responsibility you will only get partial results. The main object is not so much saving the Scout Leader trouble as to give responsibility to the boy, since this is the very best of all means for developing character.

The Scout Leader who hopes for success must not only study

what is written about the Patrol System and its methods, but must put into practice the suggestions he reads. It is the doing of things that is so important, and only by constant trial can experience be gained by his Patrol Leaders and Scouts. The more he gives them to do, the more will they respond, the more strength and character will they achieve.

The Movement is a jolly fraternity.

Aids, WB, 20

The Scout Uniform

I have often said, 'I don't care a fig whether a Scout wears a uniform or not so long as his heart is in his work and he carries out the Scout Law.' But the fact is that there is hardly a Scout who does not wear uniform if he can afford to buy it. The spirit prompts him to it.

The same applies naturally to those who carry on the Scout Movement, the Scout Leaders and Commissioners; there is no obligation on them to wear uniform if they don't like it. At the same time, they have in their positions to think of others rather than of themselves.

Personally, I put on uniform, even if I have only a Patrol to inspect, because I am certain that it raises the moral tone of the boys. It heightens their estimation of their uniform when they see it is not beneath a grown man to wear it; it heightens their estimation of themselves when they see themselves taken seriously by men who also count it of importance to be in the same brotherhood with them.

Smartness in uniform and correctness in detail may seem a small matter, but is of value in the development of self-respect, and means an immense deal to the reputation of the Movement among outsiders who judge by what they see.

It is largely a matter of example. Show me a slackly dressed Troop and I can 'Sherlock' a slackly dressed Scout Leader.

You are the model to your boys and your smartness will reflect itself in them.

It doesn't matter how poor you are, you can at least be clean and tidy. It doesn't cost you any more.

ATM, 158

The code of the knight is still the code of the gentleman today.

I: CHARACTER

'A nation owes its success, not so much to its strength in armaments, as to the amount of character in its citizens.'

'For a man to be successful in life, character is more essential than erudition.'

So character is of first value whether for a nation or for the individual. But if character is to make a man's career for him, it ought to be developed in him before he starts out, while he is still a boy and receptive. Character cannot be drilled into a boy. The germ of it is already in him, and needs to be drawn out and expanded. How?

Character is very generally the result of environment or surroundings. For example, take two small boys, twins if you like. Teach them the same lessons in school, but give them entirely different surroundings, companions, and homes outside the school.

Put one under a kindly, encouraging mother, among clean and straight playfellows, where he is trusted on his honour to carry out rules of life and so on. On the other hand, take the second boy and let him loaf in a filthy home, among foul-mouthed, thieving, discontented companions. Is he likely to grow up with the same amount of character as his twin?

There are thousands of boys being wasted daily through being left to become characterless, and therefore, useless wasters, a misery to themselves and an eyesore and a danger to the nation.

They could be saved if only the right surroundings or environment were given to them at the receptive time of their lives. And there are many thousands of others who may not be placed on quite so low a level (for there are wasters in every class of life), but who would be all the better men and more valuable to the country and more satisfactory to themselves if they could be persuaded, at the right age, to develop their characters.

Here, then, lies the most important object in the Scout training: to educate; not to instruct, mind you, but to educate, that is, to draw out the boy to learn for himself, of his own desire, the things that tend to build up character in him.

So, let us consider a few of the qualities, moral and mental, that go to make **Character**, and then see how the Scout Leader can get the boy to develop these for himself through Scouting.

Fair Play

The idea of fair play is above all the one which can be best instilled into boys and leads them to that strong view of justice which should be part of their character, if they are going to make really good citizens.

This habit of seeing things from the other fellow's point of view can be developed in outdoor games where fair play is essential. During the game the strictest rules are observed which means self-restraint and good temper on the part of the players, and at the end it is the proper form that the victor should sympathize with the one who is conquered, and that the opponent should be the first to cheer and congratulate the winner.

This should be made the practice until it becomes the habit.

A further valuable aid to the training in fairness is the holding of debates amongst the boys on subjects that interest them and which lend themselves to argument on both sides. This is to get them into the way of recognizing that every important question has two sides to it, and that they should not be carried away by the eloquence of one orator before they have heard what the defender of the other side has to say on the subject, and that they should then weigh the evidence of both sides for themselves before making up their minds and deciding which part they should take.

Discipline

Discipline cannot be got by repressive measures, but by encouragement and by educating the boy first in self-discipline and in sacrificing of self and selfish pleasures for the benefit of others. This teaching is largely effective by means of example, by putting responsibility upon him and by expecting a high standard of trustworthiness from him.

Discipline is not gained by punishing a child for a bad habit, but by substituting a better occupation, that will absorb his attention, and gradually lead him to forget and abandon the old one.

The Scout Leader should insist on discipline, and strict, quick obedience in small details. Let the boys run riot only when you give leave for it, which is a good thing to do every now and then.

So often it happens that if you try and do a good turn to someone else, the luck comes to you.

YFBS, 141

Sense of Honour

The **Scout Law** is the foundation on which the whole of Scout training rests.

Its various clauses must be fully explained and made clear to the boys by practical and simple illustrations of its application in their everyday life.

There is no teaching to compare with example. If the Scout Leader himself conspicuously carries out the Scout Law in all his doings, the boys will be quick to follow his lead.

This example comes with all the more force if the Scout Leader himself takes the Scout Promise, in the same way as his Scouts.

The first Law, namely, *A Scout's honour is to be trusted*, is one on which the whole of the Scout's future behaviour and discipline hangs. The Scout is expected to be straight. So it should be very carefully explained, as a first step, by the Scout Leader to his boys before taking the Scout Promise.

The investiture of the Scout is purposely made into something of a ceremony, since a little ritual of that kind if carried out with strict solemnity, impresses the boy; and considering the grave importance of the occasion, it is only right that he should be impressed as much as possible. Then it is of great importance that the Scout should periodically renew his knowledge of the Law. Boys are apt to be forgetful, and it should never be allowed that a boy who has made his solemn promise to carry out the Scout Law should, at any time, not be able to say what the Law is.

Once the Scout understands what his honour is and has, by his initiation, been put upon his honour, the Scout Leader must entirely trust him to do things. You must show him by your action that you consider him a responsible being. Give him charge of something, whether temporary or permanent, and expect him to carry out his charge faithfully. Don't keep prying to see how he does it. Let him do it his own way, let him come a howler over it if need be, but in any case leave him alone and trust him to do his best. Trust should be the basis of all our moral training.

Giving responsibility is the key to success with boys, especially with the rowdiest and most difficult boys.

Help the boy to become self-reliant, resourceful, to 'paddle his own canoe'; that is, to look ahead and shape his own course in life.

Aids, WB, 53

Playing the Game

Self-reliance

When training the South African Constabulary I used to send the men out in pairs to carry out long distance rides of two or three hundred miles to teach them to fend for themselves and to use their intelligence.

But when I had a somewhat dense pupil he was sent out alone, without another to lean upon, to find his own way, make his own arrangements for feeding himself and his horse, and for drawing up the report of his expedition unaided. This was the best training of all in self-reliance and intelligence, and this principle is one which I can confidently recommend to Scout Leaders in training their Scouts.

Of all the schools the camp is far and away the best for teaching boys the desired character-attributes. The environment is healthy, the boys are elated and keen, all the interests of life are round them, and the Scout Leader has them permanently for the time, day and night, under his hand. In camp the Scout Leader has his greatest opportunity for watching and getting to know the individual characteristics of each of his boys, and then applying the necessary direction to their development; while the boys themselves pick up the character-forming qualities incident to life in camp, where discipline, resourcefulness, ingenuity, self-reliance, handcraft, woodcraft, boat-craft, team sense, nature lore, etc., can all be imbibed under cheery and sympathetic direction of the understanding Scout Leader. A week of this life is worth six months of theoretical teaching in the meeting room, valuable though that may be.

The Scout Method

Enjoyment of Life

Why is Nature Lore considered a key activity in Scouting? That is a question on which hangs the difference between Scout work and that of the ordinary boys' club.

It is easily answered in the phrase: 'We want to teach our boys not merely how to get a living, but how to live'; that is, in the higher sense, how to enjoy life.

As the wonders of nature are unfolded to the young mind, so too its beauties can be pointed out and gradually become recognized. When appreciation of beauty is once given a place in the mind, it grows automatically in the same way as observation, and brings joy in the greyest of surroundings.

If I may diverge again, it was a dark, raw, foggy day in the big gloomful station at Birmingham. We were hustled along in a throng of grimy workers and muddy travel-stained soldiers. Yet, as we pushed through the crowd, I started and looked around, went on, looked round again, and suddenly had a good eye-filling stare before I went on. I don't suppose my companions had realized it, but I had caught a gleam of sunshine in that murky hole such as gave a new pleasure to the day. It was just a nurse in brown uniform with gorgeous red-gold hair and a big bunch of yellow and brown chrysanthemums in her arms. Nothing very wonderful you say. No, but for those who have eyes to see, these gleams are there even in the worst of gloom.

It is too common an idea that boys are unable to appreciate beauty and poetry; but I remember once some boys were being shown a picture of a stormy landscape, of which Ruskin had written that there was only one sign of peace in the whole wind-torn scene. One of the lads readily pointed to a spot of blue peaceful sky that was apparent through a rift in the driving wrack of clouds.

> *The Arabs have a saying: 'None but the base and ungrateful refuse generosity'; but this does not mean that he will take a reward for being kind to you. To offer a tip is to insult him, and I hope that Boy Scouts will take it in the same light.*

> YKE, 37

Development of Outlook: Reverence

Development of outlook naturally begins with a respect for God, which we may best term 'Reverence'.

Reverence to God and reverence for one's neighbour and reverence for oneself as a servant of God, is the basis of every form of religion. The method of expression of reverence to God varies with every sect and denomination. What sect or denomination a boy belongs to depends, as a rule, on his parents' wishes. It is they who decide. It is our business to respect their wishes and to second their efforts to inculcate reverence, whatever form of religion the boy professes.

There may be many difficulties relating to the definition of the religious training in our Movement where so many different denominations exist, and the details of the expression of duty to God have, therefore, to be left largely in the hands of the local authority. But there is no difficulty at all in suggesting the line to take on the human side, since direct duty to one's neighbour is implied in almost every form of belief.

Religion can only be 'caught', not 'taught'. It is not a dressing donned from outside, put on for Sunday wear. It is a true part of a boy's character, a development of soul, and not a veneer that may peel off. It is a matter of personality, of inner conviction, not of instruction.

The Scout Leader can in every case do an immense amount towards helping the religious teacher, just as he can help the schoolmaster by inculcating in his boys, in camp and club, the practical application of what they have been learning in theory in the school.

In denominational Troops there is, of a rule, a Troop Chaplain, and the Scout Leader should consult with him on any questions of religious instruction. For the purpose of its religious training, a service or class may be held, called a 'Scouts' Own'. This is a gathering of Scouts for the worship of God and to promote fuller realization of the Scout Law and Promise, but supplementary to, and not in substitution for, regular religious observances.

Many of our Troops, however, are interdenominational, having boys of different forms of belief in their ranks. Here the boys should be sent to their own clergy and pastors for denominational religious instruction.

Other Troops in slums and less-chance areas have lads of practically no religion of any kind, and their parents are little or no help to them. Naturally, these require different handling and methods of training from those boys in whom religion has been well grounded.

Here, again, Scouting comes very practically to the aid of the teacher, and has already given extraordinarily good results.

The way in which Scouting can help is through the following:

(*a*) Personal example of the Scout Leader.
(*b*) Nature study.
(*c*) Good Turns.

(*a*) **Personal example.** There is no doubt whatever that in the boy's eyes it is what a man *does* that counts and not so much what he says.

A Scout Leader has, therefore, the greatest responsibility on his shoulders for doing the right thing from the right motives, and for letting it be seen that he does so, but without making a parade of it. Here the attitude of elder brother rather than of teacher tells with the greater force.

(*b*) **Nature study.** There are sermons in the observation of Nature, say, in bird life, the formation of every feather identical with that of the same species 10,000 miles away, the migration, the nesting, the colouring of the egg, the growth of the young, the mothering, the feeding, the flying power: all done without the aid of man, but under the law of the Creator; these are the best of sermons for boys.

The flowers in their orders, and plants of every kind, their buds and bark, the animals and their habits and species; then the stars in the heavens, with their appointed places and ordered moves in space, give to every one the first conception of Infinity and of the vast scheme of his Creator where man is of so small account. All these have a fascination for boys, which appeals in an absorbing degree to their inquisitiveness and powers of observation, and leads them directly to recognize the hand of God in this world of wonders, if only someone introduces them to it.

The wonder to me of all wonders is how some teachers have neglected this easy and unfailing means of *education* and have struggled to impose Biblical *instruction* as the first step towards getting a restless, full-spirited boy to think of higher things.

(*c*) **Good Turns.** With a little encouragement on the part of the Scout Leader the practice of daily Good Turns soon becomes a sort of fashion with boys, and it is the very best step towards making a Christian in fact, and not merely in theory. The boy has a natural instinct for good if he only sees a practical way to exercise it, and this Good Turn business meets it and develops it, and in developing it brings out the spirit of Christian charity towards his neighbour.

This expression of his will to good is more effective, more natural to the boy, and more in accordance with the Scout method than his passive acceptance of instructive precepts.

Sacrifice is the salt of service.

RTS, 221

Self-respect

In speaking of the forms of reverence, which the boy should be encouraged to develop, we must not omit the important one of reverence for himself, that is self-respect in its highest form.

This, again, can well be inculcated through nature study of a preliminary step. The anatomy of plants, or birds, or shellfish may be studied and shown to be the wonderful work of the Creator. Then the boy's own anatomy can be studied in a similar light; the skeleton and the flesh, muscle, nerves, and sinews built upon it, the blood flow and the breathing, the brain and control of action, all repeated, down to the smallest details, in millions of human beings, yet no two are exactly alike in face or finger prints. Raise the boy's idea of the wonderful body which is given to him to keep and develop of God's own handiwork and temple; one which is physically capable of good work and brave deeds if guided by sense of duty and chivalry, that is by a high moral tone.

Thus is engendered self-respect.

This, of course, must not be preached to a lad in so many words and then left to fructify, but should be inferred and expected in all one's dealings with him. Especially it can be promoted by giving the boy responsibility, and by trusting him as an honourable being to carry out his duty to the best of his ability, and by treating him with respect and consideration, without spoiling him.

Loyalty

In addition to reverence to God and to one's neighbour, loyalty to the country is essential.

Loyalty to country is of the highest value for keeping one's views balanced and in the proper perspective. The external signs, such as saluting the flag, standing for the National Anthem, and so on, help in promoting this, but the essential thing is the development of the true spirit which underlies such demonstrations.

Loyalty to himself on the part of the boy – that is, to his better conscience – is the great step to self-realization.

Loyalty to others is proved by self-expression and action rather than by profession. Service for others and self-sacrifice must necessarily include readiness to serve one's country should the necessity arise for protecting it against foreign aggression; that is the duty of every citizen. But this does not mean that he is to develop a bloodthirsty or aggressive spirit, or that the boy need be trained to military duties and ideas of fighting.

Sunday is a day of rest; loafing is not rest.

SFB (26th), 244

II: HEALTH AND STRENGTH

The value of good health and strength in the making of a career and in the enjoyment of life is incalculable. That is pretty obvious. As a matter of education one may take it to be of greater value than 'book-learning' and almost as valuable as 'Character'.

We in the Scout Movement can do much by giving to the boys some of the training in health and personal hygiene, which is so essential to their efficiency as citizens.

Our task should be to get the boys to be athletic-minded, at the same time showing them that they must first build up their bodily health before they can safely take up strenuous physical exercises. This would be by proper plain feeding, and hygienic care of themselves in the matter of cleanliness, nose breathing, rest, clothing, regular habits, continence, and so on. We must avoid making them introspective by thinking of themselves liable to illness, etc., but hold up fitness for sport as the aim of health training.

With only half an hour per week in the ordinary Scout Troop meeting it is not possible for us to give formal physical training, but what we can do is to teach the boy to be PERSONALLY RESPONSIBLE TO HIMSELF FOR HIS HEALTH, how to secure it and keep it; also we can teach him a few exercises that will help him to develop his strength if he will practise them in his own time; and we can interest him in outdoor activities and games as being not only amusement for him but of practical value in making him sound, strong and healthy for life.

Health of body involves health of nerves and health of mind. Here our character training meets the physical.

The Scout Method

Be Fit!

Studies have shown that there is an immense percentage of unfit men among our citizens who, with reasonable care and understanding, could have been healthy efficient beings. Some of the reports on the health of school children show that one in every five suffers from defects that will prevent him from being efficient in after-life: defects, mind you, which might have been prevented.

These returns are immensely suggestive, and point at once to the need and the remedy; if we took the boy in time, tens of thousands could be saved every year to become strong and capable citizens instead of dragging out a miserable semi-efficient existence.

It is a matter of national as well as individual importance.

When I talk of walking I mean sprightly walking, not sloppy slouching.

RTS, 118

Organized Games

One of the objects of Scouting is to supply team games and activities which can promote the boy's health and strength and help to develop his character. These games have to be made attractive and competitive, and it is through them that we can inculcate the elements of pluck, obedience to rules, discipline, self-control, keenness, fortitude, leadership and unselfish team play.

Examples of such games and practices are: climbing of all sorts, ladders, ropes, trees, rocks, etc.; stepping-stones and plank-walking competitions; 'Spotty-face' for strengthening the eyesight; ball throwing and catching; boxing; wrestling, swimming, skipping, hopping fights, relay racing, cock-fighting, folk-dancing, action songs, etc. These and many other activities open a wide and varied programme of competition for Patrol against Patrol, which an imaginative Scout Leader can apply in turn to develop the physical points required.

Such vigorous Scout games are to my mind the best form of physical education, because most of them bring in moral education as well, and most of them are inexpensive and do not require well-kept grounds, apparatus, etc.

It is important to arrange all games and competitions, as far as possible, so that all the Scouts take part, because we do not want to have merely one or two brilliant performers and the others no use at all. All ought to get practice, and all ought to be pretty good. We in the Scouts can show every boy – town or country – how to be a *player* of games, and so to enjoy life and at the same time to strengthen his physical as well as his moral fibre.

It should be 'the thing' for the boys never to bear envy or to mention unfairness of judging or of the opponent's tactics when their team is defeated, and whatever disappointment they may feel they should only show cordial praise for the other side. This means true self-discipline and unselfishness, and it promotes that good feeling all round which is so much needed for breaking down prejudices.

Character is largely a matter of environment and training and, later on, of experience. Character is formed more by the environment outside the school walls than by the instruction within them. That environment may be for good and at the same time it may very easily be for bad.

GG, 184 and 185

Physical Exercises

Physical exercises are an intensive form of development where you cannot get good or frequent opportunity of games, and may well be used in addition to games, provided that:

1. They are not made entirely a drill, but something that each boy can really understand and want to practise for himself *because of the good that he knows it does him.*

2. The instructor has some knowledge of anatomy and the possible harm of many physical drill movements on the young unformed body. The six body exercises given in *Scouting for Boys* can be taught without any danger to the lad by Scout Leaders who are not experts in anatomy, etc. (These exercises should be done by the Scout himself – once he has learned the proper actions and breathing – in his own time, at home, and should not become a routine part of a Troop meeting.)

We should do everything to get the boy to interest himself in steadily exercising his body and limbs, and in practising difficult feats with pluck and patience until he masters them!

It is a good plan, for instance, for each Troop to adopt certain standards for simple exercises like 'standing high jump', 'hop, step and jump', 'putting the bag', and so on, so that each individual

Scout can try to increase his own ability and reach a higher standard.

Then a team uniform of sorts is an attraction to the boys, promotes *esprit de corps* in his athletic work, and incidentally involves changing his clothes before and after playing, encourages a rub down, a wash, cleanliness.

> *I may say that I always wear shorts, myself, winter and summer, and I never seem to have a cold. You might as well expect to get cold from having your face and hands exposed.*

> MFB, 58

The Out-of-Doors

Oxygen for Ox's Strength. I once saw some very smart physical drill by a Scout Troop in their headquarters.

It was very fresh and good, but, my wig, the air was not! It was, to say the least, 'niffy'. There was no ventilation. The boys were working like engines, but actually undoing their work by sucking in poison instead of strengthening their blood.

Fresh air is half the battle towards producing results in physical exercises and it may advantageously be taken through the skin as well as through the nose when possible.

Yes, that open-air is the secret of success. It is what Scouting is for: to develop the out-of-doors habit as much as possible.

I asked a Scout Leader once, in a great city, how he managed his Saturday hikes, whether in the park or in the country?

He did not have them at all. Why not? Because his boys did

330

not care about them. They preferred to come into the meeting room on Saturday afternoons!

Of course they preferred it, poor little beggars; they were accustomed to being indoors. But that is what we are out to prevent in the Scouts – our object is to wean them from indoors and to make the outdoors attractive to them.

In the Scouts especially, if we adhere to our proper *métier*, we ought to make a big step in this direction.

The open-air is the real objective of Scouting, and the key to its success. But with too much town life we are apt to underlook our object and revert to type.

We are not a club, nor a Sunday school, but a school of the woods. We must get more into the open for the health, whether of the body or the soul, of Scout and of Scout Leader.

The camp is what the boy looks forward to in Scouting, and is the Scout Leader's great opportunity.

The camp cannot fail to grip every boy with its outdoor life and taste of the wild, with its improved cooking expedients, the games over woodland or moor, the tracking, the path-finding, the pioneering, the minor hardships and the jolly camp fire sing-songs.

I used the expression 'camp life'. Keep in mind that **'camp life' is different from 'living under canvas'**.

I was shown a pattern schoolboy camp not long ago where there were rows of tents smartly pitched and perfectly aligned, with a fine big mess marquee and well-appointed cooks' quarters. There were brick paths and wooden bathing houses and latrines. It was all exceedingly well planned, and put up by the contractor. The officer who organized it all merely had to pay down a certain sum and the whole thing was done. It was quite simple and businesslike.

My only complaint about it was that it wasn't camping. Any ass, so to speak, can live under canvas where he is one of a herd with everything done for him; but he might just as well stop at home for all the good it is likely to do him.

In Scouting we know that what appeals to the boys, and is at the same time an education for them, is real camping: that is, where they prepare their own encampment even to the extent of previously making their own tents and learning to cook their own food.

Then the pitching of tents at separate sites and selected nooks, by Patrols, the arranging of water-supply and firewood, the preparation of bathing places, field kitchens, latrines, grease and refuse pits, etc., the use of camp expedients, and the making of camp utensils and furniture, will give a keen interest and invaluable training.

A Tenderfoot talks of 'roughing it in camp'; but living in camp for a Scout who knows the game is by no means 'roughing it'.

SFB, OFP, 14th

My ideal camp is one where everybody is cheery and *busy*, where the Patrols are kept intact under all circumstances, and where every Patrol Leader and Scout takes a genuine pride in his camp and his gadgets.

In a small camp so very much can be done through the example of the Scout Leader. You are living among your boys and are watched by each of them, and imitated unconsciously by them, and probably unobserved by yourself.

If you are lazy they will be lazy; if you make cleanliness a hobby it will become theirs; if you are clever at devising camp accessories, they will become rival inventors and so on.

But don't do too much of what should be done by the boys themselves, see that they do it; 'when you want a thing done don't do it yourself' is the right motto.

We want not only really healthy and clean camps, carried out in accordance with the local instructions, but camps where the boys can employ the nearest approach to a backwoodsman life and adventure.

> *Scouts are always tidy, whether in camp or not, as a matter of habit. If you are not tidy at home, you won't be tidy in camp; and if you're not tidy in camp, you will be only a tenderfoot and no Scout.*

SFB, OFP (12th), and GG, 120 (for Guides)

Swimming, Boating, Signalling

Swimming. The advantages of swimming among other forms of physical training are these:

The boy delights in it, and is keen to learn.
He gets to enjoy cleanliness.
He learns pluck in attaining the art.
He gains self-confidence on mastering it.

He develops his chest and breathing organs.

He develops muscle.

He gains the power of saving life and looks for opportunities of doing it.

Boat rowing also is an excellent muscle developer, and appeals very greatly to the Scout. It is only allowed after he has qualified in swimming, so induces a good lot of boys to train themselves in that line.

Signalling. Signalling practice, while it is educating the boy's intelligence, is at the same time giving him valuable physical exercise hour after hour in body-twisting and arm work, and in training the eye, but it is a practice which should be taken out-of-doors, so that it does not degenerate into a mere indoor exercise devoid of utility, purpose or romance.

The effort of body balance develops mental balance.

GG, 39

Personal Hygiene

Cleanliness inside as well as out is of prime importance to health.

That rub down with a damp rough towel, where baths are impossible, is of very big importance to inculcate as a habit in your boys. Also, the habit of washing hands before a meal and after the daily rear. The need for scrupulous cleanliness may well be inculcated by the practice of 'Kill that fly', not merely as a useful public service which Scouts can perform, but also as a means of introducing them to the minuteness of disease-germs as conveyed on flies' feet, and yet of such effect as to poison people.

Temperance: Temperate eating is almost as necessary with the boy as temperate drinking with the man. It is a good lesson in self-restraint for him to curb his appetite, both as regards the quantity and the nature of his food — few have fathomed the extent of a boy's capacity when it comes to tucking away food of whatever variety. The aim to be held out to him is fitness for athletics.

Temperance thus becomes a moral as well as physical detail of training.

Non-Smoking

Somebody once wrote an improved edition of *Scouting for Boys* and in it he ordered that 'Scouts are on no account to smoke.' It is generally a risky thing to order boys not to do a thing; it immediately opens to them the adventure of doing it contrary to orders.

Advise them against a thing, or talk of it as despicable or silly, and they will avoid it. I am sure this is very much the case in the matter of unclean talk, of gambling, of smoking, and other youthful faults.

It is well to establish a good tone and a public opinion among your boys on a plane which puts these things down as 'what kids do, in order to look smart before others'.

Playing the Game

Handicapped Scouts

Through Scouting there are numbers of crippled, deaf and dumb, and blind boys now gaining greater health, happiness and hope than they ever had before. Most of these boys are unable to pass all the ordinary Scout tests, and are supplied with special or alternative tests.

Many of these boys are by no means easy to deal with, and demand far more patience and individual attention than ordinary boys. But the result is well worth it. The testimony of doctors, matrons, nurses and teachers — *who in the majority of cases are not Scouts themselves* — to the good done to the boys, and through the boys to the Institutions, by Scouting, is overwhelming.

The wonderful thing about such boys is their cheeriness and their eagerness to do as much in Scouting as they possibly can. They do not want more special tests and treatment than is absolutely necessary. Scouting helps them by associating them in a world-wide brotherhood, by giving them something to do and to look forward to, by giving them an opportunity to prove to themselves and to others that they can do things — and difficult things too — for themselves.

Through badge work, where applied with discrimination, we can offer to the dullest and most backward boy a handicap that gives him a fair chance with his better-off or more brilliant comrade, and we can put into him ambition and hope, and the sense of achievement which will carry him on to greater ventures.

The Scouter, October 1923 (rep. BPO, 108)

The boy of initiative is the boy who will be picked for the job.

Aids, WB, 80

III: HANDCRAFT AND SKILL

Proficiency badges are established with a view to developing in each lad the taste for hobbies or handicrafts, one of which may ultimately give him a career and not leave him hopeless and helpless on going out into the world.

The badges are merely intended as an *encouragement* to a boy to take up a hobby or occupation and to make some sort of progress in it; they are a sign to an outsider that he has done so; they are *not intended to signify that he is a master* in the craft he is tested in. If once we make Scouting into a formal scheme of serious instruction in efficiency, we miss the whole point and value of Scout

337

training, and we trench on the work of the schools without the trained experts for carrying it out.

But the object of the badge system in Scouting is also to give the Scout Leader an instrument by which he can stimulate keenness on the part of every and any boy to take up hobbies that can be helpful in forming his character or developing his skill.

The examination for badges is not competitive, but just a test for the individual. The Scout Leader and the examiner must therefore work in close harmony, judging each individual case on its merits, and discriminating where to be generous and where to tighten up.

Some are inclined to insist that their Scouts should be first rate before they can get a badge. That is very right, in theory; you get a few boys pretty proficient in this way; but our object is to get *all* the boys interested. The Scout Leader who puts his boys at an easy fence to begin with will find them jumping with confidence and keenness, whereas if he gives them an upstanding stone wall to begin, it makes them shy of leaping at all.

At the same time, we do not recommend the other extreme, namely, that of almost giving away the badges on very slight knowledge of the subjects. It is a matter where examiners should use their sense and discretion, keeping the main aim in view.

The aim of the proficiency badge is to encourage self-education on the part of the boy in a subject which interests him.

HQG, January 1916 (rep. BPO, 60)

The Scout Method

Intelligence

Observation and deduction are the basis of all knowledge.

The importance of the power of observation and deduction to the young citizen can therefore not be overestimated. Children are proverbially quick in observation, but it dies out as they grow older, largely because first experiences catch their attention, which they fail to do on repetition.

Observation is, in fact, a habit to which a boy has to be trained. Tracking is an interesting step towards gaining it. Deduction is the art of subsequently reasoning out and extracting the meaning from the points observed.

When once observation and deduction have been made habitual in the boy, a great step in the development of character has been gained.

The value of tracking and tracking games can thus readily be seen. Tracking out-of-doors and lectures on tracks and tracking in the meeting room should be encouraged in all Scout Troops.

The general intelligence and quick-wittedness of the boys can very considerably be educated by their finding the way with a map, noticing landmarks, estimating heights and distances, noticing and reporting details of people, vehicles, cattle, by the reproduction of Sherlock Holmes stories in scenes, and through numerous other Scout practices. Signalling sharpens their wits, develops their eyesight, and encourages them to study and to concentrate their minds. First aid instruction has also similar educative value.

Winter evenings and wet days can be usefully employed by the Scout Leader reading the principal items of news in the day's newspaper, illustrating them by map, etc. The getting up of plays and pageants bearing on the history of the place is also an excellent means of getting the boys to study, and to express themselves without self-consciousness.

By 'efficiency' I don't mean mere money-making skill, but a general intelligence and capability to live a free, prosperous and happy life.

WCH, 158, and GG, 190

Self-Expression

Our Art badge is devised to lead boys on to express their ideas graphically from their own observation or imagination without attempting thereby to be or to imitate artists. By encouraging drawing, however crude, on the part of the youngster, he can be led on to recognize beauty in colour or in form, to realize that even in sordid surroundings there may yet be light and shadow, colour and beauty.

A further stage in his education can be brought about by getting him to practise mental photography, that is to notice the details of a scene or incident or person, and fix these in his mind, and then to go and reproduce them on paper.

This teaches observation in the highest degree. Personally I have found by practice that one can develop a certain and considerable power in this direction.

Rhythm is a form of art which comes naturally even to the untrained mind, whether it be employed in poetry or music or in body exercises. It gives a balance and order which has its natural appeal. In the form of music it is of course most obvious and universal. The Zulu War Song when sung by four or five thousand warriors is an example of rhythm, in music, poetry and bodily movement combined.

The enjoyment of rendering music is common to all the human family. The song as a setting to words enables the soul to give itself expression which, when adequately done, brings pleasure both to the singer and to his hearer.

Through his natural love of music the boy can be linked up with poetry and higher sentiment as by a natural and easy transition. It opens a ready means to the Scout Leader of teaching happiness to his lads and at the same time of raising the tone of their thoughts.

Play-acting also ought to form part of every boy's education for self-expression.

Singing and acting are excellent for training in self-expression. Also they mean good teamwork, everybody learning his part and doing it well, not for applause for himself but for the success of the whole show.

Aids, WB, 84

At school I was encouraged to do a lot of play-acting and I have thanked my stars ever since that I did so. For one thing it taught me to learn yards of stuff by heart; also accustomed me to speak clearly and without nervousness before a lot of people; and it gave me the novel joy of being someone else for a time.

It led one to know the beauties of Shakespeare and other

authors, to feel, while expressing them, the emotions of joy and sorrow, love and sympathy.

Above all it gave one the pleasure and happiness of giving pleasure to other people at times when they needed it.

Many Troops are giving entertainments in the winter months and are thus not only earning satisfactory additions to their funds, but are giving good training to their boys and pleasure to others.

Life is a game rather than a period of slavery, and it is a good game if played hopefully; but it is not a game of cribbage. It is rather a game of football where you must expect a few knocks and tumbles in the mud, but these should not choke you off jumping up and going at it again with a cheery determination to play the game for your side and not all for yourself.

Message to Rover Scout meeting at Gilwell, January 1932

From Hobby to Career

Hobbies, handcraft, intelligence and health are preliminary steps for developing love of work and ability to carry on, which are essential to successful work. The second stage is fitting the young worker to the right kind of work.

The best workers, like the happiest livers, look upon their work as a kind of game: the harder they play the more enjoyable it becomes. H. G. Wells has said: 'I have noticed that so-called great men are really boys at heart, that is, they are boys in the eagerness of their enjoyment of their task. They work because they like to work, and thus their work is really play to them. The boy is not only father to the man, but he is the man and does not disappear at all.'

Ralph Parlette says truly: 'PLAY is *Loving* to do things, and WORK is *Having* to do things.'

> *A joyful home, coupled with the ability to serve others, gives the best happiness.*
>
> RTS, 20

> *A Scout is active in doing good, not passive in being good.*
>
> SFB, DE, 232

IV: SERVICE TO OTHERS

The attributes which we have so far been studying, as tending to make our boys into manly, healthy, happy working citizens, are, to a great extent, selfish ones designed for the good of the individual. We now come to the fourth branch of Scout training, through which, by developing his outlook, the boy gives out good to others.

Selfishness

If I were asked what is the prevailing vice in the world, I should say: Selfishness. You may not agree with this at first sight, but look into it and I believe you will come to the same conclusion. Most crimes, as recognized by law, come from the indulgence of selfishness, from a desire to acquire, to defeat, or to wreak vengeance. The average man will gladly give a contribution to feed the poor and will feel satisfied that he has then done his duty, but he is not going to dock himself of his own food and good wine to effect a saving for that purpose.

To Eradicate Selfishness: the Good Turn Habit

The Scouting practices tend in a practical way to educate the boy out of the groove of selfishness. Once he becomes charitable he is well on the way to overcome or to eradicate the danger of this habit.

The Promise that a Scout makes on joining has as its first point: 'To do my duty to God'. Note that it does not say, 'To be loyal to God', since this would merely be a state of mind, but to *do* something, which is the positive, active attitude.

The main method in the Scout Movement is to give some

form of positive training rather than merely to inculcate negative precepts, since the boy is always ready to *do* rather than to *digest*. Therefore, we put into his activities the practice of Good Turns in his daily life as a foundation of future goodwill and helpfulness to others. The religious basis underlying this is common to all denominations, and we, therefore, interfere with the form of none.

> *Scouting is a Brotherhood: a scheme which, in practice, disregards differences of class, creed, country and colour, through the undefinable spirit that pervades it, the spirit of God's gentleman.*

> Aids, WB, 90

The boy can then realize better that part of his 'Duty to God' is to take care of and develop as a sacred trust those talents with which God has equipped him for his passage through this life; the body with its health and strength and reproductive powers to be used in God's service; the mind with its wonderful reasoning, memory and appreciation, which place him above the animal world; and the soul, that bit of God which is within him, namely, Love, which can be developed and made stronger by continual expression and practice. Thus we teach him that to do his Duty to God means, not merely to lean on His kindness, but to do His will by practising love towards one's neighbour.

The minor Good Turns, which are part of the Scout's faith, are in themselves the first step. Nature study and making friends with animals increase the kindly feeling within him and overcome the trait of cruelty which is said to be inherent in every boy (although, personally, I am not sure that it is so general as is supposed). From these minor Good Turns he goes on to learn first aid and help to the injured, and in the natural sequence of learning how to save life in the case of accidents, he develops a sense of duty to others and a readiness to sacrifice himself in danger. This again leads up to the idea of sacrifice for others, for his home and for his country, thereby leading to patriotism and loyalty of a higher type than that of merely ecstatic flag-waving.

In the Promise I purposely put the 'duty to God' as a concrete form of active work that a boy can understand.

An attitude of mind like 'loving God' is not comprehensible to the average small boy, whereas he can understand that doing his Good Turn is a form of service to God.

From a letter to Mr Power, undated but 1920s.

In SAA (same idea, SYM, 63)

Service for the Community

The teaching of service is not merely a matter of teaching in theory, but the development of two distinct phases: the inculcation of the spirit of goodwill, and the provision of opportunity for its expression in practice.

The teaching is mainly through example, and the Scout Leader gives exactly the right lead in his patriotic dedication of self to the service of the boy, solely for the joy of doing it, and without thought of material reward.

The Scout Method

The opportunity for practice is given by the Scout Leader suggesting to his boys special service projects.

Public services offer the best opening for practical training in sense of duty to the community, patriotism and self-sacrifice through expression.

The work of Scouts during peace and during wars in voluntarily taking up arduous duties in service of their country is in itself a proof of the keenness of the lads to do good work, and of their readiness to make themselves efficient where they see a good object. In this direction lies a powerful means of developing on practical lines the ideal of citizenship.

Ulterior Effect

The repression of self and development of that love and service for others, which means God within, bring a total change of heart to the individual and with it the glow of true Heaven. It makes a different being of him.

The question becomes for him not 'What can I *get*?', but 'What can I *give* in life?'

No matter what may be his ultimate form of religion, the lad will have grasped for himself its fundamentals, and knowing them through practising them he becomes a citizen with a widened outlook of kindliness and sympathy for his brother men.

With character and a smile the boy will overcome evils in his way.

Aids, WB, 94

TO SUM UP

The whole object of our Scouting is to seize the boy's character in its red-hot stage of enthusiasm, and to weld it into the right shape and to encourage and develop its individuality, so that the boy may educate himself to become a good man and a valuable citizen for his country.

By so doing we may hope to take a useful part in bringing strength, both moral and physical, to the nation.

But in developing national aspirations there is always the danger of becoming narrow and jealous of other nations. Unless we avoid this we bring about the very evil we are anxious to escape.

Fortunately in the Scout Movement we have Brother Scouts organized in almost every civilized country in the world, and we have formed already the tangible nucleus of a World Brotherhood. And the potentialities of this are being supplemented by the wider development of the co-operative sister Movement, the Guides.

In every country the purpose of the Scouts' training is identical, namely, efficiency for Service towards others; and with such an object in common, we can, as an International Brotherhood in Service, go forward and do a far-reaching work.

In our training of the boy we develop the individual in both spirit and efficiency to be an effective player in his national team of citizenhood. Acting on the same principle in the case of a nation, we should try to develop the right spirit and efficiency for helping that nation to work effectively in the team of nations.

If each, then, plays in its place, and 'plays the game', there will be greater prosperity and happiness throughout the world, there will be brought about at last that condition which has so long been looked for, of

Peace and Goodwill among men.

NOTES

1 *Scouting For Boys, The Wolf Cub's Handbook,* and *Rovering to Success.*

2 This expression (also the title of a book by B.-P. published in 1939) is probably an echo of Frederick Marryat (1792–1848), British naval captain and novelist: 'Every man paddle his own canoe' (*Settlers in Canada,* ch. 8).

3 Original text: *grousers.*

4 Such activities are suggested in *Scouting for Boys.* [Note by the Author.]

Part III

On Peace

Friendship is like a boomerang; you give out your friendship to another chap and then to more and more and they give you their friendship in return. So your original friendship and goodwill, as it goes to others, increases in strength and brings back this good will to you in return, just as the boomerang comes back to its thrower.

SRW, 98–9

International Brotherhood

The different foreign countries – some twelve there are – which have adopted Scouting for their boys are now forming a friendly alliance with us for mutual interchange of views, correspondence, and visits, and thereby to promote a closer feeling of sympathy between the rising generations.

International peace can only be built on one foundation, and that is an international desire for peace on the part of the peoples themselves in such strength as to guide their Governments.

If the price of one Dreadnought were made available to us for developing this international friendliness and comradeship between the rising generations, I believe we in the Scouts would do more towards preventing war than all the Dreadnoughts put together.

Headquarters Gazette, December 1911

The Other Fellow's Point of View

Justice and fair play do not always form part of our school curriculum. If our lads were trained as a regular habit to see the other fellow's point of view before passing their own judgement on a dispute, what a difference it would at once make in their manliness of character!

Such lads would not be carried away, as is at present too commonly the case, by the first orator who catches their ear on any subject, but they would also go and hear what the other side has to say about it, and would then think out the question and make up their own minds as men for themselves.

And so it is in almost every problem of life; individual power of judgement is essential, whether in choice of politics, religion, profession, or sport, and half our failures and three-quarters of our only partial successes among our sons is due to the want of it.

We want our men to be men, not sheep.

And, in the greater proposition of international Peace, it seems to me that before you can abolish armaments, before you can make treaty promises, before you build palaces for peace delegates to sit in, the first step of all is to train the rising generations – in every nation – to be guided in all things by an absolute sense of justice. When men have it as an instinct in their conduct of all affairs of life to look at the question impartially from both sides before becoming partisans of one, then, if a crisis arises between two nations, they will naturally be more ready to recognize the justice of the case and to adopt a peaceful solution, which is impossible so long as their minds are accustomed to run to war as the only resource.

In the Scout Movement we have it in our power to do a very great thing in introducing a practical training in justice and 'fair play', both through games and competitions in the field, and through arbitrations, courts of honour, trials, and debates in the clubroom.

HQG, June 1912

On Peace

Don't be attracted by glitter, but go for the thing you're good at.

Weekly Thought in *The Scout*, 23 November 1935

Overseas Scouts

My recent tour round the world showed me how strong is already that feeling of *brotherhood* throughout our Movement. Whether it was in Africa or Australia, Canada or New Zealand, America or Malta, Scouts felt that they were with and of us in the parent Movement at home, and I was impressed with the idea that, if this sentiment were only promoted, it would mean an immense deal for the strengthening of the bonds of our Empire, and even beyond that, for the assurance of peace in the world through a better understanding and fellowship between the nations. Internally and locally our brotherhood is already doing good in that direction. Counties in England are often fairly jealous of each other, provinces in Ireland can nearly be at war; States in overseas Dominions can be suspicious or envious between themselves, just from want of a little broadmindedness or a common tie. It is a failing that cannot be cured by preaching to the present men, but it may be prevented in the next generation by eradication, that is by bringing the mass of the boys into sympathy and mutual touch through the feeling of brotherhood. Local racial differences run strong, and are hard to wash out in such instances as between Boer and Briton in South Africa, French and British in Canada, Eurasian and White in India, Maltese and British in Malta, between the eight nationalities in Shanghai, and so on. But it struck me very forcibly in the course of my visit to these countries that the Boy Scout Movement, young as it is, is already doing a good deal in that direction.

Boys of whatever origin are equally attracted by Scouting: once they find themselves in the same uniform, under the same Promise, working for the same ends, inspired with the same ideals, and competing in the same games, they forget their respective little differences and feel that they are brother Scouts before all. If a sufficient number of them are encouraged to take up Scouting, this must in the next generation go a considerable way to abolishing the present absurd jealousies between localities. If the ties of the brotherhood can be strengthened by mutual interchange of correspondence and of visits, a further link will be forged for consolidating our Empire by the development of personal sympathy and sense of comradeship between the manhood of all the different overseas States and the Mother Country.

Should the Scout Movement develop on to a more general

footing, then I have no doubt whatever that the same principle of 'brotherhood' will extend its influence for good among those who will be the men of the different nations within the next few years, and must, of necessity, prove a genuine factor for the maintenance of peace where they are in *personal* touch and sympathy with each other.

HQG, June 1913

Life is too short for arguing.

HQG, August 1914 (rep. BPO, 53)

The Promise of a Closer Bond[1]

It needs no great stretch of the imagination to see in this the promise of a closer bond between ourselves and our Empire across the Seas, and a stronger guarantee of future peace between nations when their men begin to look upon each other as members of one brotherhood instead of as hereditary enemies.

Introduction to the Exhibition's souvenir book *Boy Scouts and What They Do: Imperial Scout Exhibition* 1913

Anti-War, but not, therefore, Anti-Military

I had, last month, a most interesting conference with a number of members of the Peace Society and of the Society of Friends. They wanted to understand better the ideals underlying the Boy Scout training.

I gave to the meeting a general outline of our work and aims, and invited questions and suggestions from those present. In reply to some of these, I made it plain that though we were against war, we were not, therefore, against self-defence.

Also, I pointed out that you cannot do away with war by abolishing armies; you might just as well try to do away with crime by abolishing the police. What would be the result in either case?

As regards war with civilized nations, that is, no doubt, a brutal and out-of-date method of settling differences. But there are still, even in Europe, many nations only partly civilized. It is all a matter of education and character, and mutual knowledge and regard for each other. The only way towards bringing about universal peace in Europe is not by trying to cure the present generation of their prejudices, not even by building palaces for peace conferences, but by educating the next generation to better mutual sympathy and trust and the larger-minded exercise of give-and-take.

The only really practical step so far taken to that end is in the Boy Scout Movement, where, with our brotherhood already established in every country and getting daily into closer touch and fellow-feeling by means of correspondence and interchange of visits, we are helping to build the foundation for the eventual establishment of common interests and friendships which will ultimately and automatically bring about disarmament and a permanent peace.

HQG, April 1914

On Peace

There is a wide-spread disease prevalent just now and most of us suffer from a touch of it: the disease of swollen head. We are apt to think that our particular kind of politics or society or whatever we happen to be interested in is the one really important thing in the world.

The best antidote to this disease is to take a peep into the vastness of the Universe or into the ancient history and evolution of our own earth and its livestock.

Then do our heads subside and in all humbleness we realize that we are but little pawns in the great game of Nature. We are here for a short time on earth to take our share with our fellow living creatures in carrying out the great plans (which are so far beyond our comprehension) of our Creator.

From B.-P.'s preface to a book on Nature Lore, c. 1925, in SAA

Scouting and the League of Nations

The League of Nations is a splendid thing to have been evoked for statesmen to make; we men in the street cannot tell what its actual worth is until it has been tried; but, for God's sake, let us try it and see if there is anything in it! [*Applause*]

But one feels that however well you may make a machine, every part beautifully fitted and arranged for running on the road, there is one thing necessary to make it go: the spirit. It is the spirit that is going to make that League of Nations grow; but it must be the spirit that is within the people, if they mean it to go, and it is that spirit of brotherhood we want to press.

If many of the nations who have taken up Boy Scouts and Girl Scouts would only develop our Movement on a sufficient size, a very large leaven of the next generation would be impregnated with that spirit of true brotherhood, and if we once get that established, that machine, the League of Nations, must go and will go, and there can be no danger of its ever being interrupted in its work. [*Applause*]

Address to a US audience, May 1919

(BSA Microfilms, 01012)

Automatic Internationality

It has possibly hardly struck many a Scoutmaster that in his work with his Troop the results are extending far beyond his comparatively limited area, that his efforts are being watched, results noted, and his example followed by others in countries across the sea. But so it is; and out of such beginnings an international sympathy and understanding is growing up.

Many excellent movements have been thought of and urged upon the world for all they were worth: but in spite of the pressing they have not appealed so widely as their promoters had hoped and have ended in smoke. Other movements have sprung up almost of their own accord to meet some need, and have grown and flourished exceedingly. You and I know of one, at any rate, that has done so. Again it is a case of the natural as opposed to the artificial. It is this natural automatic growth of a movement that speaks to its vitality and its possibilities. Nations differ in their characteristics to a marvellous degree considering their relationship in the human family, and although modern communication with its interchange of literature, manufactures, personal visits, etc., ought to have made a vast difference by now, it hasn't done so. We are still very much strangers to each other.

A League of Nations is to be formed to make us better friends through force of law. I hope it may. But there is another league of nations very much in embryo at present but growing up *automatically*, and that is in the brotherhood of the Boy Scouts. And since its growth is entirely natural and not forced in any way, there is immense promise about it.

At the Jamboree[2] we shall, I hope, get the first general expression. Representatives of twenty-six foreign nations will be among us, and I need not go further than suggest what tremendous ulterior importance may attach to the occasion.

A very real responsibility attaches to each one of us because it is on what we do, what we say, and almost what we think that these different countries will fashion the future line of their Scout work. I think the meeting for interchange of ideas comes just at the right moment. Although we British Scouts are not yet by any means at the highest attainable standard, we are sufficiently well grounded to give the right impression; and the foreign Scouts, while fairly well started, are not as yet so matured that they cannot alter and adapt their methods where they may have gone a little off the line.

So that even if the Jamboree did nothing towards enthusing the boys, towards educating the public, or towards bringing help to the Scoutmasters, yet it would be worth while if through bringing together the representatives of foreign countries in the one ideal of good citizenship, it should have promoted that spirit of fraternity and mutual goodwill without which the formal League of Nations can only be an empty shell.

HQG, June 1920

Why worry about individual training? Because it is the only way by which you can educate. You can instruct any number of boys, a thousand at a time, if you have a loud voice and attractive methods or disciplinary means. But that is not education.

Aids, WB, 48

The Olympia Challenge[3]

Brother Scouts, I ask you to make a solemn choice. Differences exist between the peoples of the world in thought and sentiment, just as they do in language and physique. The war has taught us that if one nation tries to impose its particular will upon others, cruel reaction is bound to follow. The Jamboree has taught us that if we exercise mutual forbearance and give and take, then there is sympathy and harmony.

If it be your will, let us go forth from here fully determined that we will develop among ourselves and our boys that comradeship, through the world-wide spirit of the Scout Brotherhood, so that we may help to develop peace and happiness in the world and goodwill among men.

Brother Scouts, answer me: will you join in this endeavour?

B.-P.'s closing speech at the 1st World Scout Jamboree,
Olympia, London
7 August 1920
The Jamboree Story, p. 15

Scouts breathe through the nose, not through the mouth.

SFB, OFP (2nd)

'Tempora mutantur et nos in illis'[4]

'It is glorious to feel that my country is the greatest on earth; that our soldiers were in war the bravest and ever victorious against all odds; that our women are the most beautiful in the world; as also it is with our country and its scenery and climate; that in art and science, in manufacture and invention, it is the men of our nation who have led the way. And when one looks at the people of other countries, how strange and eccentric they are.'

That is the kind of talk that most of us have heard; but to which nationality did the speaker belong? Was he Briton or Italian, German or American, Chinese or Swede?

In truth he may have been any one of them, since people of all countries have been apt to give expression in that way to their patriotic pride.

Playing the Game

During the past centuries each country has been striving individually to build itself up with its own methods and its own industry. it has not as a rule looked far outside its own border.

But now that is all changed, a new era in the history of humanity has set in; with improved methods of communication and trade these individualities have all become merged in common interests and communities have become interdependent in their finance as in their manufacture; so that for the prosperity of each the peace and goodwill of all is nowadays essential.

The world-wide crash of war has roughly shaken us all and made us awake to the newer order of things. No longer is one nation better than another. Whether through mutual self-sacrifice, loyal support or brave opposition a sterling respect for each other has been engendered; the war has warned us that under the modern conditions of material and intellectual development we ought to re-form ourselves and make better use of the blessings of civilization; otherwise this hellish punishment of brute strife, of which we have had a taste, will overwhelm us in the end.

If we realize this and shape our actions accordingly, then indeed, out of the evil of war great good may come; but it is essential that we should seize and make the best use of the opportunity before it has passed away.

It has been formulated by our legislators, but it cannot have complete success until it possesses a soul: the *spirit* of the people.

The League of Nations is at any rate one step in that direction. Fortunately the lesson of the war among the nations has been reflected in a minor degree in the Boy Scout Movement by the Jamboree.

Here, for the first time, we have seen with our own eyes the international development of our Brotherhood and we have realized that the true spirit of Scout comradeship inspires it, a spirit which recognizes no difference of country, creed, colour or class, a spirit which may eventually contribute to the soul of the League of Nations.

Thus a field of immense possibilities has become opened to us. While, therefore, we are building up, each for the good of our country, our own individual national associations of Boy Scouts and Girl Guides as a school of young citizens, let us keep ever before us the still greater aim of promoting the comradeship with our Brother Scouts in other lands.

In this way we may help in no mean degree to bring about that mutual unity and goodwill which will make the world an assured home of peace, happiness and prosperity for all.

Jamboree, January 1921

Never say die till you are dead. Struggle on against any difficulty or danger, don't give in to it, and you will probably come out successful in the end.

YKE, 154

Playing the Game

'Prevention Is Better than Cure'[5]

In a community the prevalence of crime is a sign of bad citizenship. Police are organized for its suppression. The more efficient the police force, the less there is of crime.

At least that is apparently the idea that is most commonly accepted.

But if one looks below the surface it would seem that the *prevention* of crime rather than its *suppression* would show the better community.

This is rather a matter of the development of higher character in its individual members than one of organization of repressive force.

The higher character of a people is the outcome of education and religion; it is brought about through the development of unselfishness and sense of duty.

The balance-sheet of the community cannot be audited as 'satisfactory' where the cost of making good citizens, through the medium of its education and church, is exceeded by the *per contra* cost of punishing its bad citizenship through the medium of police and prisons.

The whole aim of the Boy Scout and Girl Guide Movement is to help education and the churches in their promotion of character for higher and better citizenship.

An arresting fact, which holds within it infinite promise, is that this movement is a spontaneous growth and not a planned organization. It has sprung from the natural desires of the young people, and has not been imposed upon them as a syllabus of instruction. The results have been immediate both as regards numbers and effects, in spite of the absence of trained directors and notwithstanding all the difficulties incident to the war.

Nor has this growth confined itself to the country of its origin; in the short twelve years since its birth, it has spread to every civilized country in the world.

It already numbers well over a million members, and is growing every day. It has become the nucleus of an international Brotherhood, and this opens a vista of still further-reaching promise and possibilities.

What applies to the community applies with equal truth in international relations. It cannot be considered a well-ordered world where peace has to be enforced by police.

The League of Nations is a police force for suppressing war and as such is a valuable step, but its *prevention* is the better aim, and this can only come from the mutual goodwill and understanding of the peoples themselves.

If we reflect that we members of the human family are only here on this earth together for a short span of life, we realize that petty differences and fighting for little selfish ends are out of place in the Creator's scheme of things.

With the understanding which is ours we ought to rise above these and look wider, so that love and mutual kinship should 'guide our feet into the way of peace'.

This may seem altogether too visionary and ideal, however desirable, but with the example before us of the unlooked-for that has happened and is happening in the Boy Scout Movement, one cannot but feel hopeful of a practical outcome if the right steps are taken in this direction.

Doubtless the elder generation as a whole, brought up as it has been to think in terms of fighting whether politically or on the field of battle, may be hard to convert to this broader plane of thought, but with the oncoming generation of future citizens still in the malleable condition of youth, with all its enthusiasms in full blast and with its class snobbism as yet unborn, a tremendous field of promise lies before us.

Jamboree, April 1921

> *A Scout must never be a snob. A snob is one who looks down upon another because he is poorer, or who is poor and resents another because he is rich. A Scout accepts the other man as he finds him, and makes the best of him.*

SFB, OFP (4th), YKE, 36, and in part (for Guides), GG, 66

International Outlook

In developing our patriotism we must not forget the danger of getting it perverted into a narrow nationalism. It is right to be proud of your country, but not to gas about it to the disparagement of others, or to boost it on to a higher pedestal than it actually deserves. Your best patriotism is to help to raise your country's efficiency so that it can take its place adequately in the team of nations of the world. The Great War has demonstrated a thing to which people were formerly blind, and that is that all countries are now very dependent on each other in the details of their trade and commerce, that only by mutual good will and co-operation can the world be prosperous and happy.

One country may have the raw materials, but another has the

means of manufacturing them, while a third can do the finishing process, and a fourth can best utilize the articles when finished. The cotton grown in India is manufactured in Manchester, finished in Belgium, and used in East Africa. This kind of thing goes on in every direction, including the food supply from a producing country, through a supplying country, to a devouring country. Britain produces more coal and iron than it needs, but not sufficient beef and corn, and so it exchanges surpluses with other countries.

Interlocked as they were in this way, a war between two great countries immediately dragged in others, until the greater part of Europe was scrapping in a dogfight. Millions of men were killed, nations ruined, and the whole world put in a state of unrest for years. After this ghastly experience, let us hope that there will be greater security in the future, and that better statesmen will be at the head of affairs in all countries.

The League of Nations and the International Court of Law have now been formed to prevent such a thing happening again. But Leagues and Courts and regulations are of little use if they haven't got the heart and support of the people behind them. You can muzzle and chain up dogs, but there will be no real certainty of peace until they are good pals and contented. It isn't the muzzles that matter so much as the tempers of the dogs.

So the duty of the citizens in each State is to get more into mutual touch and sympathy with those of other States, through interest in their history and doings, and through interchange of visits, etc. Once mutual goodwill and personal friendship come to be established throughout the citizenhood of the various countries, it should be the best guarantee of all against war in the future.

Rovering to Success, 1922, pp. 164–5

There is Scouting and so-called Scouting; for true Scouting we must dig down, we must get at the meaning that underlies it and develop the spirit that gives it life.

HQG, October 1921

Human Body as God's Handiwork

I think if every fellow studied a little of his own body and how it works he would quickly gain a new idea of the miraculous handiwork of God and would realize how He is actually active in your body as well as in your mind.

And when, as some of you have done, you see these wonderful bodies of His with all their complicated, beautifully fitted living mechanisms smashed, destroyed or maimed by man-made bombs and shells in man-made battles over man-made villainies, you will feel that there is something wicked and profane about war.

Rovering to Success, 1922, pp. 190–91

I see no harm in worshipping God with your body as well as your mind. When you get up in the morning you ought to pray for guidance to do what is right during the day and you ought also to exercise the muscles and organs of your body in order to keep yourself healthy and well.

YFBS, 75

On Peace

A Practical Step towards Peace

At a time when the world is thirsting for peace it is the duty of every one of us to try and help to that end if we possibly can. I cannot help thinking that in the Scout Movement a tremendous opportunity lies before us, the possibilities of which have not perhaps as yet suggested themselves fully to some of us.

I mean the opportunity of substituting for war propensities a tendency to peace and goodwill by developing a mutual feeling of brotherhood among the rising generation of all countries.

No practical step has hitherto been taken in the direction of securing permanent peace beyond the formal League of Nations and opportune treaties between Governments.

But we all realize that something more than this is needed in the direction of the education of the hearts of the nations. This cannot be carried out in the case of the old who have their tendencies already formed. It is the oncoming generation – both boys and girls – who should be taught that they are members of the human family and that, when complications arise between them, they should think in terms of peace instead of as formerly in terms of war.

In the Boy Scouts and Girl Guide Movements, whether consciously or unconsciously, we are already doing much to this end.

Jamboree, July 1922

Divine Service, prayers, hymns, and especially addresses to boys should be as short as possible.

Note written in 1909 and published in *The Scouter*, May 1939

A Universal Brotherhood of Service[6]

The war showed us how close below the surface lie the primitive savage instincts of man in spite of our boasted civilization. At the same time it proved what splendid qualities of courage and self-sacrifice are inherent in the human character. This suggests that education in the past has not been devised on the best lines for fully utilizing the good that exists to eradicate the evil, and that scholastic training alone does not go deep enough to produce more than a veneer on the mass of the people. There is still something lacking to raise higher the standard of manliness, good citizenship and enjoyment of life among the majority.

The Scout Movement is an attempt to assist education in this direction by catching the boys in out-of-school hours and developing in them character, health, and technical skill, so that each shall become an efficient and high-toned individual. The aim of that efficiency, however, is not so much for his own promotion as for the ability better to serve the community.

Jamboree, October 1922

Giving responsibility is the key to success with boys, especially with the rowdiest and most difficult boys.

Aids, WB, 52

The Peoples Can Learn from Each Other

Today I have been to visit a plot of sacred ground where lie buried a number of Indian soldiers who gave their lives for our Empire in the Great War. Over each, a white marble tomb bears the name of him it commemorates, together with the simple epitaph from the Quran: 'For God we are, to God we go'.

And may that same text not be a healthy guide to all of us in adjusting ourselves to life? 'For God we are'; whatever may be our creed or country, as servants of God our main concern is to carry out His will during the short term that we live upon this earth, ere 'to God we return'.

And God's service? What is it to the ordinary man? Does not conscience, apart from all books and doctrines, tell us? Does it not say that for the sons of any country helpfulness and goodwill to our fellow men is the highest service and of all things the most satisfying?

The pursuit of this service means repressing our little personal ambitions and putting them in the second place whether they be for power or riches or political ends; they count for very little when 'to God we go'. The active doing of good, more even than passive kindness of thought, must be our first aim. And this is at the base of all true religion; so no sectarian differences need divide us.

Some Indians whom I have met seem over eager to adopt Western ideas. Others of the opposite extreme believe that India has nothing to learn from other countries.

The truth is that we all have much that we can adopt with advantage one from another. Through the international training and relationship of Scouting, the future generation in all countries is being brought up with a new outlook on citizenship.

Citizenship is not the outcome of politics or art or commerce, but of character and sense of service for the community, that is, of manly honour, self-control, chivalry and broad-minded outlook, of putting others first and self second.

The Scouts, whose training is all to this end, form a worldwide brotherhood, actuated by the same ideas, under the same Law and the same Promise.

India, by adopting Scouting, is taking its rightful place as a nation in this international brotherhood – a brotherhood not formed for war preparation nor for political ends nor for commercial development, in any one particular country, but solely as a brotherhood of goodwill and service for our fellow men.

From the preface to *Scouting for Boys in India*, June 1923

If you ever feel tempted to bet on a dog or horse or on cards, take hold of yourself and think of the Eleventh Scout Law: 'A Scout is not a mug.'

The Scout, July 28, 1934

On Peace

World Patriotism

One result of the Great War has been to develop national aspirations in a number of small States which had previously been absorbed by greater Powers.

Simultaneously in various parts of the world other States have been growing up from small beginnings, through peaceful evolution, under the impulse of honest national endeavour.

This means that in most countries there has come a fresh accession of patriotism. The danger is that this patriotism might take a narrow course and make each country think only of itself and its own standing and welfare.

Nations, like individuals, have yet to learn that the greatest obstacle to progress, prosperity and happiness is selfishness. Self-seeking is at the root of most of our troubles whether personal, collective or national.

One of the prime needs of today is a practical education in

unselfishness – and that is why Helpfulness and Service for others figure so largely in the programme of Scouting and Girl Guiding.

'Goodwill and Co-operation' is the watchword of our Movement, and when this comes to be really established in practice in a nation, when the common good is promoted by all irrespective of the interests of class, party or creed, when we all give out instead of grasping in – then shall we see Peace and Prosperity ruling in our land. But nowadays the prosperity and peace of a country do not depend altogether on their organization within her boundary but rather on her relations with other countries, her neighbours around her.

Therefore the patriot who truly wants to help his country must go wider in his patriotism than the mere boosting up of his own land; he must extend that goodwill to the other nations which go to make up the citizenhood of the world.

It is due to ourselves that we of the human race should, after the late cataclysmic outbreak of bad temper on our part, cultivate among us a world *esprit de corps*.

In addition to merely trying to make our respective countries, as we describe it, 'fit for heroes to live in',[7] we should go further and make the state of the world such that we, as a world family, can be proud of it.

You may say 'it is all very well to enunciate ideals, we want something practical; an ounce of practice is worth a ton of precept'.

Therefore may I urge that the Boy Scout and Girl Guide training is a practical step in the direction needed. August next year is fraught with great possibilities as an example of such training.

In England there will be gathered a great concourse of contingents of Scouts from every part of the British Empire overseas. These will come from States which form the Commonwealth of British speaking nations, to meet their brothers in competitions, camps and conferences.

Just as Scouting forms the school for individual efficiency which is then harnessed for the service of others, so this rally will form for these young nations a school of national patriotism and its connection with the wider patriotism of Empire.

But greater than this school will come the University of the following week when there will be held, in Denmark, our great international Rally.

This will form a school for the still wider application of the same principle; where patriots of the different nations, while training their boys to be the better citizens for their individual countries, will give them also the further and higher ambition to be worthy members of the world brotherhood through goodwill and co-operation with their neighbours.

And is not this, after all, the bringing into effective operation of the basic principle of our religion, no matter what form of it we profess, namely, the developing of a higher, unworldly outlook in the love and service of God, and, secondly, on the human side, in the love and service of one's neighbour?

Thus every man and woman who takes part in our work with this motive of higher patriotism in view is doing a work that tends both in principle and detail to humanize the world, to render the highest possible service by helping to bring about that which God has asked for, His reign of Peace and Goodwill among men.

Jamboree, October 1923

Playing the Game

You 'play the game' not only to amuse yourself, but so as to help your side to win.

That, after all, is the main duty of a Scout — to 'play the game'.

WCH, 33

Deference to Other Religions

A Mahomeddan Guider comes to England and addresses a lot of Girl Guides on religion, in the course of which she quotes Mahomet as the one divine teacher. This in spite of the fact that her audience are believers in Christ. How would you regard her action? As tactless, as insulting, as fanatical? At any rate it wouldn't be exactly polite or in accordance with our law of courtesy.

Yet I have known Christian Guiders as well as Scouters do exactly the same thing with Jews or Hindoos or people of other beliefs present, and these on their part have sat under it, too polite to raise objections but none the less made uncomfortable by it.

Once, at a mixed gathering at a 'Scout's Own' a speaker carefully avoided much reference to Christ and was accused by some there of 'denying Him'. His defence was that he was rather following Christ in that he was showing Christian deference to the feelings of others who, equally with himself, were sons of one Father, under whatever form they rendered homage to God.

Quoted, Wade, p. 45

On Peace

Scouting and the League of Nations

A friend who is closely conversant with the methods of the League of Nations sent me lately his congratulations on the fact that the League had passed a resolution inviting the Governments of all member-nations to facilitate as far as possible the interchange of visits between Boy Scouts, Girl Guides, and students of the various countries. He considered this a particularly high tribute to our work and ideals, more especially as the students had only been included in the recommendation as an afterthought.

The resolution was primarily framed on the deserts of the Scout Movement. He said that the League realized the value of our training because in its own work it is occasionally liable itself to feel the want of the Scout upbringing among its own members. Why?

Because no country, so far as he knew, had as yet included in its school curriculum the one quality which above all others is most needed among mankind to-day, and which alone the Scout and Guide movement has taken up as the aim of its training, namely, self-denial in *Service for others*.

Jamboree, January 1924

One of our tenets is to extend our goodwill and toleration so that we pay no regard to differences of class or country or creed.

LVL, 304

379

Playing the Game

The War in Afterthought

Most of us, I think, realize that the Great War, now that we can look at it in more just perspective, was a discredit to all the nations who took part in it, a reflection alike on our civilization, our education and our religion.

When we remember that we descended to the primitive instincts of savagery, that we prostituted our scientific talents to devising more effective methods of manslaughter, that though we professed to be Christians in principle we did not accept the guidance of Christ in practice: these are facts that might well cause us to hang our heads in shame.

The war that was to have ended war has left the world in a worse state than before; with more nations in rivalry with one another, with more armed men in the Empire than ever before, with unrest and suspicion between countries and internally between sections and parties. It was not a satisfactory episode.

But the war showed that we yet possess among us good qualities of gallantry and self-sacrifice and virtues, which if employed definitely for peace in place of war should go far to make this world a fairer and a happier one to live in.

Jamboree, July 1924

Scouts are brothers whenever they meet all over the world. They have their
secret signs by which they recognize one another, and they are helpful and
hospitable to all. A Scout would give you the best of his food and accommo-
dation, but he would not expect you to pay him any more than he would
expect you to spit in his face for it. A Scout will sacrifice his life to save his

'pal' or even to save a stranger . . . especially if the stranger is a woman or a child.

YFBS, 12

Let's Rise to the Occasion and Look Wide

If we rise to the occasion we Guides have it in our power to contribute something towards making a new life for the suffering world. But if we allow things to slip back we shall be missing a great opportunity.

The present unsatisfactory conditions in the world are the after effects of the war – that war that was to have ended wars. Trade, industry and commerce are upset, unsettled conditions prevail, and unrest and dissatisfaction exist in most European countries, as one result of the war.

Then also we have more nations in rivalry with one another than there were before, and more armed men in the world ready for war than have ever existed in history.

Playing the Game

We civilized peoples, with our education and our Churches, have little to be proud of in having permitted this reversion to primitive methods of savagery for settling our disputes. The Great War was a great disgrace.

And we seem to be doing little to counter that disgrace, to extract some good out of the evil done, to get some return for the sacrifices made. One looks in vain for a real effort on the part of constituted authority, apart from the League of Nations, to remedy matters.

Schools merely continue their teaching of academic history, largely restricted to the more creditable doings of their own particular country, and with little regard to that of other nations.

Also, by preparing young people to make successful careers for themselves they encourage self-interest as a guiding principle, instead of putting service to others in the forefront.

Thus we have internal warfare of class against class, and party against party.

Similarly, the Churches agree to disagree on minor points of form, to the detriment of the spirit, instead of showing the example which is so badly needed to-day of mutual goodwill and co-operation.

The new generation, growing up in such atmosphere, come to regard this jealousy and unrest as a normal condition of things, whereas we who have seen happier times know it to be abnormal and – provided that it be adequately faced – remediable.

Not only is it remediable, but out of the present ruin a foundation may be constructed on which to build a finer edifice.

It is here that we in the Scouts and Guides have our opportunity for doing a great human good not only in our own several countries, but, if we act in co-operation, for the world.

To oust existing evils a change of heart was needed for the coming generation. But an earthquake was required to bring it about.

The earthquake has happened. The war and its upset of old ideas has given the opportunity for implanting entirely new ones. Buddha has said: 'There is only one way of driving out Hate in the world and that is by bringing in Love.' The opportunity lies before us where in place of selfishness and hostility we can infuse goodwill and peace as the spirit in the coming generation. If the schools and churches are slow to take advantage of it we in the Girl Guides at any rate can prove, by example, that such a step is possible. That it should come through the women is not only right, but is likely to be the more effective.

The war proved that women can take responsibility and their definite share in the work of the world. In doing this they gained a new footing in the estimation of the men. They now naturally take their place in their councils and in the government of the country. They are the recognized advisers of the men. Also, they have the further influence over the character and future lives of their sons.

In a word, they are definitely and truly becoming GUIDES in the world.

Therefore, Guiders, if we look wide and sympathetically we can note and fill in chinks that are left open in the school education, and we can put the basic principles of religion into action among our girls, so that what they give out will be of the best standard.

It may seem fantastic to imagine that a few thousand girls

spread about the world, as ours are, can do much in producing universal peace and happiness, but if we so train those girls that each one is in herself not merely a well-badged Guide but a real apostle of goodwill and service, we shall go a good way in helping to achieve that end.

Our aims and methods give us the line: our success and expansion to date give us the hope.

But, as I have said before, it behoves us to look wide.

Happily, the internationality of our sisterhood gives us a broadened outlook, but if you see any organizers or imitators trying to narrow our methods to suit their particular section you can warn them that their effort will fail. It is only by ever widening and seeing with others' eyes that we can succeed.

Therefore, keeping our higher aim ever before us, let us make the best use of the opportunity afforded by this conference to compare our experiences, to offer our suggestions to the common stock, and to co-ordinate our efforts so that we can go forward together, inspired with confidence to extract good out of evil and to make a new and a happier world for those who are to come after us.

> Speech of welcome at the Foxleave, Hampshire
> World Guide Conference,
> 16 July 1924

Here are . . . a really mixed lot, but all grinning the cheery Scout smile and all jolly together, forgetting their differences of race, colour and creed, and looking on each other as brothers in the one family, all playing the great game of Scouting together.

SRW, 28–9

On Peace

The Jamboree in Denmark: a Great Success

No one could have foreseen five years ago what we have now seen in this camp – viz., boys of different nations who were then at desperate war together now living together in cheery comradeship. This fact alone should be an inspiration to continue to foster that comradeship and to strengthen our net of Scouting and spread it yet wider. Here lies before the leaders, before every member in fact of our brotherhood, a wonderful opportunity of vast and far-reaching promise for the future peace and happiness of the world.

Jamboree, October 1924

A Utopian Dream?

If all men had developed in them the sense of brotherhood, the habit of giving first consideration to the needs of others, and of putting their own personal ambitions, pleasures or interests second to these, we should have a very different world to live in.

'A Utopian dream,' some would say, 'but merely a dream, and therefore not worth trying for.'

But if we dreamed, and never stretched forth to grasp the substance of our dreams, we should never make progress.

Address to a Canadian educational conference, quoted in: Lord Hampton, *Scouting Sketches*, Pearson, London, 1925, pp. 20–21

A fellow who is not straight at starting is pretty sure to go on being crooked for the rest of his career.

YKE, 80

The Religious Aim of Scouting

The aim of the Boy Scout and Girl Guide Movements is now generally understood to be that of making happy, healthy, helpful citizens. In this material age, with distractions and pleasures more than ever accessible, the training of the spirit is becoming correspondingly difficult, and is too largely neglected. Our object in the Scout Movement is to give such help as we can in bringing about God's Kingdom on earth by inculcating among youth the spirit and the daily practice in their lives of unselfish goodwill and co-operation.

By the term 'God's Kingdom' I mean the prevalence of love in the world in the place of dominance of selfish interest and rivalry such as at present exists.

Self is the first aim of all too many individuals just as it is of every so-called patriotic 'nation'. The promotion of self means, ultimately, war. It is the rule of the devil in the world. Its antithesis, love, such as would express God's rule in the world, has not so far been brought about; and so we have class against class, party against party, country against country, and even religion against religion, in all the so-called Christian nations of the world.

On Peace

That reconstruction after the European War has not come up to expectation, largely because, in striving after economic and material results, the spiritual side has been largely neglected.

[B.-P. goes on to describe the role of Scouting in promoting a sense of religion and Duty to God.]

With the coming of goodwill and co-operation the petty discords that have divided the nation will cease, classes and creeds will no longer profess to be brothers while acting as enemies and dividing the house against itself. With goodwill and co-operation nation will sympathize with nation, and politicians will find it no longer possible to drag into war peoples who are disposed to be friendly to one another. They will find that it is the will of the people which counts. We have seen in our experience how national patriotism carried to the extreme makes for war with other nations in spite of the efforts of statesmen to check it.

From the Address to the Joint Conference of Scout
and Guide Commissioners, 2 July 1926 (reprinted in
Scouting and Youth Movements, 1929, pp. 58–67)

Never ask others to do what you would not do yourself.

Weekly Thought in *The Scout*, 2 November 1935

Playing the Game

Scouting as an International Brotherhood

The development of the Boy Scout and Girl Guide Movements has not been limited to our own country or Empire. Every civilized country in the world has adopted the training, and adopted it spontaneously, without propaganda or urging from the parent country.

Scouting was not a year old before other countries had formed their branches. Some 'patriots', anxious for their country's weal, said: 'Can't you patent it and so prevent rival nations from taking it up?' Others said: 'No need to worry, it is too British to appeal to foreigners.' That both points of view were at fault has been amply proved in later years; for out of the two million Scouts and Guides in training throughout the world we in the British Empire number only some five hundred thousand.

Those opinions were spoken in the 'good old days' before the Great War had changed all our ideas on nationality. In twenty-one short years the Scout and Guide training has spread to forty-two different countries about the world, and has proved its potentiality as a factor in world peace.

Scouting and Youth Movements, 1929, pp. 75–7

Giving rein to your temper is not only a nuisance to others, but is also generally damaging to your own cause. If in an argument you are right, there is no need to lose your temper; if you are in the wrong, you cannot afford to lose it.

LS, 67, and (in part) RTS, 88 and 234, and LVL, 315

Scouting for World Peace

I read somewhere lately a question to the following effect: Why did God send the Great War? Why did a beneficent Almighty permit millions of the best of His creation to be maimed, millions killed, and many millions more of innocent women and children to be reduced to misery and suffering, and the whole world to be plunged into a state of unrest and ill-will?

May it not have been intended as an object lesson, such as could be read by the least imaginative of us, that those who profess and call themselves Christians are as yet still pagans not practising what they profess, still actuated by material rather than spiritual aims?

If this be so, have we learned the lesson and tried to profit by it?

More men are under arms in the world to-day than before the war. The Churches are still at arm's length from one another.

Playing the Game

An international solution has been started in the League of Nations; but in the suggestions for disarmament and pacts of peace all parties approach each other still with suspicion and with a main eye to their respective mutual interests.

If all this be true one feels bound to reiterate what one has so often said before and what the Archbishop of Canterbury so aptly emphasized at our Jamboree, namely that it is a change of spirit in the people that is essential before we can hope for a possible solution of our problems.

A spirit of mutual friendship and trust, and the Christian spirit of love must be brought into general practice if we are to carry out the lesson of the war.

You cannot teach an old dog new tricks. It is difficult to get those who fought in the war to become wholehearted converts to loving their enemies. Human nature is there and we are human.

Our hope must lie with the oncoming generation, with its international likes and dislikes as yet unformed.

We in the Scouts have had the luck to make a definite step in this direction, and a successful one as far as it has gone.

The movement is comparatively small, but on sound lines capable of expansion to form a telling influence in the world, if we only take hold and press on with it.

This change of spirit is the biggest need in the world to-day; and it is the highest thing to aim for, since it is a definite step towards bringing God's rule to earth – a rule of peace and good-will among men.

Call to your mind that last parade at Arrowe Park when the boys of all nations came by arm in arm regardless of difference of country, class or creed. If the Golden Arrow has brought this mes-

On Peace

sage home to our hearts let us not lose time, but utilize to the best of our power the opportunity which the Jamboree has given us and press forward in the coming year, each man of us in his own sphere to extend our movement still further afield and to develop in the boys a closer comradeship and friendliness with their brothers of other nations.

Jamboree, January 1930

Needlework is good for all of us; it rests and calms the mind. You can think peacefully all the worries of Europe whilst you are stitching. Sewing generally solves all the toughest problems, chiefly other people's.

GG, 142

After Ten Years

The first international Jamboree of the Boy Scouts, held in London in 1920, was an eye-opener to most people, whether inside or outside the Movement, as to the degree to which Scouting had spread throughout the world.

For some years past the different countries had been working out their schemes of Scout training, based on the same principles and differing only in the smallest details one from another, but, owing to the Great War with its consequent restriction of communications, the internationality of the Movement was only realized – even by those working within it – when the boys came together from their twenty-five or so different countries, and showed themselves to be possessed of an identical spirit – the spirit of brotherhood and goodwill.

Playing the Game

As a direct outcome of this Jamboree our International Bureau was formed ten years ago, with its international journal, and, later its Hostel in Switzerland for international camping; leading to the frequent interchange of visits and correspondence between the Scouts of the various countries and to meetings such as those which many of us remember in Denmark and in Sweden, the World Jamboree at Birkenhead two years ago and the Rover Moot at Kandersteg which is now assembling.

Following very close behind the Scouts came the Girl Guides with their international developments. They too, have held their World Camps and Conferences, and they too have formed their World Bureau for the promotion of international guiding with its great ideal of unity and its determination to break down in the oncoming generation prevailing differences between classes, creeds and countries, and to bring about in their place peace and good-will in the world.

We who are in the Movement to-day in its early stages have before us the opportunity and responsibility of initiating a step of profound importance to the future of the world.

Never before in the world's history has there been greater need for such a step.

The Great War brought into being more nations than ever existed before. All of these are filled with patriotic enthusiasm for their own flag and have armed themselves to defend it. Thus it has come about that the Great War, which was to have ended all wars, has actually brought more armed men into being, and more up-to-date methods of man-killing, than ever existed before in the history of the world.

One antidote to this dangerous condition is, while retaining our patriotism for our own country, not to allow our enthusiasm to turn it into an obsession such as will make us think that our own country is the only pebble in the beach. We must recognize with kindly eye that there are other peoples around us – and good ones all.

Thus the great antidote to ultra-national feeling is goodwill and friendliness towards other nations. But a still greater and more powerful antidote is to recognize that however great our country, be it Empire, Kingdom or Republic, there is a greater dominion yet and that is the Kingdom of God.

The Kingdom of God means a rule of love and goodwill in the world, not merely at home between friends but also abroad among the other pebbles in the beach.

If that rule could once get its hold over us all, then, and only then, could there be peace in the world.

War is the Devil's work through a narrow self-conceit.

Peace is God's work through love for all.

So there lies a glorious work for every member of our brotherhood, whether Scouter, Rover, Scout or Cub – namely to give his help in any way that he can towards promoting friendliness and goodwill among the different nations of the world.

We who are working in the early stages of this big world-wide move have got to look ahead. We want to look at it, not in its present embryo stage, but as it may be twenty or thirty or a hundred years hence if we go about its organization with a big wide-minded view before us.

Let us aim for the time when each country has got not merely a certain number, but a *definite proportion*, of its young men and boys actuated by the same ideal of goodwill and co-operation.

This cannot be achieved without the careful laying of foundations but it is not an impossibility. It may mean sacrifices here and there but if the greater object be kept in view these will be small in comparison.

Let us look back on the past years with thankfulness but let us also look forward, keeping ever before us this vision of a brotherhood where the members are prepared to sink minor differences of race, religion and rank, and to go forward hand in hand to the great future which lies before them in helping to build up peace and happiness in the world.

Jamboree, July 1931

Go to bed early and get up early, and sleep with the windows open.

WCH (15th), 214

What I Want to See at Gödöllö

There is a general agreement among the leaders of thought in the world to-day that if the League of Nations is to effect its aims in producing peace it is essential that it should have behind it the will of the peoples to that end.

This means that the prevailing traditional prejudices and ill-will between countries must be dropped and that in their place mutual goodwill and understanding must be cultivated.

It is difficult for us of the passing generation to change all at once lifelong ideas which have become habitual with us, but it could be done with the coming generation. Indeed it would be inexcusable, if not worse, were we to neglect the opportunity and bring up our children to harbour the same enmities and jealousies that we hold.

It is right to teach them patriotism and love for their country, but let us remember all the time that there is the danger – and a very prevalent danger – of overdoing it and of producing a narrow-minded form of patriotism, a patriotism which only sees one's country's point of view without regard to the interests and aspirations of our neighbours.

It is this kind of selfish outlook which brings about wars. Under modern conditions countries are no longer independent but are inter-dependent. The world therefore needs, and Christianity demands, a new spirit in its peoples, the spirit of large-minded mutual toleration and whole-hearted friendliness.

I think we all agree on that: but how to bring it about is another question.

I believe it is here that we Scouters, by means of our Movement, can if we wish make a definite contribution to that end.

Also, backed as we are by the ever-growing complementary movement among the young womanhood in most countries, that contribution would in the course of a few years be a really powerful one.

Most of us were originally attracted to Scouting on account of its educational recreation for the boys of our respective countries. But its gradual adoption in so many parts of the world opened up the possibility of its becoming a world brotherhood.

The international Jamboree of 1929 showed this to be not merely a visionary hope but already an established fact. There one saw the body of the brotherhood in actual existence, merely need-ing the spirit to make it a living force.

I gave out there the 'Golden Arrow' as the symbol of the spirit of active goodwill to be fostered in every land where Scouting exists.

That spirit must be one which recognizes no differences of class or creed or country, or political party, a spirit which refuses to look back and closes the door on the past enmities and injus-tices of our fathers, and which looks forward and opens the way to peace and prosperity for our sons by bringing them together in a new atmosphere of mutual goodwill and amity.

Four years have elapsed since that Jamboree.

At our next Jamboree at Gödöllö I shall watch to see how far this spirit has been inculcated in that time.

In my inspections and visits to the camps I shall not be so much interested in the details of camping or the efficiency or the smartness of the different contingents, as I shall be in noting how far the Scouts have been inspired with the spirit of true brother-hood by their leaders.

It is by their expression of that spirit that they will be judged.

If this more broadminded form of patriotism has been brought about in these four years then indeed I shall rejoice, for that is to me the test of the success or otherwise of our world movement.

My brothers, therein seems to me to lie the highest form of patriotism.

The future safety and welfare – nay the very life – of our respective countries depends upon their keeping the peace with one another in the coming years.

If, therefore, we mean to serve the best interests of our coun-tries and prevent further disastrous warfare our aim must necessarily be to sink any personal prejudices we may hold and bring up the next generation as friends and not as foreigners to one another.

But there is yet a higher call to us. I cannot but feel that the wider growth of our Movement, from its original lesser game of *Scouting for boys*, has been no man-made invention, but has been a God-sent evolution, sent as an opening where, if we only use it aright, we Scouters can help directly, both in inspiring the boys and by giving the example to others, towards bringing about that which all nations are praying for to-day, namely, Peace and Goodwill in the world.

Jamboree, April 1933

All promises are important things and should never be broken, but when you promise on your honour to do a thing you would rather die than break such a promise.

SFB (26th), 47

See Things from your Neighbour's Point of View

Playing the Game

But to me the most striking revelation about the whole gathering [at the Australian Jamboree], and the most satisfactory, was the remarkable spirit of *friendliness* shown to one another by all the different races assembled there. There was continual interchange of mutual helpfulness and acts of cheery comradeship. There was realization on the part of the boys of the brotherhood of the World Movement to which they belong.

What a contrast to the mutual suspicion and ill-feeling just now prevailing between the politicians in Europe. This seems to be largely the outcome of narrow super-nationalism and fear, further fomented by a cheap press looking for sensational headlines, all dangerously contributing to precipitate war, without any real reason for it. Yet if education or religion had led these same men or their peoples to practise mutual trust and goodwill, there would be no danger. With proper education of the boy there should be little need for prisons or physicians; with proper education of the nations there should be no need for armies or navies.

Education is hard-put to it nowadays to train the young how to live when social evolution and conditions of life are changing so rapidly, but it is evident that much of the traditional school training is out of date, also that, generally, the human race is not yet civilized. It is not particularly creditable to us or to our upbringing that we still have to revert to primitive methods for settling our disputes. Many countries are teaching their sons patriotism, but too often it is a false patriotism, one which contents itself with waving flags and boosting its own country above others. A wider and more generous spirit is needed for the truer patriotism, which, by exercise of unselfish give and take, brings all sections and factions together in a united whole and which can then extend that spirit

On Peace

and look wide beyond its own borders, or its own particular interests, and see with an understanding eye the aspirations of others.
It will see things from its neighbour's point of view as well as from
its own, and will co-operate rather than prepare to fight him.

From a message broadcast from San Francisco,
in *Jamboree*, July 1935 (also BSA Microfilms, 01006)

*It is perfectly astonishing to see how few boys are able to run. The natural,
easy light step comes only with the practice of running. Without it the poor
boy develops either the slow heavy plod of the clod-hopper or the shuffling
plodding of the city man (and what a lot of character is conveyed in the gait
of a man!).*

Aids, WB, 65

The Value of the Jamboree

I look forward with special hope to our coming Jamboree. It will
show how during the past eighteen months our Movement has
been building and expanding a new spirit of toleration between
nations through their rising generations.

All people in all countries wish for peace, happiness and prosperity.

They have recent object lessons before them to show that none
of these things are gained by war; and that on the contrary war
brings misery and ruin to all.

Yet they persist in war and are even now spending vast sums in
preparing for fighting.

399

Playing the Game

In spite of their so-called civilization, in spite of the teachings of religion, they revert to primitive savagery and a savagery made all the more savage by scientific invention. It is a mad world!

Yet if they will look the other way, as some will do at our Jamboree, they will there find another object lesson in our minor experiment, showing that amity and goodwill between nations is not only possible but is becoming easy and practicable.

Already, in the few years that we have been promoting it, mutual friendship has been established by the Boy Scouts and Girl Guides in fifty different countries – and many millions of those who have been Scouts and Guides in their time now form a leaven in the different populations of men and women who disregard minor differences and past quarrels, but look forward to a future of happiness and prosperity for all through mutual amity and fellow-feeling.

We have here in embryo a universal army or police force of Peace to which the different armies of war will have eventually to surrender.

It may take time before that dream is realized, but this and other Jamborees are all minor steps to that worthwhile end.

So let us promote them with whole-hearted energy.

Jamboree, July 1937

Education through fear and suppression has been all too common and has wrecked many and many a life.

A father asked me recently how he should correct his son of lying; he had whacked him until he was tired, without avail. My reply was: 'Better whack yourself for having made him a liar.'

It is fear that starts the lying habit. Education lies in encouraging the

boy to give out his best and truest self-expression in work and in words,
and not in suppressing and 'disciplining' him.

HQG, April 1921

Are we not Going Too Far?[8]

Mussolini, in explaining to me his reasons for absorbing the Boy
Scouts of Italy into his general scheme for training the whole of
the oncoming generation, said that unity was essential in a nation
if it was to hold its own, and the only way to get unity in a nation
already divided against itself in parties, sects and clans, was to get
hold of the young and train them to one common ideal. In his
case this was defence of their country.

Thus unity is being promoted in more than one country by
enforcement and the repression of individual ideas and initiative,
nominally for the good of the whole. But the danger is lest such
unity is but a surface unity not coming from the heart of the
people.

In more democratic countries where freedom of the individual
is still a treasured possession there yet lies the danger of liberty
being turned into licence, where politicians and extremists may,
through mass suggestion, lead adherents into divergent paths of
thought and action, thereby dividing a nation against itself.

With regard to this question of wider patriotism there is little
doubt that this last Jamboree has marked a great step forward in
the development of international friendship among the boys.

The question has arisen in some minds whether we are not
going too far in that direction. What may be the outcome of it,

etc. I want to remind you in this case, as indeed in what I have been saying of the original principles of our Movement, *all the steps in our history have been of automatic growth* — not merely the problems, but the steps in growth and development. For instance, you can remember that it was not I who urged Scouting to the boys. It was only suggested to me to write a book, and the boys took it up for themselves. I wrote a book for certain institutions for boys, but boys outside those institutions took up Scouting on their own account. It was an automatic growth.

Then, no propaganda was sent to foreign countries when we were busy with this Scouting at home, but within a very short time many countries took up Scouting and now, after thirty years, countries over practically all the civilized world have taken up Scouting: another automatic growth. The whole thing is a natural growth, and therefore a natural movement and not an artificial organization made by rules and regulations. Of course, a few basic rules are necessary here and there, but they ought to be limited to the very basic ones, without refinements of little rules to cover every kind of possible questions in the future.

This eagerness of the boys to meet each other, and the assiduity with which they keep up their mutual acquaintance afterwards by letter are surely signs which we must not, and indeed cannot, ignore.

August 1937

Manuscript, SAA (BSA Microfilms, 01003),
collated with the versions given in Reynolds,
1950, pp. 181–2, and J. S. Wilson, *Scouting Round the World*, London, Blandford Press, 1959, pp. 101–2.

On Peace

For the boy a uniform is a big attraction, and when it is a dress such as backwoodsmen wear it takes him in imagination to be directly linked up with those frontiersmen who are heroes to him.

The uniform also makes for brotherhood, since when universally adopted it covers up all differences of class and country. The Scout uniform, moreover, is simple and hygienic.

LVL, 284–5

An Experiment in Training for Peace[9]

Though the numbers [of Scouts and Guides in the countries visited by the Goodwill Cruise] were not great if compared with the totals of other larger countries, the universal enthusiastic spirit of brotherhood was a revelation to all of us on board and one which was at once touching and vastly impressive. Moreover it made one *think.*

Playing the Game

In the past no kind of training had been given to young people regarding their neighbours in other countries. In the schools, history lessons taught them of the wars in which from time to time we had fought against them; geography lessons told of the products of the different countries, such as hides and tallow, but nothing of the more important product – their people.

Thus the outlook of young people was largely insular and this was further narrowed by the exaltation of national sentiment under the guise of patriotism. Consequently foreign races came to be looked down upon and not exceedingly liked. Any further information regarding the doings of foreigners was supplied by politically minded newspapers.

But with the advent of improved communications came the international development of commerce, tourism, sport and art, thus mutual appreciation has gradually come into being internationally among the adults. This appreciation was further developed on to a close understanding when the Scout and Guide Movement came to be adopted by the fifty different countries who have now imbibed its spirit and who practise its tenets.

The younger generation, undeterred like their elders by political or traditional differences, have accepted wholeheartedly the idea of mutual relationship in a widespread brotherhood. We have at the moment some four millions of Scouts and Guides about the world, not counting the backing of many more millions of young adults who have been through the training.

Among these the interchange of visits and correspondence with their foreign neighbours has become a popular item in the programme of their activities. From Great Britain alone, on an average, some 8,000 boys visit their brothers abroad in a year.

On Peace

Latterly, school journeys have also been added to foreign going pilgrimages for the young, whereby they gain a practical insight into geography and the realization that Britons are not the only pebbles on the beach.

But the Scouts are apt to go further than this; through interchange of visits, mixing and living with their opposite numbers in camp and on hikes together, also through international rallies (called Jamborees) and cruises, the personal touch is established and expanded into comradeship.

A further innovation lies in the fact that this form of education for peace is not confined to the boys, but is also practised by those more important people – the future women of the nation. The Girl Guides have their international camping place in Switzerland and are in no way behind their brothers in their keenness to make friends among their foreign sisters.

It is this glorious enthusiasm which expanded itself so definitely in each country on two last cruises which with its warmheartedness touched one deeply and with its obvious sincerity gave one to realize that this experiment in training the oncoming generation to think and live in terms of peace is not without promise of having far-reaching effects as the Movement continues to grow. That is why as I said above he would be pretty hard-boiled who did not feel something of the inspiration and hope conveyed in this latest insight into the spirit of the Movement.

SAA Archives, September 1938
(BSA Microfilms, 00966)
(a shorter version in *Jamboree*, October 1938)

Playing the Game

Damn the Rules! Call it an experiment!

To someone objecting to one of his suggestions as being against
the Rules. Quoted in Reynolds 1957, 74

A Mountain Dream

Enforced solitary leisure spent among mountain tops is so good
for the soul that every man would be the better for such 'retreat' if
he forced himself to take it occasionally.

The quiet meditation, remote from the rush and unrest of
ordinary life, cleanses the mind, and gives it ease and inspiration.

Sitting here, unperturbed by press headlines, and looking at
Mount Kenya with his hoary old head standing four square as
ever, one sees the clouds come and cover him for a time, and
though they bring thunder and storm, they drift away again, leaving him standing there unmoved in the sunshine, as he has stood
through thousands of years of similar passing showers.

So too, on a larger scale, this world is, from time to time, disturbed by clouds of war and unrest, but these pass away and,
together with them, thank goodness, the agitators who brought
them about; and the old world wags on unmoved as it has done
for thousands of years through similar nightmares.

So you say to yourself, why get rattled about troubles that you
can't prevent? But can't you?

Browning says:[10] 'God's in His Heaven; all's right with the
world.'

But a certain head-hunting tribe says that this is not so. Their

406

belief is that the devil has for the present got possession of the world, and when that possession is over God's reign of peace will come.

The devil's agents are, after all, merely men, and it is therefore possible for man also to counter his devilments, and to bring about that reign of Peace and Goodwill which is the reign of God.

Here seems the opportunity – indeed the duty – for every individual to take his share in preventing recurrence of those evils.

It is in such crusade that I see a goal open to Scouters and Old Scouts.

My mountain says 'Look wider; look higher; look further ahead, and a way will be seen.'

Don't let the technical outweigh the moral. Field efficiency, backwoodsmanship, camping, hiking, good turns, Jamboree comradeships are all means, not the end.

The end is CHARACTER – character with a purpose.

And that purpose, that the next generation be sane in an insane world, and develop the higher realization of Service, the active service of Love and Duty to God and neighbour.

The Scouter, March 1939

When I am Prime Minister, I will make it obligatory that before a man can be elected to Parliament he should have travelled round the world at least once.[11]

RTS, 166

Playing the Game

Don't Be Discouraged

A happy New Year to you all, Brother Scouters, and may 1940 bring to us all the world peace for which we all long, and which we in the Scout Brotherhood, at any rate, have made one of our main objectives.

Even though the more spectacular side of our work, the Jamborees and Peace Cruises of happier times, is in abeyance for the duration [of the war], there is still that most important part of our programme – the quiet, regular instilling into our boys by example and practice of the habits of goodwill, toleration and understanding of others. These, if implanted in our Scouts of to-day, will in the future make war an unthinkable thing. So don't be discouraged. Good Scouts have never been so much needed in the world as they are to-day, and those of you who are turning them out may rest content that you are making to the future of the world a valuable contribution.

Jamboree, January 1940

I have before me a guiding 'banner with its strange device'[12] in the shape of an envelope, which some little lady addressed to me with nothing more on it than the letters 'B. P'. But for me it has a hidden meaning. Would that everyone had such a reminder before them, applicable as it is to all circumstances, whether of peace or war, of life or of death: BE PREPARED.

From a letter to A. M. S. Methuen, the publisher, dated 20 January 1901, quoted in Reynolds 1942, 121

Sowing the Seed

I read in the Bombay *Scout Gazette* for February this sentence:

'The long-expected war has come at last with all its devastating calamities, and it cannot be helped.

'The Scout Movement, an institution of Peace and Service, pledged itself to serve its generation, tried its utmost through its different organizations, but failed.'

I am sorry, but I do not quite agree that it has failed.

On the West Coast of Africa, in a place then known as the 'White Man's Grave', I met a missionary who told me that the average life of his predecessors in that spot had been four years, and he expected that this would be about the length of his own life there.

I started to argue why waste the life and knowledge he possessed in trying to convert a few illiterate natives, when he might be employing his talents more usefully, for a long term of years, among his own heathen fellow countrymen in the slums of England. But he felt 'called' to this work, and said that though he would not live to see the fruits of his labours he was sowing the seed which would ultimately ripen and produce good fruit in due season.

The beginnings of any great development must naturally be small. The Christian religion itself started with only a tiny group of men who had faith, and from them, after some hundreds of years, it spread through Europe; and only now, two thousand years later, was it beginning to make its appeal to untutored peoples about the world.

Scouting is by comparison as yet in its early babyhood, it has to grow for many generations before it can have gained sufficient hold on the minds and actions of men generally to secure Peace. But we are on the right road, and already showing the way. Only a sprinkling of Scouts about the world have as yet reached man's estate, but they are well distributed among the different nations. The seed has been widely sown. More and more boys are growing up in their thousands to be the fathers of yet more Scouts in their millions.

Most of us who have been sowing the seed will not in the nature of things be here to see the harvest; but we may well feel thankful, indeed jubilant, that our crop is already so well advanced as it is, considering the very short time that has elapsed since its original sowing.

But it means that if that harvest is eventually to come, our job in the meantime is to see that the growing crop is adequately tended, that the boys now in our hands have the higher aims of Scouting so instilled into them that these become their principles for their·lives, and not only for their own lives but for the lives of the sons they ultimately father into the world.

On Peace

But this instillation cannot be done by preaching, it can only be impressed through example and through such steps as appeal to the boyish instinct and temperament.

Hence Scouting!

Patience is needed at this stage on the part of the trainers. Patience is hard to practise; you are eager to see immediate results; but I think patience can be acquired if you look forward to the ulterior aim and realize how necessary must be the intermediate steps. But one blessing about training Scouts is that even while the ultimate aims may seem as far off as the moon, you are all the time giving Happiness, fresh interests and Character to each individual you are privileged to have as your disciple.

I have heard Scouters lamenting that they cannot find enough war work for their Scouts, but I should not worry too much about that, valuable though it is for the boys.

You are, or can be, preparing them for helping in the greater cause of Peace.

Look forward. The existing world war-quake is a man-made catastrophe, and can only be redeemed by man. Our present generation is out to effect this by defeating force by force. On the next generation will lie the duty of bringing about Peace through peaceful actions.

No one knows what form that Peace will take. Federal Unions, Economics, resuscitated Leagues of Nations, United States of Europe, and so on, are variously suggested; but one thing is essential to general and permanent peace of whatever form, and that is a total change of spirit among the peoples, the change to closer mutual understanding, to subjugation of national prejudices, and the ability to see with the other fellow's eye in friendly sympathy.

Playing the Game

But although it will be difficult to get men of the present generation entirely to change their spots, we Scouters have two great assets to help us in impressing these ideas on the minds and actions of their oncoming successors. We have young and mouldable minds to deal with, and secondly the war, instead of hampering us in our work, actually gives us object lessons with which to ram home our points.

For instance, the splendid courage of our seamen of all kinds and of our airmen and soldiers, without glorifying militarism, can inspire the boys on their part also to deeds of gallantry and sacrifice of self. The presence of our overseas brothers from all parts of the Empire can give them fuller appreciation of their membership of our great Commonwealth, and its high aims which bring us together.

By contrast the exhibition of brute force now being exercised ruthlessly against weaker people will rouse in them a yet stronger instinct for justice and fair play. The appalling suffering of their own Fellow Scouts in other countries will touch them very nearly, and will excite their fuller personal sympathy and friendship for those boys, although of different nationalities.

These friendships can be more fully developed, if Scouters set their minds to it, through increased interchange of correspondence, pen-palships, visits, hospitality to refugees, study of maps and histories of other countries, and by reminding the boys that we are all Sons of the same Father, Whose direction to us is 'Love your neighbour.'

Such training in friendship has no precedent outside our own Brotherhood, but if the unprecedented chaos of war is to be settled in peace, unprecedented steps to that end are not only justifiable but essential.

Hatred, born of war, and revengeful feeling, will naturally be weeds in the path with many boys.

But as your plants grow up from the seeds which you have sown labelled 'Broad-minded outlook', 'Love', and 'Desire to bind up the wounds of war', such weeds will eventually be choked and Goodwill and Peace will be your harvest!

The Scouter, April 1940

It is on St George's Day that I myself make a point of re-reading Scouting for Boys *in order to refresh my memory as to what it contains.*

HQG, March 1919

A Lesson in Being Prepared

The war, with its day-to-day developments, has taught us, if anything were needed to do so, the value of our motto, to 'Be Prepared', not only for what is probable but for what might in any way be possible. The fate of Holland falling into the grasp of the Nazis must recall by contrast, to many of us the picture of the great peace and happiness which centred round our camp three years ago at the Jamboree at Bloemendaal. That was a wonderful experience for all of us. On the conclusion of that great Rally I had reminded the boys that it was, in all human probability, the last time that many of us would see each other. I was, of course, thinking of my own declining years compared with their rising into strength and manhood. Little did I or anyone then imagine the possibility that only three years later the reverse would be the case, that I should be living and so many of them dead. They were Dutch, Norwegians, Finns, Danes, Czechs, as well as British boys, and among these were numbers who, though growing up with the spirit of mutual goodwill that was to make peace in the world, are now laid low by the fell stroke of brute force against national freedom.

Considering the short period of our existence, the Scout crusade had already made remarkable progress in the world, and the Rally at that Jamboree seemed to strengthen and consolidate the right spirit in the coming generation and so to consummate all that we had hoped for in its world expansion. Then has come this crushing setback of the war. But I look on it as only a temporary setback. The war is bound to end with the triumph of Freedom, and though it may take some years to materialize I am confident that the steps we have taken in the development of international goodwill will then prove their value as a practical aid towards peace.

Though the war may have killed very many of our dear comrades and companions of that camp it has not killed all, and it has not killed the spirit. You Scouters and Scouts who still live will carry on that same spirit, and will now develop it with all the greater force when you realize that you are taking up the torch which was dropped by those who have been struck down.

Few of those comrades of ours could have foreseen that within a short time, they would be fighting and giving their lives for their country, but we do know that through 'Being Prepared' as Scouts they were the better able to face their fate with courage and good cheer. As your tribute to their memory it is open to you to make goodwill and friendship for brother Scouts abroad your aim more directly than ever before.

When the war is over and the bullies of the world have been defeated we must Be Prepared for establishing peace, a peace that will ensure for ever the end of war.

How this will be carried out in detail none can say, but one point of principle is certain and that is that the road to peace will be the more easy and effective where the young men and women of different countries are already good friends and comrades, as in the Scouts and Guides.

So let us Be Prepared with steadfastness for what may befall in the war, and afterwards do our part in bringing about the essential spirit for peace.

The Scouter, September 1940

THE FOUNDER'S PRAYER[13]

Father of us all, We meet before Thee here to-day, numerous in the lands we come from and in the races we represent, but one in our Brotherhood under Thy Divine Fatherhood.

We come before Thee with hearts grateful and gladdened by the many blessings Thou hast granted us and thankful that our Movement has prospered as acceptable in Thy sight. In return we would lay on Thine Altar, as our humble thanks-offering, such sacrifice as we can make of self in service for others. We ask that during our communion here together we may, under Thy Divine Inspiration, gain a widened outlook, a clearer vision of all that lies open before us and of our opportunity. Thus we may then go forth with strengthened faith to carry on our mission of heightening the ideals and powers of manhood, and of helping through closer understanding to bring about Thy happier Rule of Peace and Goodwill upon Earth.

On Peace

NOTES

1 The Imperial Scout Exhibition held at Bingley Hall, Birmingham, 2–9 July 1913, was the first Scout event with substantial participation from abroad.

2 The First World Jamboree, held at Olympia, London, 30 July–7 August 1920.

3 B.-P.'s parting message at the First World Jamboree.

4 Opening article of the first issue of the journal of the International Bureau. The verse quoted by Baden-Powell ('Times change, and we change with them') exists in different versions ('*Tempora mutantur, nos et mutamur in illis*', or '*Omnia mutantur . . .*'). Apparently a quotation from Harrison, *Description of Britain* (1577), Pt LII, ch. 3. Also quoted in John Omen (1560–1622), *Epigramata*, where it is attributed to Lothar I (787–855).

5 A common proverb.

6 B.-P.'s speech at the Sorbonne on the occasion of the second International Scout Conference in Paris (22 July 1922).

7 A quotation by Lloyd George (1863–1945): 'What is our task? To make Britain a fit country for heroes to live in' (speech, 24 November 1918).

8 B.-P.'s address to the Ninth International Conference, The Hague, August 1937 (probably his last public address).

9 A comment on the third (and last) Goodwill Cruise of British Guiders and Scouters on the ship *Orduna* (8–23 August 1938).

10 Robert Browning (1812–89), one of the greatest English poets of the nineteenth century, was also a close friend of B.-P.'s mother Henrietta, and for this reason was always one of B.-P.'s preferred authors. The quotation is from *Pippa Passes*, part 1.

11 'Travel, in the younger sort, is a part of education: in the elder, a part of experience' (F. Bacon, *Essays*, XVIII, 'Of Travel').

12 '. . . A youth, who bore, 'mid snow and ice / A banner with the strange device, / Excelsior!' (H. W. Longfellow, 1807–82, *Excelsior*).

13 Written by the Founder for use in international events. Supplied by the World Scout Bureau. A similar text is published in Heather, 97–8.

Sources and Abbreviations

a) Books

AA	*African Adventures* (1937)
AD–AC	*Adventures and Accidents* (1934)
Aids (1919)	*Aids to Scoutmastership*, 1919 edition
Aids, WB	*Aids to Scoutmastership*, World Brotherhood Edition (1944)
ATM	*Adventuring to Manhood* (1936)
ATS	*Aids to Scouting, for NCO and Men* (1899)
BBA	*Birds and Beasts of Africa* (1938)
BPO	*B.-P.'s Outlook*: Selection from *The Scouter* (1957 edition)
BSBS	*Boy Scouts Beyond the Seas* (1913)
CI	*Cavalry Instructions* (1885)
DP	*The Downfall of Prempeh* (1896)
GG	*Girl Guiding* (1966 reprint of the 1938 edition)
IM	*Indian Memories* (1915)
LS	*Life's Snags and How to Meet Them* (1927)
LVL	*Lessons from the 'Varsity of Life* (1933)
MAAS	*My Adventure as a Spy* (1915)
MFB	*Marksmanship for Boys* (1915)
MSK	*More Sketches of Kenya* (1940)

Sources and Abbreviations

OWF	*An Old Wolf's Favourites* (1921)
PYOC	*Paddle Your Own Canoe* (1939)
QTW	*Quick Training for War* (1914)
RTS	*Rovering to Success* (1959 reprint of 1922 edition)
SFB, OFP *	*Scouting for Boys*, original fortnightly parts (1908)
SFB (26th) *	*Scouting for Boys*, 26th edition (1951)
SFB, DE *	*Scouting for Boys*, 34th edition (Definitive Edition, 1963)
SFB, WB *	*Scouting for Boys*, World Brotherhood Edition (1946)
SIW	*Sport in War* (1900)
SRW	*Scouting Round the World* (1935)
SYM	*Scouting and Youth Movements* (1929)
WCH †	*The Wolf Cub's Handbook*, 17th edition (Definitive Edition with notes, 1977)
WCH (15th)	*The Wolf Cub's Handbook*, 15th edition (1960)
WSCD	*What Scouts Can Do* (1921)
YFBS	*Yarns for Boy Scouts* (1909)
YKE	*Young Knights of the Empire* (1916)

b) Periodicals

HQG	*Headquarters Gazette* (Leaders' magazine, 1909–22)
The Scout	Boys' magazine, 1909–40

* For *Scouting For Boys*, the Original Fortnightly Parts are quoted wherever possible (number of Camp Fire Yarn given); second choice is the 1963 Definitive Edition, and third choice is the 1946 World Brotherhood Edition.

† For *The Wolf Cub's Handbook*, the 1977 Definitive Edition is quoted wherever possible.

The Scouter   Leaders' magazine, 1923–40
Jamboree   International Bureau magazine, 1920–40
The Wolf Cub   Cubs' magazine, 1919–22

c) Archives

BSA Microfilms Boy Scouts of America Archives, Texas
SAA   Scout Association Archives, London

d) Other Sources

Beaumont   Marguerite de Beaumont, *The Wolf That Never Sleeps*, London, 1953
BPBB   *The Baden-Powell Birthday Book*, compiled by M. Hall from the writings of Robert Baden-Powell, 1st Baron Baden-Powell of Gilwell, Collins, London and Glasgow, 1964 (the book contains a quotation for every day of the year: the day is given for quotations taken from it)
Heather   Heather Baden-Powell (King), *Baden-Powell: A Family Album*, Alan Sutton, Gloucester, 1986
The Jamboree Story *The Jamboree Story, The Full Story of the Eight World Jamborees of the Boy Scout Movement*, published by the Boy Scout International Bureau, London 1957
Reynolds 1942   E. E. Reynolds, *Baden-Powell*, London, 1942

Sources and Abbreviations

Reynolds 1950   E. E. Reynolds, *The Scout Movement*, London, Oxford University Press, 1950

Reynolds 1957   E. E. Reynolds, *Boy Scout Jubilee*, London, Oxford University Press, 1957

Wade   E. K. Wade, *27 Years with Baden-Powell*, London, Blandford Press, 1957

Baden-Powell: A Chronology

Place	Date	Age	Details
England	1857		Born 22 February at 6 Stanhope Street (now 11 Stanhope Terrace), London.
England	1864	7	Stayed in Cornwall and sketched Mousehole.
England	1866	9	Voyaged with brother from London to Isle of Wight in a steamer.
France	1868	11	Stayed at Biarritz.
Spain			Did his first lithograph of San Sebastián, Spain.
England			Went to school at Rose Hill, Tunbridge Wells.
Scotland	1870	13	Won scholarship to Fettes College, Edinburgh.
England			Nominated also for Foundation at Charterhouse. Went to Charterhouse, London, as Gownboy Foundationer.
England	1871	14	Joined the school choir.

Baden-Powell: A Chronology

Place	Date	Age	Details
England	1872	15	Won the school's prize for French. Took part of Bob Nettles in the play *Parents and Guardians* at Charterhouse Theatricals.
England	1873	16	School moved from London to Godalming, Surrey.
England	1874	17	In the Wimbledon Rifle Team, and Football 2nd XI.
England	1875	18	Wimbledon Rifle Team, and Football 1st XI. In the 6th Form.
England	1876	19	Left Charterhouse in May. Unattached student at Oxford University, after failing entrance examinations for Balliol and Christ Church colleges. Passed Army Examination, 2nd for Cavalry, 4th for Infantry, out of over 700 candidates. Opted for Cavalry. Appointed Sub-Lieutenant, 13th Hussars.
India			Joined the Regiment in Lucknow as a Sub-Lieutenant.
India	1877	20	With Regiment at Lucknow. Garrison Course for Lieutenant.
India	1878	21	Passed Garrison Course, 1st Class with 'extra' certificate for reconnaissance.

Playing the Game

Place	Date	Age	Details
			Promoted to Lieutenant, antedated to 1876.
England			Sick leave to England in December.
England	1879	22	Passed Hythe Musketry Course, 1st Class with 'extra' certificate.
India	1880	23	Returned to India to the 13th Hussars and accompanied the Regiment to Afghanistan.
Afghanistan			Employed making maps of the battlefield of Maiwand.
Afghanistan	1881	24	Kendahar Campaign and Quetta Station under Sir Baker Russell.
India	1882	25	Marched from Quetta to Muttra (900 miles). Appointed Assistant Adjutant.
India	1883	26	At Muttra. Appointed Musketry Instructor. Appointed Station Staff Officer. Won Kadir Cup for pig-sticking. Published *On Vedette*.
India	1884	27	Promoted to Captain. Attached to Duke of Connaught's staff at Meerut. Published *Reconnaissance and Scouting*.
South Africa			Moved with Regiment to South Africa.
South Africa	1885	28	Published *Cavalry Instruction*. Carried out special reconnaissance of Natal border.

Baden-Powell: A Chronology

Place	Date	Age	Details
			Big-game shooting trip, Inhambane, Mozambique.
England			Sailed for England.
			Quartered at Norwich.
Russia	1886	29	Resigned Adjutancy.
			Attended Russian manoeuvres at Krasnoe Selo, and got run in as a spy.
England			Went up for Staff College Examination but went down with fever.
			On duty at Royal Military Tournament in London.
England	1887	30	AAG Dover manoeuvres.
France			Visited French and German battlefields.
Germany			
England			Sent to Aldershot by Lord Wolseley to superintend trials of Cavalry machine guns.
South Africa			To South Africa as ADC to General Smyth, commanding troops.
South Africa	1888	31	Campaign in Zululand against Dinizulu.
			Acted as Military Secretary and Intelligence Officer to GOC.
			Promoted to Brevet Major.
South Africa	1889	32	Shooting trip to Knysna, Swaziland.
England			Military Secretary to Acting Governor of South Africa.
			Home on sick leave.

Playing the Game

Place	Date	Age	Details
			Secretary to Sir F. de Winton's Anglo-Boer Mission to Swaziland. Published *Pig-Sticking*.
Malta	1890	33	Left South Africa with General Smyth and went as his Military Secretary to Malta.
Malta Italy	1891	34	Intelligence officer in Malta. Attended Italian manoeuvres. Examined and reported to War Office on defences of Messina Straits, south side.
Albania, Greece Turkey, Algeria			Visited these countries.
Tunisia Italy	1892	35	Visited Tunis. Attended Italian manoeuvres, in the Valley of Aoste. Examined and reported to War Office on defences of Messina Straits, north side.
Bosnia, Herzegovina, Austria			Visited Bosnia, Herzegovina, Austria, Montenegro.
Tunisia, Algeria Ireland	1893	36	Visited Tunisia and Algeria. Rejoined 13th Hussars at Cork, Ireland. Manoeuvres at Curragh.
Ireland	1894	37	Passed Veterinary Course. Passed examination for Lieutenant Colonel. Brigade Major Cavalry Brigade at Curragh manoeuvres.

Baden-Powell: A Chronology

Place	Date	Age	Details
England			Brigade Major Cavalry Brigade at Churn manoeuvres.
			Acted as guide to Swazi chiefs at Aldershot.
Ireland	1895	38	Squadron Commander, Dundalk and Belfast.
Gold Coast			Ashanti expedition, commanding native levy.
			Star and Brevet Lieutenant Colonel.
England	1896	39	Returned home.
			In May was appointed Chief Staff Officer.
Matabeleland			Matabeleland Expedition under Sir Frederick Carrington.
			Mashonaland.
			Carried out scouting in Matopo Hills.
			Commanded column on Shangani River.
			Appointed Brevet Colonel.
			Published *The Downfall of Prempeh*.
England	1897	40	Returned home.
Ireland			Rejoined 13th Hussars in Dublin as Squadron Commander.
India			Appointed to command 5th Dragoon Guards in India.
			Joined them at Meerut, India.
			Published *The Matabele Campaign*.
			Awarded the Matabele Medal.
India	1898	41	Commanding 5th Dragoon. Guards.

Playing the Game

Place	Date	Age	Details
			Commanded Brigade of Cavalry for manoeuvres.
			Visited troops at the front attacking Tochi Pass under General Bindon Blood.
			Visited Kashmir on leave.
Nepal			Shooting trip to Nepal.
			Moved Regiment to Sialkote.
England	1899	42	Home on leave.
			Published *Aids to Scouting*.
South Africa			Appointed to raise and command North-West Frontier Force in anticipation of the Boer War.
			Boer War, defence of Mafeking for 217 days (7 months).
South Africa	1900	43	Mafeking relieved.
			Commanded column in Northern Transvaal, South Africa. Published *Sport in War*.
			Promoted to Major General by order of the Queen.
South Africa	1901	44	Organized South African Constabulary.
England			Home on sick leave.
Scotland			Received CB and King and Queen's Medals from King Edward VII at Balmoral Castle.
			Returned to South Africa.
South Africa	1902	45	Inspector-General, South African Constabulary.
			Boer War ended.

Baden-Powell: A Chronology

Place	Date	Age	Details
England	1903	46	Appointed Inspector-General of Cavalry, Great Britain.
USA, Canada			Visited USA and Canada.
Germany			Attended German Imperial manoeuvres in Dresden.
France, Austria			Inspected Cavalry establishments, Saumur, Hanover and Vienna.
England	1904	47	Inspector-General, Cavalry.
France			Attended French Cavalry manoeuvres.
England			Organized Cavalry School at Netheravon, Wiltshire.
England	1905	48	Started *Cavalry Journal.*
Italy			Inspected the Cavalry Schools of Tor di Quinto and Pinerolo.
East and South Africa	1906	49	Accompanied the Duke of Connaught on tour of inspection, East Africa and South Africa, as Inspector-General, Cavalry.
Belgium			Visited Belgian Cavalry in Brussels.
Egypt	1907	50	As Inspector General, Cavalry, visited East Africa, Egypt and Sudan.
Sudan			
England			Published *Sketches in Mafeking and East Africa.* Exhibited 125 drawings at Bruton Street gallery. Exhibited bust of Captain John Smith in Royal Academy.
Holland			Visited Holland.

Playing the Game

Place	Date	Age	Details
England			Held the experimental camp for twenty boys at Brownsea Island, Dorset. Promoted to Lieutenant General.
England	1908	51	Published *Scouting for Boys*. Appointed to command Northumbrian Territorial Division. Scout Movement started and spread to Australia and New Zealand. Attended Scout camp at Humshaugh, Northumberland. Founded *The Scout* newspaper. Travelled, inspecting troops, throughout Northern Division.
Brazil, Argentina Chile	1909	52	Visited the three countries.
England			Boy Scout Rally at Crystal Palace. Published *Yarns for Boy Scouts*.
Scotland			Received KCB and KGVO from King Edward VII at Balmoral Castle.
England	1910	53	Retired from Army as Lieutenant Generalwith a Reward for Meritorious Service. Started Girl Guides.
Canada USA			Visited Canada and USA organizing Scouts.
Chile			Received Order of Merit of Chile.
France			Visited Paris.
Russia			Visited Russia where he was received by the Tzar.
Scotland			Received Honorary DCL, Edinburgh University. Published *Scouting Games*.

Baden-Powell: A Chronology

Place	Date	Age	Details
England	1911	54	King George V reviewed Boy Scouts in Windsor Great Park.
Norway			Visited Norway and Sweden.
Sweden			Interview with King and Crown Prince of Sweden.
England			House Warden of Mercers' Company.
			Started Buckhurst Scout Farm.
			Received Coronation Medal.
Panama	1912	55	World tour organizing and inspecting Scouts.
USA, West Indies			
Japan, Australia			Gave forty-one addresses to public,
South Africa			sixty-three speeches and sixty-nine addresses to a total of 70,280 people
Norway			Visited Norway.
England			Met and married Olave St Clair Soames.
			Scouts presented motor-car.
			Received Royal Charter for Scouts.
			Created a Knight of Grace of St John of Jerusalem.
			Published *How Girls can Help to Build Up the Empire*.
Algeria	1913	56	Toured with Olave in Algeria, Malta and Naples.
Malta, Italy			
England			Set up home at Ewhurst, Sussex.
			Master of Mercers' Company.
			Birth of first child, Arthur Peter Baden-Powell.
			Birmingham Scout Exhibition and Rally.
			Published *Boy Scouts Beyond the Seas*.

Playing the Game

Place	Date	Age	Details
England	1914	57	Queen Alexandra's Scout Rally at Horse Guards Parade. Outbreak of First World War. Reorganized Girl Guides. Organized Scout coast-watching and war services. Mother died. Published *Quick Training for War*.
France, Belgium	1915	58	Visited British front in France and Flanders.
England			Daughter Heather born.
France			Olave accompanied Baden-Powell to France and started the Calais Scout Hut.
England			Published *Indian Memories My Adventures as a Spy*, and *Marksmanship for Boys*.
Scotland, Ireland			Visited Scouts in Ireland and Scotland and toured England in a small car. Chairman of the Girl Guides Association under Charter of Incorporation.
England	1916	59	Returned with Olave from France. Closed Scouts' Farm. Girl Guide Conference at Matlock, Derbyshire. Olave elected Chief Commissioner. Inauguration of Wolf Cub section. Published *The Wolf Cub Handbook*, *The Wolf Cub* newspaper and *Young Knights of the Empire*.

Baden-Powell: A Chronology

Place	Date	Age	Details
England	1917	60	Daughter Betty born.
			Moved house to Little Mynthurst, Surrey.
Scotland			Inspected coast-watching and other Scouts throughout Scotland.
England	1918	61	Inspected Scout flax-gathering camps.
			Queen Alexandra reviewed Girl Guides, Hyde Park, London.
France			Member of War Museum Committee.
Spain			Visited British front and Scouts in
Portugal			France, Spain and Portugal.
England			Armistice signed.
			Bought Blackacre estate near Bentley, Hampshire, which he renamed Pax Hill.
			President of Camping Club of Great Britain.
			Published *Girl Guiding*.
England	1919	62	Moved into Pax Hill.
Canada			With Olave visited Canada and the
USA			USA.
England			Published *Aids to Scoutmastership*.
			Started Gilwell Park Training Centre for Scout Leaders.
			Awarded Order of Alfonso II.
England	1920	63	First World Scout Jamboree at Olympia, London. Acclaimed Chief Scout of the World.
Greece			Received Orders of Redeemer of
Portugal			Greece and Christ of Portugal.

Playing the Game

Place	Date	Age	Details
England			Started Scout International Bureau (now known as the World Scout Bureau).
			Obtained Royal Charter for the Girl Guides.
			Published *Brownies or Bluebirds*.
England	1921	64	Created Baronet in January.
India			With Olave visited India at invitation of Viceroy to organize Scout and Guide Movement.
Burma, Ceylon Palestine, Egypt			Also visited Burma, Ceylon, Palestine, Egypt.
France			Visited France to see Scout camps in devastated areas.
Denmark			Received Order of Dannebrog (Denmark).
Belgium			Received Order of Commander of Crown of Belgium.
England			Published *What Scouts Can Do* and *An Old Wolf's Favourites*.
Belgium	1922	65	Visited Scouts in Belgium; also met King Albert.
England			Published *Rovering to Success*.
			Posse of Welcome for the Prince of Wales by 60,000 Scouts at Alexandra Palace.
France			Created Commander of Legion of Honour (France).
Switzerland			Addressed International Scout Conference, Paris and International Education Conference, Geneva.

Baden-Powell: A Chronology

Place	Date	Age	Details
England	1923	66	Awarded GCVO.
Canada, USA			With Olave visited Canada to address the National Council of Education. Received Honorary LLD, Toronto and McGill Universities. Visited Scouts in the USA.
England			President Old Carthusian Club. Honorary DCL, Oxford University. Republished *Pig-Sticking*.
England	1924	67	Ill with whooping-cough for months.
Germany, Belgium, Channel Islands			Visited Cologne and Ypres; also the Channel Islands.
England			Commanded 13th/18th Hussars at King's Review at Aldershot. Attended Imperial Jamboree at Wembley.
Denmark			Attended Second World Scout Jamboree near Copenhagen.
England			First World camp of Girl Guides at Foxlease.
France	1925	68	Visited Pyrenees and Norway.
Norway			
Switzerland			Opened International Scout Chalet at Kandersteg.
England			Commanded 13/18th Hussars at King's Review, Aldershot for second time.
USA	1926	69	Toured in USA to nine centres and attended Second Girl Guide World Conference in New York.

Playing the Game

Place	Date	Age	Details
England			Founded the World Bureau for Girl Guides.
			Fiftieth year in 13th Hussars.
			Visited the Regiment and was presented with silver salver.
South Africa			Visited South Africa with Olave for Scout and Guide inspection.
South Africa	1927	70	Completed tour in South Africa.
England			Awarded GCMG.
			Published *Life's Snags*.
Sweden			Attended National Scout Jamboree, Sweden.
Afghanistan	1928	71	Met King Amanullah of Afghanistan and inspected Boy Scouts.
Hungary			Attended Girl Guide World Conference in Hungary.
Poland			Received Polish Order of Polonia Restituta.
Ireland			Visited Scouts in Irish Free State and in Wales.
Wales			Family camping tour in Wales.
Gibraltar	1929	72	Cruised in *Duchess of Richmond* to the Isles of the Blest with Olave, Heather and Betty.
Majorca			
Belgium			Visited Belgium, Luxembourg and France with Peter.
Luxembourg			
France			
England			Attended Third World Scout Jamboree at Arrowe Park, near Birkenhead.

Baden-Powell: A Chronology

Place	Date	Age	Details
France			Boy Scouts presented Rolls-Royce car ('Jam Roll'), a caravan ('Eccles'), a portrait and £3,000.
			Raised to peerage and created Lord Baden-Powell, 1st Baron of Gilwell.
			Received Honorary LLD, Liverpool University.
Hungary			Awarded Order of Merit, Hungary.
Czechoslovakia			Awarded Order of White Lion, Czechoslovakia.
Greece			Awarded Order of Phoenix, Greece.
England			Family camping tour in Worcestershire.
			Freedom of the City of London conferred.
West Indies	1930	73	Visited West Indies, Bermuda and New York.
USA			
England			Attended Third Girl Guide World Conference at Foxlease. Olave created World Chief Guide.
			Family camping tour in Wessex.
Switzerland			Visited International Scout Chalet, Kandersteg, Switzerland.
New Zealand	1931	74	With Olave visited New Zealand, Australasia and South Africa.
Australia			
Tasmania			
South Africa			
Austria			Attended Fifth International Scout Conference of Scout Leaders, Baden, Vienna.
			President of Austria conferred Austrian Order of Merit.
Switzerland			Attended Rover Scout Moot at Kandersteg, Switzerland, with Peter.

Playing the Game

Place	Date	Age	Details
Switzerland	1932	75	With Olave attended opening of International Girl Guide Chalet at Adelboden, Switzerland. Visited Swiss Scouts' camp.
Holland			Visited the national camp of Dutch Scouts at The Hague. Awarded Order of Orange of Nassau of Holland.
Lithuania			Awarded Grand Cross of Gedimanas, Lithuania.
England			Olave created Dame Grand Cross of Order of the British Empire.
Malta Gibraltar	1933	76	With Olave visited Scouts and Guides in Malta and Gibraltar.
Italy			Also visited Italy; met with Mussolini and also with Pope Pius XI. Saw the Balilla and their training schools.
Hungary			Attended the Fourth World Scout Jamboree in Godöllö, Hungary.
Sweden			Awarded the Grand Cross of Order of Sweden.
Latvia Estonia Finland Poland Lithuania			Awarded the Grand Cross of Order of Three Stars of Latvia and Red Cross of Estonia. Visited Holland, Poland, Lithuania, Latvia, Estonia, Finland, Sweden and Norway during the Scout and Guide Cruise on the SS *Calgaric*.
England			Published *Lessons from the 'Varsity of Life* Received the Freedom of Pontefract.

Baden-Powell: A Chronology

Place	Date	Age	Details
England	1934	77	At home for five months recovering from a serious internal operation.
Malta			Visited (along with 670 Scouters and
Gibraltar			Guiders) Scouts and Guides in Malta,
France			Gibraltar, Nice, Algiers and Lisbon
Algeria			during the Scout and Guide Cruise on
Portugal			the SS *Adriatic*.
Ceylon			With Olave attended National
Malaya, Java			Jamboree in Australia, en route visited
Port Darwin			Scouts and Guides in Ceylon, Malaya,
Thursday Island			Java, Port Darwin and Thursday Island.
Australia			
England			Published *Adventures and Accidents*.
New Zealand	1935	78	Visited New Zealand, South Sea
South Sea Islands			Islands, Canada, Newfoundland and
Canada			the USA inspecting Scouts and Guides.
Newfoundland			
USA			Visited the President of the USA at the White House, returning home in the SS *Majestic*.
			Peter Baden-Powell married Carine Boardman.
Sweden			Attended World Rover Moot in Sweden.
Kenya, Uganda			Left for Kenya, Uganda, Tanganyika,
Tanganyika			Zanzibar and Rhodesia.
Zanzibar			
South Africa			Attended National Scout Jamboree at East London, Rhodesia, South Africa.
England			Published *Scouting Round the World*.

Playing the Game

Place	Date	Age	Details
South Africa	1936	79	Revisited Mafeking with Olave and family.
St Helena Ascension Island			Returned to England via St Helena and Ascension Island.
England			Attended Commissioners' Conference at Norwich.
			Scout and Guide Dinner of Welcome, London.
			Betty Baden-Powell married Gervas Clay at Bentley.
France			Awarded the Grand Cordon of Legion of Honour (France).
			Visited Scouts and Guides in Paris.
England			Published *Adventuring to Manhood*.
India	1937	80	Sailed (January) for India and attended the first All-India Scout Jamboree in Delhi; the Viceroy and 4,000 Scouts present.
			Spent eightieth birthday with 13th/18th Hussars, last mounted ceremonial parade of the Regiment.
			Saw the Kadir Cup Competition.
England			Returned to England.
			Inspected Scouts on duty at the Coronation of King George VI.
			Awarded Coronation Medal of George VI.
			Inspection of Scouts by the King and Queen at Windsor.
			Awarded the Order of Merit.

Baden-Powell: A Chronology

Place	Date	Age	Details
Holland			Visited Holland for the Fifth World Scout Jamboree and the International Conference at The Hague.
England			Awarded the Wateler Peace Prize by the Board of the Carnegie Institute for his services to World Peace and promoting international goodwill through the Scout Movement.
England			Silver Wedding Anniversary dinner in London. Members of the Scout and Guide Movements contributed to a present to the two Chiefs. The gift included a number of pieces of silver and a cheque for over £2,600. Published *African Adventures*.
Kenya			Sailed for Kenya. Built Paxtu at Nyeri, Kenya.
England	1938	81	Returned to England. Gazetted out of the army after sixty-two years' service.
Iceland			Visited (with 470 Scouters and
Norway			Guiders) Iceland, Norway, Denmark
Denmark			and Belgium during the Scout and
Belgium			Guide Cruise on the SS *Orduna*.
England			Published *Birds and Beasts in Africa*.
Kenya			Left Pax Hill for the last time and returned to Kenya, sailing on the *Llandaff Castle*.
Kenya	1939	82	Remained in Kenya.

Playing the Game

Place	Date	Age	Details
			Family reunion of children and grand-children at Paxtu.
			Published *Paddle Your Own Canoe*.
			Exhibited sketches at Officers' Art Society, London and Kenya Art Exhibition, Nairobi.
Kenya	1940	83	Published *More Sketches of Kenya*.
			Began *Snaps and Scraps*.
England			Heather Baden-Powell married John King at Bentley.
Kenya	1941	84	Died on 8 January.
			Military funeral and burial at St. Peter's Churchyard, Nyeri, on 9 January.
England			Memorial Service at Westminster Abbey, London, on 27 January.